The Knights Hospitaller

The Knights Hospitaller

A Military History of the Knights of St John

John C. Carr

Pen & Sword
MILITARY

First published in Great Britain in 2016 by
Pen & Sword Military
an imprint of
Pen & Sword Books Ltd
47 Church Street
Barnsley
South Yorkshire
S70 2AS

ISBN 978 1 47385 888 6

A CIP catalogue record for this book is available from the British
Library

Typeset in Ehrhardt by
Mac Style Ltd, Bridlington, East Yorkshire
Printed and bound in the UK by CPI Group (UK) Ltd, Croydon,
CRO 4YY

Pen & Sword Books Ltd incorporates the imprints of Pen & Sword
Archaeology, Atlas, Aviation, Battleground, Discovery, Family
History, History, Maritime, Military, Naval, Politics, Railways, Select,
Transport, True Crime, and Fiction, Frontline Books, Leo Cooper,
Praetorian Press, Seaforth Publishing and Wharncliffe.

For a complete list of Pen & Sword titles please contact
PEN & SWORD BOOKS LIMITED
47 Church Street, Barnsley, South Yorkshire, S70 2AS, England
E-mail: enquiries@pen-and-sword.co.uk
Website: www.pen-and-sword.

Contents

Prologue: The Pope's Divisions

W hen Winston Churchill, Franklin Roosevelt and Joseph Stalin met at Yalta in February 1945 to order the post-Second World War world, the American delegation included Ed Flynn, a Democratic politician who wielded great influence in New York, especially over Irish-American Catholics. According to a widely circulated (but so far undocumented) story, Flynn suggested to Stalin that he approach Pope Pius XII to bring him into the general global rearrangement.

The pontiff, of course, was not included in the cast of Stalin's plans for a global socialist utopia, and the sarcasm was clear in his reply: 'How many divisions has the Pope?'[1]

We don't know what Flynn had to reply to that, but the question does have an answer. The pope has indeed had his divisions – or, more accurately his division. If it hasn't fought in any wars for the past couple of hundred years, in that time it stayed close to the action. The Sovereign Military Hospitaller Order of Saint John of Jerusalem, Rhodes and Malta, known as the Knights Hospitaller or Hospitallers for short, is the oldest continuously-operating military-religious organization in the world. Originating in Jerusalem around the middle of the eleventh century, the Hospitallers were a mainstay of the popes' military reach at a time when the Roman Catholic Church, as a major political power, had to have a corresponding military power at its disposal. For hundreds of years the Hospitallers were at the forefront of the major battles of Christendom against militant Islam. Time after time they were driven from their homes, only to find others. They are still around today, and though they no longer bear arms, their discipline and faith are uneroded.

The active heyday of the Knights Hospitaller lasted almost from their founding in the eleventh century up to the end of the eighteenth century, when their fighting importance declined, to gradually give way to charitable and religious functions. The reference to Saint John in the Order's formal name reflects its origin as administrators of the Saint John the Baptist hospice that served pilgrims arriving in mediaeval Jerusalem.

John the Baptist is an apt figure to be named after. The four gospels describe him as a charismatic hermit-preacher in the Jordan Valley in the time of Christ. From what the Bible and the historian Josephus tell us, John was a powerful character 'who urged the Jews to strive towards perfection and exhorted them to deal justly with one another and walk humbly with God'. Here, in a line, is the ideal of spiritual and social discipline combined. John the Baptist's stern sense of duty and morality fuelled his fierce denunciation of the court of Herod Antipas, deputed by Rome to administer a quarter of Roman-held Palestine. Herod had John beheaded in the Castle of Machaerus at a desolate spot east of the Dead Sea. Thus was created the martyr who would inspire and give his name to an international army.

From their inception the Knights Hospitaller have served the Roman Catholic Church in both warlike and peaceful ways. Of course, here an old philosophical conundrum arises – how can a religious organization employ a military one whose duty often is to kill on the field of battle? There are ways of answering that question, but they don't belong in a military history except where the issue impinges on strategy, tactics, leadership and battlefield conduct. The object of this book is to chronicle and examine the battles which the Hospitallers waged through their history, against a wider historical and political background, and leave philosophical conclusions to the reader.

The full history of the Knights of Saint John is not easy to research. Volumes of archives have been lost or destroyed, and large gaps separate the known periods of Hospitaller history, i.e. between the Outremer and Rhodes periods and between Rhodes and Malta. The early part of that history, from the origins of the Order in the eleventh century to its expulsion from the Middle East at the end of the thirteenth, is tightly bound up with the history of the Crusades and can only be told in that context. The Rhodes period (1309–1522) has its own narrative, but as a leading authority, Anthony Luttrell, has remarked, 'serious Hospitaller history before 1530 is no-one's history'.[2] What that means is that the historian must make do with scattered and often conflicting material. The picture becomes clearer after 1530, when the Knights settled in Malta.

The siege of Malta of 1565, though a resounding triumph against Islamic power in the Mediterranean, was the last such great feat of arms by the Order. The struggle indeed went on sporadically until Napoleon Bonaparte expelled the Hospitallers from Malta in 1798. After that date, and by the time the Order settled in Rome in 1834, its military profile began to blur and blend into the peaceable charity works that characterize it today. They are in Rome still, quietly headquartered in a stately palazzo in Via Condotti which has the privilege of constituting a sovereign state. There, beneath the red and white banner of the eight-pointed Hospitaller cross, the work of the Knights of Saint John goes on.

Thanks mainly to the help of Sean Lovett, head of the English section of Vatican Radio in Rome, I was able to enter the sanctum sanctorum of Via Condotti for research into the Hospitallers' later years. Marianna Balfour, the Order's public relations director, was encouragingly helpful, as was the entire library staff, especially Valérie Guillot, who performed feats of photocopying beyond her ordinary call of duty. Henry Sire, a Professed Knight, provided plenty of material on the recent history of the Order and cleared up a few vague issues such as how much influence the popes have actually had over the Order and the vexed question of 'copycat-orders' in Europe and America. These may flaunt the emblem of Saint John on the Internet and employ the term 'knights' but they are of dubious legality.[3] They have nothing at all to do with the genuine 900-year-old Sovereign Military Order of the Hospitallers that bears a global humanitarian burden demanding fully as much selflessness and dedication as that of the fighting knights of ages past.

The initial idea of writing this book occurred to me while I was in Rhodes in September 2013 helping to produce tourism documentaries for the Internet. Though I had visited the island before, this time I was able to get my first comprehensive look at the Knights' fortifications and preserved Old Town. Philip Sidnell, my commissioning editor at Pen & Sword, eagerly seconded the project, as his own ancestry has something of the Knights of Malta in it. As I discovered while working on my previous book for Pen & Sword, *Fighting Emperors of Byzantium*, telescoping many centuries of detailed military history into a moderate-sized volume carries its risks, mainly those of misinterpretation and generalization. In the text I employ the terms Knights Hospitaller, Knights of Saint John and Knights of Malta fairly interchangeably, depending on context. Though I have made every effort at accuracy and objectivity, I hope any remaining errors are not too eye-watering. Finally, I must point out that the Order has had no hand in the research and writing of the text, and therefore the conclusions I draw and judgements I make are completely my own.

JCC
Athens, January 2016

List of Illustrations

Chapter 1

Unfinished Business

Richard I on the march – Saladin stalks the Crusaders – the Hospitallers in 1192 – the Battle of Arsuf – arrival at Jaffa

Late August is no season for an army of foot soldiers to be slogging down the Palestinian seaboard. The searing heat regularly tops 40 degrees Celsius – in the shade – and reduces much of the countryside to a parched brown carpet of sand and scrub. And when a soldier is carrying weapons and kit, and very likely weighed down by armour in the bargain, progress has to be very slow. True, the blue Mediterranean Sea on the right might offer the chance for a cooling dip or two, but water of a different kind – drinking water – is a constant and urgent necessity. And getting it is a problem; the dusty hills to the left, where a precious few springs bring slivers of brackish water from the Lebanese mountains, seethe with Muslim raiding bands.

This was the scene in the high summer of 1191 as King Richard I of England led his 15,000 Crusaders down the Palestinian coast. The march was slow going, but that did not bother Richard as long as he could keep his force tightly formatted and in defensive posture. Naval ships scudding offshore carried much of the necessary fresh water plus most of the food supply to replenish the ten days' rations carried by each man. The march began at dawn on 22 August 1191 from Acre (now Akko) on the coast of what is now northern Israel. Richard planned to lead the army on a sweltering 120km slog south along the coast to Jaffa, near what is now Tel Aviv. From there he planned to strike inwards to the Palestinian heartland to measure swords with the Muslims under Sultan Salah-ad-Din of the Ayyubid dynasty – or Saladin, as he was by then universally known. Once Saladin was dealt with, the road would be open to Jerusalem, the holy centre of Christendom, which had fallen into Saladin's hands four years before, triggering an outburst of Western holy indignation that had ignited the Third Crusade. That was the plan.

Every man in Richard's army expected him to eject Saladin from Jerusalem after a rest and regrouping at Jaffa. Yet the king himself seemed to lack a clear-cut idea of what his later moves would be. As he was not known to be a dithering character, and his strategic abilities were second to none, the most likely explanation is that he was keeping his options open. Let's get to Jaffa first, he seemed to be thinking, and see what Saladin's moves have been in the meantime. Jaffa was vital anyway as a naval supply point. Perhaps if the sultan could be tempted into attacking that port, he could be defeated there, and then Jerusalem would be the Crusaders' for the taking.

Above all, the Crusader army had to be kept moving. Made up largely of English and French volunteers and soldiers of fortune, it had been living it up in Acre for about six weeks. Acre had been taken after a two-year siege in which great deeds of desperation and bravery were performed by both sides. After that Herculean effort many Christian soldiers were understandably reluctant to leave their 'good wines and good girls, some very beautiful', in what was the equivalent of the big city for the perils of a new campaign.[1] Richard employed a mixture of cajolery, prayer and threats to move some of the more reluctant pleasure-addicted soldiers, but move they eventually did.

The first stage of the march was a 20km wheel around a wide bay to Haifa, the next stop. The formation kept as close to the sea as possible, its right flank literally at the water's edge. The left flank kept wary eyes out for Saladin's forces that at any moment could come galloping and yelling out of the coastal plain bounded by the Belus River to the north and the Kishon to the south. Everyone knew that the Muslims, though unseen, were shadowing Richard's every move. Richard himself took up position at the rear of the column to make sure that it moved in compact formation with no straggling at the back, and possibly also to encourage latecomers with his presence. He thus found himself riding alongside one of his best-trained, battle-hardened and dedicated corps, the Knights Hospitaller.

The Hospitallers and the other Military Order, the Knights Templar, who rode and marched in the vanguard of Richard's army had plenty of reason to want to settle accounts with Saladin. The memory was still painfully fresh of July 1187, when more than a hundred Hospitaller and Templar prisoners taken after the fall of Jerusalem were hacked to death in Saladin's presence. The Muslims had no use for them alive as they largely rejected the chance to be ransomed and refused the offer to convert to Islam, preferring to die in the Christian cause.

Much as the Hospitallers and Templars itched to avenge the atrocity, Richard was taking no chances on this campaign. At forced-march pace, he reckoned he could make the distance to Jaffa in five days, but he resisted the temptation to speed up. Besides being foolish in the Middle East summer, fast marching tended to loosen an army formation, and with the Muslims ever-present, that was an unacceptable risk. There was also the fleet offshore to coordinate with; the heavily-laden twelfth century transports needed to regularly offload supplies to smaller craft that would ferry provisions and arms to the army ashore. Moreover, the weeks of wine, women and song in Acre must have softened up the soldiery somewhat, so a serious march needed to go easy in the initial stages. In fact, the whole of 24 August was spent encamped on the south bank of the Belus River as Richard patiently waited for stragglers to catch up.

Richard could take heart in that now, and only now, could he run the Third Crusade unhindered. Joining him at first had been Philip II Augustus, the king of France, and German Emperor Frederick I (Barbarossa). In June 1190 Frederick had fallen off his horse in mid-stream in Asia Minor and drowned, essentially taking the Germans out of the campaign, while a year later Philip Augustus, who had set out on the Crusade with fervour, appeared to have tired of the whole business and after helping the English king capture Acre, set sail for home. Philip said he considered the Acre campaign to have fulfilled his holy vow to recapture some of the Holy Land for Christendom, and felt he was more needed at home, where his throne was none too secure. But Richard did not quite buy that explanation, suspecting that Philip Augustus wanted to be back in France to consider possible moves against the English; after all, Richard held more of France than Philip Augustus did, and that could not sit well with any Frenchman. The silver lining, however, was that Richard was now in sole command of operations and he could pretty much do what he saw fit, yet he never ceased to worry about what the French might be up to back in Europe.

As a military corps, Richard's contingent of Hospitallers was about half a century old. About the middle of the twelfth century they had expanded from their original occupation of providing aid and medical care to Christian pilgrims in Jerusalem to donning armour and cultivating the arts of war. By the time of the Third Crusade the Latin states in Palestine were short of manpower, a shortage that was answered by knightly volunteers, mostly from France. The Hospitallers, as devout and well-trained fighting monks, owed more of an allegiance to the Christian faith rather than to one specific ruler, and appeared not to make an issue of who was commanding them. Their morale was certainly high. At the siege of Acre the Order had its own catapult, and had probably contributed to the cost of another one felicitously dubbed God's Own Sling.[2] Three days after starting out from Acre, Richard felt he could leave the Hospitallers at the rear and move up to the front of the column. On this march the Hospitallers appear to have been under the general command of Duke Hugh III of Burgundy, whose French troops had refused to follow their king back to France.

The Crusader army consisted of three divisions: the vanguard, including the Knights Templar; the centre, consisting of English and Norman troops and including the exiled King of Jerusalem, Guy de Lusignan, hoping to be reinstalled at home on the lances of his troops; and the rear, led by Hugh of Burgundy. The Crusader standard flew defiantly above the host on a tall pole on a wagon drawn by four big horses, a banner that devout observers likened to 'the root of Jesse signifying the descent of Jesus from the royal line of David'[3] and meant to be fully and intimidatingly visible to the Muslim bands that jabbed at the left flank from time to time. The raiders were compared to desert flies, buzzing close and stinging, and swatted away only to return again and again. A few careless Crusaders and their valuable horses were lost by such swatting. Though progress around the bay was slow, Richard expected to make Haifa by evening of Sunday, 25 August. But sometime in the afternoon, when visibility was reduced – probably by gusting dust or sea mist – the rear and central divisions lost contact with each other. The ever-watchful Muslim cavalry under al-Adil, Saladin's brother, charged out of the haze and into the gap. Men and horses went down, supply wagons were overrun; the attackers reached the beach, where one knight named Evrart (under Bishop Hubert Walter) beat off the enemy with his sword in his left hand, as his right hand had been sliced off. Richard wheeled his horse and sped rearwards to the scene; seeing him racing up, the Muslims fell back. Saladin's eldest son, al-Malik al-Afdal, imagined that he had come close to rounding up the entire Hospitaller column, and needed just a few more troops to do it. But Saladin's intention from the first was probably a hit-and-run thrust rather than a full-scale assault. He had to content himself with executing a captured Hungarian count.

When the march resumed on 28 August the Templars and Hospitallers retained their positions in the van and rear respectively, but Richard had decided on a tighter formation to prevent mishaps like the one of three days before. First, the troops themselves were considerably lightened; many had begun the march 'overburdened with food and arms'; a few had actually perished of thirst in that blazing climate. Second, the divisions were placed closer together, so that to the ever-watchful enemy in the foothills of Mount Carmel the force resembled a vast wall of chain mail against which the skirmishers' arrows proved useless; one Muslim claimed to see Crusaders with 'ten arrows in their backs' marching along serenely. As it was the left flank that was constantly exposed to danger, Richard rotated left and right regularly to even out the risk.

The men were very conscious of finally treading the soil that Christ had once trod. 'I have reached the place where God walked in the flesh', they sang as they left Haifa and entered the Plain of Sharon.[4] But there were other, rather more diabolical, elements such as venomous snakes and spiders, scorpions, and all manner of horrid imaginary beasts that were described around the campfires and made some sensitive souls so nervous that chants of '*Sanctum sepulcrum adjuva!*' ('Holy Sepulchre, help!') would echo into the warm nights. An exhausted sleep, then the men would rouse their aching limbs and move on, suffering mightily under a today-unimaginable 90lbs of armour per soldier and a sun that reached roasting temperature well before noon – and always on guard for snakes and Muslims.

With the Crusaders pressing on towards Jerusalem, Saladin stepped up his harassment. Not making his job any easier was the fact that Richard was taking his time, punctuating the march with stops of one or two days; the soldiers' energy had to be conserved for the imminent great push on the Holy City. The sultan didn't quite know what to make of this tactic; he wanted a battle soon as, by some accounts, his own forces were running short of food.[5] As Muslim squads incessantly probed the Crusaders' defences, Saladin cast about for a suitable place in which to force Richard to an encounter. He must certainly have realized how the scorching August heat had been affecting Richard's European troops for eight gruelling days. Some men fell dead of heat stroke and were buried en route; others, ill and exhausted, were put on coastal boats at the next halt.

Saladin himself, like Richard, believed in the cautious approach. He was not well, suffering from painful blisters on his legs and lower abdomen, and moreover stuck to the prescription of the Koran advising patience for 'those who fight strenuously for the cause of God'. But was he in fact patient, or unsure of what to do? On 31 August he tested the waters with a probe in force at the Dead River. On the appearance of the Arabs the Crusaders wheeled into position with a speed and precision that drew rueful admiration from the attackers, who lost one of their most renowned leaders, a Turk named Ayas the Tall, a celebrated lance fighter.[6] With the elimination of Ayas, revered by the Muslims as a 'man-eating lion … the first to bless the sneezing clouds of war-dust' for his prowess in single combat, the attack ran out of steam. Richard, true to form, galloped up to the scene of the attack, but hardly had time to weigh in when a crossbow bolt hit him in the side. Luckily, his armour took most of the impact, but for a few moments he swayed in the saddle. As with the clash south of Acre on 25 August, Richard's conspicuous courage and Saladin's wish to conserve manpower ensured that the encounter would be inconclusive. That evening the Hospitallers encamped at the mouth of the River of Reeds, aware that the Muslims were just over a kilometre upstream, washing in and drinking the same water. As they sat down to sing 'Sanctum Sepulcrum adjuva', they roasted the meat of the horses whose end had come that day, either from enemy action or exhaustion. The knights who had owned the horses were pretty much powerless to protest, but the king regulated this potentially fraught situation by ordering that the meat be given to worthy soldiers who deserved it, and that the knights be recompensed by new mounts. Besides, horsemeat wasn't bad at all.

Saladin's resistance hardened with every step the Crusaders took. Their next scheduled stop was the south bank of the Rochetaille River, another vital fresh water source. They spent 4 September at the River of Reeds, while Richard pondered his next move. He expected that Saladin would be waiting for him in force at some point between there and Jaffa, and decided on a ruse to throw him off balance: he sent messengers to contact a Muslim outpost and propose that he enter into peace talks with Saladin's brother al-Adil. The sultan himself had been reconnoitring possible battle sites, but that evening, when he was told of Richard's offer, he agreed. This, of course, was no genuine desire for peace, but a delaying tactic in order to gather as many Muslim forces as he could.

Exactly the same applied to Richard, who was in as much a mood for peace as his adversary – that is, none. The king's aim was to confuse the enemy and perhaps gain a bit of intelligence; Saladin may not have realized this, as he inexplicably left the bulk of his formation scattered to the south. Of course, the parley quickly ended in deadlock; ad-Adil furiously rejected Richard's blunt demand for a return of the whole Holy Land, which of course was never intended to be accepted, as serious negotiation was never the king's intention. No sooner had ad-Adil ridden off in a huff than Richard ordered the army to enter the Forest of Arsuf to reach the Rochetaille River. Every man in the army fully expected the enemy to set fire to the woods, but it didn't happen. However, Richard was far from complacent; directly ahead lay the open plain of Arsuf, where Saladin would surely launch his major attack.

The morning of Saturday, 7 September dawned bright as the Hospitallers, refreshed from resting at the Rochetaille River, formed up in their usual position at the rear of the formation, the Templars in the van, and the rest of the 15,000-strong army of Poitevins, Normans and English in the middle. The vulnerable left flank was commanded by Henry of Champagne. Richard himself and his chief lieutenant, Hugh of Burgundy, put together a flying squad of reserves that they could use to insert into critical sectors. All along the column the men told one another that this day was going to be no ordinary one. One of the nobles in the king's retinue named Ambroise devoutly hoped so, as he watched the army set out in a tight formation so dense that 'an apple thrown into the ranks could not fail to hit man or horse'.[7]

Before the dry plain of Arsuf, and with the foe like a gathering cloud, it's worth taking a closer look at Richard I's Hospitaller contingent as it struck camp and followed the rest of the army. From what we know of the Military Orders at the time, there were perhaps a maximum 300 Hospitallers on the Jaffa expedition. That probably was the Order's entire front-line force as we know that the Grand Master of the Hospitallers, Garnier of Nablus, rode at their head. As the Grand Master had both civil and military authority, his decision to ride with his Knights indicates that the whole Order considered itself to be in the process of moving from its headquarters in Acre to its hoped-for 'real' place in Jerusalem. The Grand Master was directly answerable to the pope in Rome, and as a new pontiff, Celestine III, had just been installed, we may imagine that a breath of fresh hope animated the devout Hospitallers.

The Knights were mostly mounted, divided by social status into brother-knights and brother-sergeants, roughly equivalent to the later distinction between commissioned and non-commissioned officers – though, as now, in the heat of battle such distinctions tended not to mean very much in terms of valour and abilities. The usual proportion of brother-sergeants to brother-knights was about four to one, which we may assume was the case at Arsuf. Accompanying the brethren-in-arms (knights and sergeants) were several score turcopoles, or auxiliary foot-soldiers recruited from local Christians including ethnic Arabs. (The term turcopole probably derives from the Greek *tourkopoulon*, or 'little Turk', a slightly derogatory term applicable to Middle Eastern locals in general and perhaps originating in Byzantium.) These turcopoles, despite the lower mercenary status accorded them, were generally good fighters and quite indispensable to any campaign.

Riding in the front rank of the Hospitallers would have been the Gonfalonier, or standard-bearer, whose role in battle was vital as the contingent's rallying-point. We don't know who the Gonfalonier at Arsuf was, but he would have had to be a valiant knight steady enough to keep the banner flying amidst the chaos of combat. Not that most of the brethren-at-arms needed any special spur to fight; all were volunteers of undoubted faith and courage, who had what it took to make the hazardous 3,000km journey from their castles and manors in England and France, overland through Byzantium or by sea through the Mediterranean, to fight for the cause of Christ. And we need not doubt that from Grand Master Garnier of Nablus on down, every Hospitaller was keen to liberate Jerusalem with his lance or die trying. Either way, he would win glory, if not in this world then in the next.

Richard himself seems to have hoped to avoid battle until his force could reach safety in an orchard on the other side of the plain. This was sensible thinking – a pitched battle of the kind Saladin was seeking would delay the march to Jaffa while causing unnecessary losses. Moreover, a battle in the fierce heat of day was not advisable. But this time Richard wouldn't be calling the shots; Saladin felt he had held himself back long enough and as the first Templars in the van of the Crusader army left the Rochetaille River behind, while the sun was still low in the eastern sky, they came face to face with 30,000 Muslims arrayed on the left of the plain in thick formation.

Saladin attacked first with several thousand of his advance guard hurtling out of the sun towards the Crusaders. The Crusaders held, keeping their general formation while beating back the attacking waves emerging from the oak woods on the left. The Muslim battle-cries, trumpets and drums were deafening. Leading the charge were fanatic turbaned black Bedouins, followed by the regular Arab regiments with their yellow banners. The sight of the black Africans struck fear into the Europeans. A fearful rain of arrows mowed down horses 'like rain or snow falling in the heart of winter', according to one soldier. The sheer impact of the attack stunned the Crusader force, draining courage from knight and ordinary soldier alike. Few expected 'to survive one hour or come out of it alive'. But Richard was never at his steadiest as at that hour, keeping the army moving despite the fierce enemy storm battering at it and expressly forbidding any counterattack that might open a fatal gap in the columns.

The Hospitallers were hit especially hard. Garnier de Nablus sent a courier speeding up to the king to plead to be allowed to counterattack on his front. The Order, he said, was 'surrounded, like a flock of sheep in the jaws of wolves'. Richard steeled himself not to seize the bait. But as the pressure on the Hospitallers became brutal, and their horses went down by the dozen under what seemed to one witness like 'the fury of all paganism', Garnier addressed a fervent prayer to Saint George, the patron saint of all Crusaders: 'All Christendom is on the point of perishing because it fears to return a blow' against the enemy, he told the saint. Spurring his horse up to the king in the centre, Garnier shouted to the king above the din of battle: 'We are in danger of eternal infamy!' and begged to be allowed to fight back. But Richard was adamant, believing that a solid defence would prevail in the end and calling on Garnier to exercise the discipline and self-restraint that his Order was renowned for.

Distressed, the Hospitaller Grand Master rode back to his men who were at their boiling point. 'Let's charge them!' the Knights pleaded. 'Let's not be called disgraceful cowards.' When soldiers express sentiments like these, whatever the circumstances, their commander is wise to heed them. Perhaps Garnier assented to a charge; perhaps he was bypassed, as the next thing anyone knew, the Hospitallers' Marshal – the strictly military commander subordinate to the Grand Master – and a Knight named Baldwin of Carew had begun the countercharge, to be followed in short order by the rest of the Hospitallers and then hundreds of other left-flank troops led by Henry of Champagne, James of Avesnes and Robert, Earl of Leicester, roaring the name of Saint George.

Saladin saw the counter-attack coming, probably before Richard himself was aware of it. By now the Templars in front had just about reached sanctuary in the Arsuf orchard. Expecting the worst of the ordeal to be over, Richard then became aware of the commotion behind him, and looked back to see the Hospitallers and others in full cry against the enemy. His hand forced, Richard had no choice but to accept the inevitable. Without waiting to even sound the trumpet for a general attack, he rode into the fray 'faster than a bolt from a crossbow' to find a scene of utter carnage. The Crusader charge had been so ferocious as to scythe the Muslim lines like grass. The whole Arab front line was mown down in one go. Severed enemy heads littered the blood-soaked ground, to be trampled by man and horse into shapeless masses of gore. The screams of the grievously wounded filled the stifling air.

Most chroniclers agree that it was perhaps four squadrons of knights, including the Hospitallers, which sent the Muslims flying from the field. Richard was modest about his own contribution, heaping all the credit on the cavalry, though the historian Ambroise claims that Richard's 'brandished sword cleared a wide path on all sides', and gives the king a good deal of the credit for the 'Turkish corpses' thickly carpeting half a square mile. The king is reported to have ridden Fauvel, his great Cypriot stallion, into the thick of the slaughter, crying, '*Adjuva nos, Deus!*' ('Help us, God!'). A body count later turned up thirty-two emirs and some 700 ordinary soldiers, most of them felled in the first furious Crusader charge. Crusader casualties, while not precisely known, are believed to have been far fewer. But one of them was the Flemish knight, James of Avesnes, who had helped lead the charge of the centre units. When his horse had been shot from under him, James had fought on foot, but, encircled by the enemy, was doomed. His body was recovered the following day, together with his shield of six diagonal red and gold stripes. His face was so blood-stained and battered as to be almost unrecognizable and he was missing an arm and a leg; around him lay fifteen dead Muslims. James of Avesnes, lionized for his courage, was buried at Arsuf, writes Ambroise, to general 'wailing and lamentation'.[8]

Shaken at this unexpected setback – and after two subsequent Arab attacks were beaten off – Saladin pulled his troops back into the foothills to ponder his next move with his son al-Afdal, all of 20 years old but already a seasoned campaigner. The sultan's first move was to send messengers to Muslim territories in the East demanding reinforcements. He knew it would take some time for his army to get over the shock, but he believed (or tried to convince himself) that he had delayed the Crusaders' march south and kept up his own morale by dictating official letters to that effect.

Richard, for his part, was in no doubt about the scale of his victory. Even though battle had been forced upon him, compelling him to alter his plans, he had displayed the flexibility and decisiveness under a sudden change of conditions that mark the truly able commander. He could be excused the note of triumphalism that colours a report he wrote nearly a month after the battle, asserting that Saladin 'lost more on that day than on any day in the previous forty years'. A slight exaggeration it may be, but over the next three days Richard's army covered the remaining distance to Jaffa without incident. The town itself was in ruins; the Muslims had razed it a year before. But as the Hospitallers pitched their tents in the surrounding vineyards and gardens, full to bursting with harvest-time fruit, figs and nuts, many must have cast their glances eastwards towards Jerusalem, some 50km away. Between them and the Holy City, however, stood a vengeful Saladin, who Richard knew 'lies in wait at a distance, out of sight like a lion in his den'.

Chapter 2

Birth of a Military Order

Knighthood and Christianity – pilgrimage – origins of the Hospital – Atsiz sacks Jerusalem – Urban II calls the First Crusade – Knights of Saint John – the Templars

He took it upon himself to help innocent people ... you look into the eyes of the children and you can't help wonder[ing] what they think and how any good person or country [could] just sit back and let them and their families be slaughtered.

The above quote comes from a friend of Konstandinos Erik Scurfield, a British ex-Royal Marine who joined the Kurdish fighters and was killed battling the Islamic State's forces in Syria on 2 March 2015.[1] It's included here as an example of the clear courage that is called forth by fighting for what one believes in; the camaraderie, as any soldier who has been in combat will affirm, is almost sacred in its intensity. Scurfield, as far as is known, had no Kurdish blood connection; yet he found in the Kurds (of whom, in an irony of history, Saladin had been one) a fighting brotherhood and a supremely important cause – to halt extreme Islamic militancy.

The sentiments expressed by Scurfield's comrade-in-arms would be very familiar to the average Knight Hospitaller of nine centuries before, who would have endorsed them to the hilt. In a Bible-reading age young aristocrats in western Europe were brought up in the noble ideals of protecting the weak and upholding the faith. These ideals could not be separated – they were parts of a single Christian doctrine and practice. Many of those so taught, of course, grew up to be despots and scoundrels, but enough of the good ones remained to take Christianity and its duties seriously. And when, sometime in the eleventh century, they heard that there was a need to protect Christian pilgrims in the Muslim-ruled Holy Land, they found a cause that could both satisfy their consciences and provide an outlet for the testosterone-fuelled instincts of healthy, well-exercised, military-age young men.

In the year 1000, as the first millennium of our era gave way to the second, the idea of pilgrimage was very popular in both the Christian and the Muslim domains. From the very earliest days of Islam, devout Muslims were enjoined to make at least one pilgrimage to Mecca during their lifetimes – the hajj, which remains technically de rigueur for all Muslims to the present day. For the Jews, their apocalyptic vision since the start of the Diaspora was firmly fixated on the holiness of Jerusalem and the goal of someday returning. European Christians, too, held Jerusalem to be the most sacred of cities; centuries of Sunday sermons in the churches, countless illustrated Biblical manuscripts and paintings, had given the images of Christ's Crucifixion and Resurrection, the 'green hill far away' of the hymns, an otherworldly permanence in the European mind, whether Greek or Latin, French or German. For centuries, tales known as miracula had circulated in western Europe and the Mediterranean, telling of visions that people had of angels commanding them to go and succour 'the poor of Jerusalem'.[2]

Thus the idea of charitable pilgrimage to the Holy Land was already an old one, when in 623 Pope Gregory I commissioned the first hospital in Jerusalem specifically to care for pilgrims. A mere nine years had passed since the Persians had massacred the city's Christian population, and the Persians were still in control, but it seems that the pilgrims nonetheless continued to come in devotion-fuelled waves. Heraclius, the crusading Byzantine emperor, had already set in motion his military plan to recapture Jerusalem, which he did with great fanfare in 630, securing the True Cross and other holy objects which were to be of good use in future Christian military campaigns. Heraclius' triumph, however, lasted just eight years; in 638 Umar, the third caliph of Islam, took the surrender of the city from the Byzantine Greeks after Muslim forces inflicted a stunning defeat on the Byzantine-Roman army at Yarmuk. News of the disaster had spread from Byzantine Constantinople, rippling across the nobilities of Europe and sowing the seed of an idea that the site of Christ's Passion, the par excellence node and focus of the Christian faith, needed to be clawed back from the unbelievers. There were, however, many far simpler folk in the West who, ignorant of wars and power politics, wished for the sake of their own souls to make the pilgrimage to Jerusalem and see for themselves where so many of the gripping stories of the Bible had been played out. Many, if not most, hoped to atone for sins. The poorer non-nobles, especially, would have had little interest in the politics of revenge. They cared little who was in charge in Palestine; their concern was to make the hazardous journey safely – and if it involved hardship, so much the better – and return with a feeling of a religious duty done. Back home, they could proudly call themselves palmers – i.e. entitled to wear crossed palm leaves from Palestine as a sign of what they had done, rather in the fashion of a campaign medal.

The papal hospital set up in the early seventh century was still standing in Jerusalem about 800, when Charlemagne added a library to it. (The French Crusaders would later cite Charlemagne as their legitimation for intervening in the region.)[3] For the next 200 years the flow of pilgrims continued unchecked, apparently undeterred by chronic political instability and the Muslim presence. The Holy Land fell under the control of the Fatimids, a Shia Muslim dynasty headquartered in Egypt. In 1005 the mad Fatimid caliph al-Hakim ordered the hospital destroyed, along with much of Jerusalem itself.

The origins of what would become the Knights Hospitaller of the Order of Saint John are shrouded in obscurity. The mists part around 1047, when Muslim visitors took note of at least one hospital operating in Jerusalem and applying medical principles common in the Islamic world but yet unknown in the West. It was about this time that a group of merchants from Amalfi in southern Italy set up a new pilgrims' hospice in Jerusalem; we are given the name of one Maurus who took the actual initiative and may have been inspired by both miracula and an awareness of the superiority of Islamic medicine.[4] The pilgrim trade was a windfall for Italian shipping companies, which may help account for the Amalfitan merchants' solicitude, though to be fair, none of our sources hints that their motives were anything but altruistic. The exact date in which the hospice was set up – on the site of the former Monastery of John the Baptist – is a matter of dispute, though it was certainly sometime between 1048 and 1070. The institution took the form of an adjunct to the Monastery of the Virgin Mary, staffed by Benedictine monks, which the Italians had built in the Christian quarter of the city.

The Amalfitan merchants needed permission from Caliph Ali al-Zahir, the head of the Egypt-based Fatimid dynasty that ruled the Muslim domains of which Jerusalem was a part. The caliph, troubled by political unrest in the Muslim world, cultivated good relations with the Christian Byzantines, which was probably how the Amalfitans had no trouble getting his permission. Besides, the Italian town of Amalfi itself was under Byzantine control at the time. For several decades the hospice operated unspectacularly but effectively, until the advent of the First Crusade at the end of the eleventh century.

The ultimate causes of the Crusades – that 'Two Hundred Years' War for the soul of man and the profits of trade'[5] – are too complex to go into here and would need several books the size of this one. But for the average bored and young western European noble with a horse and longing for adventure, what mattered was that pilgrims were bringing shocking tales back from the Holy Land telling of innocent Christians being slaughtered. In 1064 a terrible incident had occurred when Bedouin brigands had set upon a caravan of some 7,000 Dutch and German pilgrims under Arnold, the Bishop of Bamberg, and butchered two thirds of them; those who had swallowed their gold to protect it were robbed anyway by being disembowelled. The atrocity had occurred literally as the caravan had reached its destination and was before the walls of Jerusalem.[6] There was also the story of Fulk, Count of Anjou, who made the pilgrimage in atonement for burning his adulterous wife in her wedding dress, and Earl Sweyn Godwinson, the brother of England's King Harold, who made the long journey in barefoot penitence after raping an abbess: both incidentally perished en route.

By about 1070 there was more cause for concern, as power in the Muslim world passed into the hands of a new and vigorous force determined to replace the decaying Fatimids. These were the Seljuk Turks, who had swept out from central Asia and in a few short decades had imposed their will on Persia, Iraq and a great deal of Syria. In 1071 their charismatic sultan, Alp Arslan (or Heroic Lion) had shattered a Byzantine army at Manzikert (in what is now eastern Turkey), placing Constantinople and Christian Europe under direct threat. At about that time Alp Arslan, a devout Sunni Muslim, sent his general Atsiz to wrest Jerusalem from the heretic Shia Fatimids.

Respecting Jerusalem as a Muslim holy place, Atsiz preferred to starve the city into surrendering rather than shed blood. This aim duly accomplished, he set out for some mopping up operations in Egypt, but a Jewish-led uprising in the city soon called him back. This time Atsiz was in no mood for mercies. After the ladies of his harem conveniently opened the gates for him, he set his Asian nomads to murder and rob indiscriminately. One eyewitness marked 'a strange and cruel people, girt with garments of many colours, capped with helmets black and red'. Lip service to Sunni Islam these men may have paid, but it didn't prevent them from slaying at least 3,000 of their co-religionists, many of whom had taken refuge in mosques. 'They were not men but beasts', wrote the same observer. Besides burning every crop and cutting down every tree in sight, 'they despoiled the graves and threw out the bones … inflame[d] themselves with males, cut off ears and noses'.[7] Such descriptions of this new and alarming people, the Turks, were certainly embellished as they spread westward.

The idea of a Christian holy war to rectify this lamentable state of affairs was not a new one. The Byzantine Empire, in fact, had been constantly absorbed in trying to keep the Holy Land free from Persian and then Muslim control for at least 700 years, ever since Emperor Constantine the Great had sent his devout mother Helena to Jerusalem (then officially called Aelia Capitolina) to retrieve the True Cross and remodel the city into the supreme Christian sanctuary. Many generations of Byzantine emperors had fought, often personally, to maintain it. But by the late eleventh century Byzantine power had waned considerably, ceding more and more ground to Islam. About 1001 Pope Sylvester II had sent a small seaborne expedition to Syria, but nothing seems to have come of it. Some seventy years later Pope Gregory VII signalled that he heartily endorsed Byzantine pleas for military help when he said he 'would rather expose [his] life in delivering the holy places' than rule the world.

Then, in 1088, an extremely capable French Benedictine monk named Eudes (or Odo) de Lagery was elected to the throne of Saint Peter as Pope Urban II. Seven years into his pontificate, the French pontiff received a visit from legates of Byzantine Emperor Alexios I Komnenos who was seriously worried about losing any more territory to the Muslims and needed western aid. It was something of a climbdown for the Byzantine Greeks, who forty years before had split with the western Christian church after intractable quarrels over doctrine and above all the claims of Rome's popes to rule Christendom. The Greeks' vivid descriptions of Turkish atrocities (no doubt embellished for the occasion) reduced some of their hearers to tears. The animosity between what were now the Roman Catholic and Greek Orthodox churches was put aside (albeit temporarily) as Urban signalled his support for a joint Christian war against the Muslims. Urban, however, thought over the whole issue very carefully. On the one hand, the Holy Land was a long way for European armies and navies to travel; but on the other, an expedition there might well give legions of unruly Frankish and Norman nobles something to channel their warlike instincts into. Besides, the pope would be in the favourable position of being owed something by the Byzantines.

One cold day in November 1095 Urban addressed a crowd of thousands in the fields of Clermont in Auvergne. In what has been called 'the most influential speech in mediaeval history',[8] he let rip: 'An accursed race, wholly alienated from God, has violently invaded the lands of [the Greek] Christians ... They destroy the altars, after having defiled them with their uncleanliness.' After flattering those nobles present to the effect that God had 'conferred remarkable glory in arms, great bravery and strength' on the Franks, he appealed for a great and united effort by them to liberate and cleanse 'the Holy Sepulchre of Our Lord and Saviour, now held by unclean nations'. Having stirred up his listeners' emotions to fever pitch, the pope then made several cogent practical points. The civil strife that had plagued France, he claimed, was because the land 'too narrow for your large population [and] scarcely furnishes enough food for its cultivators'. In a formula employed by leaders in all ages to justify aggression, he held out an idealized image of the waiting Jerusalem, 'a land fruitful above all others, a paradise of delights', of which anyone could partake while being assured of 'imperishable glory in the Kingdom of Heaven'.

It was a powerful multi-layered message which at once struck home; cries of '*Deus li volt!*' ('God wills it!') rent the air. According to William of Malmesbury, nobles fell to their knees, followed by thousands of commoner folk prepared to be born into a new and purified life of fighting for God. For two years Urban toured France, the era's equivalent of a media star. When he returned to Rome, even the cynical Romans were swayed. He got busy organizing what in essence was a religious army in which noble officer and common soldier alike were freed from all social and financial obligations, including taxes. He emptied the jails of volunteers and promised those who fell against the infidel total remission of earthly sins. Ridiculous tales, purportedly originating in the East, told how Muhammad the Prophet had suffered an epileptic fit and been eaten by pigs. Others, rather more eagerly palatable, told of curvaceous dusky women and Arab gold waiting to reward the bold and intrepid. It was this potent admixture of devotion, simplicity and greed that pervaded the hearts and minds of the thousands who flocked to the banners of Urban's great army which prepared to set sail in August 1096.

In the meantime, what were the nascent Hospitallers in Jerusalem doing? Far from what was being perfervidly imagined in the West, the Seljuk Turkish rulers were not quite the monsters depicted in Urban's lurid narratives. We gather this from the fact that in 1081 a hospice for women pilgrims was allowed to be set up not far from the original Amalfitan facility, followed by another one for men only, under the protection of the Church of Santa Maria Latina. The Turks may have favoured the Latin institutions at the expense of the Greek Orthodox Church of the Holy Sepulchre which was too associated with the immediate enemy Byzantium, and when the more tolerant Fatimids recovered control of Jerusalem sometime in the 1090s, the hospices' survival seemed assured. The carers' way of life, described as 'semi-religious', was widely respected. At about the time the First Crusade had come within reach of Jerusalem, the only Christians whom the Muslim authorities did not banish from the city were the guardians of the hospices, headed by a devout man named Gerard.

The Blessed Gerard, as he is most often referred to, was most likely an Italian or Lombard. His surname is unknown, though we do know that he was not of noble stock and not overly impressive in appearance. The Muslims of Jerusalem, though tolerating his presence, had grievously mistreated him; a Crusader found him disfigured with 'scars of the chains that had pierced his feet and hands ... to the point at which he had lost the use of the greater part of his limbs'.[9] Yet the untiring efforts of this purported wreck of a man were 'the seed from which the Order of Hospitallers grew'.[10] And it was in that embryonic state when the 30,000 mostly Frankish troops of the First Crusade under Duke Godfrey of Bouillon, after three years of marching and fighting, stormed Jerusalem on 15 July 1099 after a forty-day resistance by the Muslims. The 1,000-strong Fatimid garrison was slaughtered by various means such as beheading, burning or being forced to hurl themselves off the great walls. In an all-too-common symptom of ancient and mediaeval warfare, babies were snatched from their mothers and dashed against walls. Seventy thousand Muslim non-combatants were butchered; the Jews were burned alive. The streets were choked with heaps of severed heads and feet. 'Wonderful things', exulted a clergyman in the Crusader army.

One wonders what Gerard's view would have been. He certainly must have witnessed the horrors, for he remained in charge when a week after the carnage the Crusaders set up the Latin Kingdom of Jerusalem and persuaded the devout and unassuming Godfrey of Bouillon to govern the state as Defender of the Holy Sepulchre. What remained of the Greek clergy was exiled, and Jerusalem slid under the direct rule of the pope. To his credit, Godfrey refused the title of king in the city that he insisted belonged only to Christ the King; but within a year he was dead and his younger brother Baldwin had no such moral scruples, styling himself King Baldwin I in 1100.

The concept of a fighting priest or monk seems to have been a uniquely western European one. The Byzantine Greeks, who were not ones to romanticize war, certainly found them oddly menacing. Anna Komnene, the daughter of Emperor Alexios I Komnenos, was horrified by the number of armed priests among the First Crusaders who, swarming into Constantinople on their way east, had no respect for the Orthodox faith or anything else beyond their narrow vision – 'a plague of locusts', she called them.[11] On the contrary, the Blessed Gerard and his co-workers steadfastly laboured along the lines of a devastatingly simple and noble ideal, that 'because every poor man and woman was Christ, he or she should not just have good treatment, but the best and most luxurious treatment possible'. Thus they admitted needy Muslims and Jews as well as Christians.[12]

For the rest of the twelfth century, the Latin Kingdom of Jerusalem, and similar Frankish-ruled portions of Middle Eastern territory dubbed the County of Tripoli, the Principality of Antioch and the County of Edessa, all ruled by French nobles, made up what was called Outremer (Beyond The Sea). From the tip of the Red Sea at Aqaba to what is now southeast Turkey, Outremer served also as the papal outpost of power in the eastern Mediterranean. Its importance to the West was both political and commercial: to keep at bay Muslim forces while building up a brisk trading network at which the Italian maritime states were becoming the masters. The Byzantine Empire to the north was tolerated, though many Crusaders made no secret of their hope of some day dragging the Orthodox Greeks, too, into the papal fold.

All, of course, was not sweetness and light in Outremer. Baldwin I, besides having to personally conduct actions against either the Seljuk Turks or the Fatimids of Egypt for almost every year of his reign, also was answerable to his barons, who were in turn jealous of their compatriots in charge of the other principalities. Clashes among them were frequent as they vied for resources and trade advantages. The king's senior clergy made clear that they owed allegiance only to the pope and no one else. The Italians demanded, and got, control of the ports of Ascalon, Jaffa, Acre, Tyre and Beirut. The local people, Christian and Muslim alike, were often so oppressed by the French nobility that many native Christians were inclined to look back on Muslim rule as a golden age.[13]

It was the nobility who provided the bulk of what were soon to become a corps of military monks. The Jerusalem hospices seemed to be a natural magnet for such men. Just how the peaceable charity of the Blessed Gerard took on an armed, quasi-military character in a mere twenty or so years remains vague; it must have been a gradual process growing out of the very practical need for an armed corps to guard incoming pilgrims from attack by bandits. The guardians of the hospices assumed an automatic 'right of legitimate' defence against any Muslim hostility.[14] The Order also seems to have benefited from donations and leases of horses, servants and weapons in previous years.[15] In those days, it would appear, the boundary between peaceable and warlike activities was far less well-defined that it is now. One might easily blend into the other as circumstances demanded.[16]

As early as 1102 Baldwin I is reported as seizing the port of Jaffa with 'some ninety knights and rather more mounted sergeants', bolstered by a piece of the True Cross. That same year the 'miserly and corrupt' Daimbert of Pisa, the Latin Patriarch of Jerusalem, was formally accused of persecuting Orthodox Christians and embezzling funds entrusted to him for the upkeep of the Jerusalem Hospital and 'the soldiers of Christ'. By 1110 King Baldwin's knights had assumed a political as well as military importance; in that year a body of them had appeared before Edessa, 'banners waving and armour gleaming in the sun', to scare off the Muslim warlord Mawdud who was threatening the city, and seemed to have a say in the final arrangements for the governance of Edessa.[17]

The Blessed Gerard was respected enough by Jerusalem's new rulers to receive generous endowments of money and property. The picture becomes clearer in 1113 when Pope Paschal II formally mustered the knights of the hospital – by now known also as the Knights of Saint John – into a formal order. The Hospitallers' second Grand Master, Raymond du Puy, is credited with giving the order a military role, that of being prepared to keep open the pilgrim routes from the coast. About 1120, two years after the Blessed Gerard's death, the Knights Hospitaller proper had emerged, dedicated to chastity, obedience and the military protection of Christians. At about this time, too, the original patron Saint John the Evangelist was subtly replaced by his namesake John the Almsgiver.[18] The Hospitallers would almost certainly have formed part of Baldwin's expedition – 500 knights and double that number of infantry – to relieve Kafartab Castle in Syria under threat from another Muslim warlord in 1115. The mere demonstration of strength was enough to make the Muslims withdraw.

The Knights of Saint John very soon had imitators. In 1118 Baldwin I sickened and died on campaign, to be succeeded by his cousin Baldwin II. Then 'certain noble men of knightly rank', William of Tyre writes, 'religious men, devoted to God and fearing Him', got together under the leadership of two knights, the Burgundian Hugh de Payens and Geoffrey de Saint Omer, and laid before the new king of Jerusalem a plan for a permanent military corps whose duties were, in addition to aiding the constant stream of pilgrims and protecting them against local threats, to defend Outremer itself. As these knights – probably eight or nine in the beginning – lived in the south wing of the royal palace near the ruins of the Temple of Solomon, once the royal permission had been secured, they styled themselves the

Mendicant Soldiers of the Temple of Solomon, soon shortened to Knights of the Temple, or simply the Templars.

Presumably this occurred with the full knowledge of the Hospitallers, though from the outset there was a subtle difference in specialization, a difference that was to become far more marked and trigger much rivalry and sometimes outright conflict. But in 1120 there seemed to be little such prospect, and Baldwin II, a battle-scarred former Count of Edessa who had adopted a few Turkish customs to ingratiate himself with the Muslim locals, eagerly endorsed the new Templar order, whose members took solemn oaths of 'perpetual poverty, chastity and obedience'. While the Hospitallers adopted black tunics with white crosses below the left shoulder, the Templars wore white with a red cross. The two colour schemes may have had a semiotic value. The Hospitallers' black was more in line with their charitable and holy work, emphasizing their self-perception as fighting monks, whereas the Templars' white and red could be seen as putting the military element first, as monkish fighters.

While the Templars proceeded to vigorously build up their order through recruitment and converting Islamic shrines into Christian places of worship, the Hospitallers mostly stuck to their own quarter south of the Holy Sepulchre. Their main hostel grew to include some 1,000 beds, staffed by four senior doctors who checked on their patients twice a day, including carrying out blood and urine tests. Any new mother in need received a bed. But the toilets – perhaps wisely in that age – were outside, so every patient who could walk was given a sheepskin coat and boots to be able to answer the calls of nature without undue discomfort in winter.[19] As for Baldwin II, he had little time to consolidate his rule before he had to rush north to Antioch to ward off an offensive by a Turkish warlord. He won the ensuing encounter – helped by the presence of the True Cross borne before him in a jewelled box – but was later captured. He spent two years as a Turkish prisoner before being ransomed in 1125.

There had long been a lurking philosophical difficulty in how to combine Christianity's insistence on peace with the practice of war. Sir Steven Runciman has stated the issue succinctly:

The Christian citizen has a fundamental problem to face; is he entitled to fight for his country? His religion is a religion of peace; and war means slaughter and destruction. The earlier Christian Fathers had no doubts. To them a war was wholesale murder. But after the triumph of the Cross, after the [Roman] Empire had become Christendom, ought not its citizens to be ready to take up arms for its welfare?[20]

The average knight is unlikely to have thought very deeply about this issue or, if he had, would have been reassured by various clergy that since heathens were something less than normal human beings, one could kill them without fear of sin. In fact there was no lack of manufactured religious justification for the Knights' militancy and readiness to shed blood. The effect of the First Crusade certainly made up many wavering minds. Like the Late Roman Emperor Constantine the Great 800 years before, the Crusaders discovered that fighting for Christ worked. The strictures and morals of early Christianity, as enshrined in the New Testament, closely resembled military-type discipline in their ultimate aim for an ordered world. After all, had not Christ Himself warned that He had come 'not to send peace but a sword?' and advised His disciples to sell their clothes if necessary to buy a sword for the tough times that would lie ahead?[21] Evil had to be fought, and physically if necessary. Further confirmation was found in Timothy 2:3–4: 'Thou therefore endure hardness as a good soldier of Jesus Christ. No man that warreth entangleth himself with the affairs of this life; that he may please him who hath chosen him to be a soldier.' It seemed to many to be the only honourable course out of the corruption and trickery of the world.

Biblical examples notwithstanding, the question of whether any religion can justify warfare is a vast one, and cannot be gone into here. Edward Gibbon tackled the issue by seriously doubting that 'the servants of the Prince of Peace would unsheathe the sword of destruction unless the motive were pure, the quarrel legitimate and the necessity inevitable'.[22] Of course, countless times the Scriptures have been wilfully misinterpreted to serve cynically secular and greedy motives, and the Crusades were no exception. Holy wars throughout the ages have always been accompanied by definitely unholy practices. The rationale has been that unbelievers or heretics have forfeited normal human rights of life and liberty, and therefore they deserve to get what is coming to them. Yet many who took the cross were tortured by doubt, until leading churchmen themselves told them they were doing right.

The Templars and Hospitallers had different ways of going about the contradictory tasks of caring and killing. The former came under the sway of the Cistercian monastic order founded by Bernard of Clairvaux in 1098. A man of vigorous and wide-ranging intelligence, Bernard insisted on a back-to-basics regime of austerity and simplicity that spread through Europe like a brush fire, claiming even popes as adherents. The Hospitallers, by contrast, hewed more to Saint Augustine's thinking, with its emphasis on personal responsibility for salvation and good works. Both, however, would have agreed with Bernard of Clairvaux that a 'reborn pure knighthood' in the service of Christ was the apex of masculine human achievement. To Bernard, action was better than thinking. More controversially, he asserted that 'the Christian glories in the death of the pagan, because Christ is thereby glorified'.[23] Himself incapacitated by chronic intestinal disease, he believed he was doing with his oratory what should be done with the sword. As Bernard's order of Cistercians gained a rapid following throughout Europe, it fed a larger potential reservoir of recruits for the Military Orders.

The Templars inaugurated their fighting career with forays from Antioch into Muslim-held Armenia; yet the Hospitallers were by no means stagnant. The Blessed Gerard died in 1120, to be succeeded as Grand Master by Raymond du Puy, a more recognizable military-style figure. In 1128 Geoffrey de Flugeac, a Crusader knight, gave them the Qalansuwa Castle on the coast north of Arsuf. This was followed by the acquisition of Bayt Jibrin in the high ground between Ascalon and the Dead Sea, donated by King Fulk, who had succeeded Baldwin II in 1131. The donations came with a thick string attached – that they be fortified. So if there had been any doubts before, the Hospitallers were now a serious military organization.[24]

At this stage the Knights of Saint John were by no means all from the knightly class; there were all manner of men, even freed serfs, who could get together the expense needed for equipment, horse and travel. An ambitious teenager could enlist as a novitiate, in the hope of becoming a full Hospitaller brother after a minimum three years. Those who actually made the eastward journey were the younger and fitter men, and those with a taste for adventure, who nonetheless were always a minority in the Order; the bulk of members stayed in Europe in the Priories that were being set up in several countries (see Chapter 11 below). Some romantic souls actually hoped for martyrdom while wearing the black tunic with the white cross, though anyone who demonstrably was running from the law or debts was debarred from joining up. And once a Hospitaller, always a Hospitaller; one couldn't resign.

The Hospitallers by now had become, along with their Templar rivals, the most reliable military units of Outremer. We hear of a knight named Gerard Jebarre being sent on a secret mission to England in 1136 to retrieve a Norman noble, Raymond of Poitiers, and install him as ruler of Antioch.[25] The Hospitallers took a further step in the militarization process in 1140, when Pope Innocent II issued his encyclical *Quam amabilis deo*, which formally assigned them the duty of defending the faith:

> The Sick are being administered a thousand kinds of services of charity. Those who are harmed by manifold constraints and dangers are getting back their old vigour, and in order to enable them to visit the places which were sanctified by the life of our Lord Jesus Christ on earth, the brethren of this house [are] always prepared to risk their life for their brothers [pilgrims] from the attacks of the infidels on their way to and fro ... These are the people whom God uses to cleanse the Oriental Church from the dirt of the infidels and to fight the enemies of the Christian name.

Based on this document, the Hospitallers were encouraged to widen their troop base by recruiting more sergeants and ordinary soldiers. The *Quam amabilis deo* enabled the order to gradually remedy a shortage of military manpower in Outremer which, despite its Frankish rule, was still a hazardous place in which to travel, as the papal encyclical points out. The dry and hilly route inland from the Mediterranean coast (corresponding roughly to the modern highway linking Tel Aviv with Jerusalem) was infested with bandits and many were the Western pilgrims who came to grief there, when their journey was almost over. But besides protecting the pilgrims, the Knights of Saint John had set their sights on a wider strategy.

For the Crusader states of Outremer to survive, their vulnerable spots had to be secured and plugged. One of these was the Buqaiah Valley between Mount Lebanon and the Syrian coast. Besides serving as a fertile food source, the valley contained the main trading route between the coast farther south and the Arab cities of Damascus and Emesa (Homs). Trade routes, however, could double as military routes, and control of the so-called Buqaiah Gap was a key security concern. With Arab-held Emesa a definite threat in the north, a fortification was required that would safeguard trader and soldier alike. Thus was built the mighty Krak des Chevaliers – still arguably the most formidable castle in the world – run by the Hospitallers as the administrative and military centre of a semi-autonomous enclave in the County of Tripoli.

Both Military Orders were by this time consolidating their internal rules and structures. It has been written that though 'each hated the other religiously',[26] their practices and chains of command were similar enough. For a while the Templars followed Bernard of Clairvaux's injunctions to cut their hair short and avoid bathing; those practices were soon honoured more in the breach than the observance, though Bernard's orders to eliminate 'pagans' were enthusiastically internalized. It was also the indefatigable Bernard who was a key mover in the resurgence of anti-Muslim feeling in Europe that was to trigger the Second Crusade. The hardships of the First Crusade a half-century before were forgotten – a new knightly generation now chafed at the bit for its slice of glory. They flocked anew to the banners in 1146 after Bernard delivered a mesmerizing speech at Vézelay in the presence of France's King Louis VII, who himself took the cross, to be followed by German Emperor Conrad III who also fell under the spell of Bernard's silver tongue. These new Crusaders, unlike the first wave, would find disciplined corps of military monks awaiting to add their service in the Holy Land.

Gibbon's view of the importance of the Military Orders in their early years is worth quoting at length:

> The firmest bulwark of Jerusalem was founded on the Knights of the Hospital of St. John, and of the Temple of Solomon; on the strange association of a monastic and military life … The flower of the nobility of Europe aspired to wear the cross, and to profess the vows, of these respectable orders; their spirit and discipline were immortal; and the speedy donation of twenty-eight thousand farms, or manors, enabled them to support a regular force of cavalry and infantry for the defence of Palestine … But in their most dissolute period the knights of the hospital and temple maintained their fearless and fanatic character: they neglected to live, but were prepared to die, in the service of Christ.[27]

Before the middle of the twelfth century, the Military Orders had become the first professional and disciplined combat units to appear in Europe and Palestine since the era of the Roman legions.

Chapter 3

Europe and the Middle East in the Twelfth Century

Knighthood in Europe – French kings – advance of the papacy under Gregory VII – Hospitallers in Spain – Byzantium – Fatimids and Seljuks – the Latin Kingdom of Jerusalem

Therefore did He lay down the law that a man accused might uphold his cause by battle, and God Himself fights for the innocent in such a combat.

The above sentence is from *The Romance of Tristan and Iseult*, an early thirteenth century romance penned by Gottfried of Strasbourg and the Anglo-Norman poet Thomas. Referring to the hero Tristan's decision to do battle for his king, it perfectly encapsulates the knightly ideal of fighting for right with God on one's side. It wasn't a uniquely French concept by any means, but in France it seems to have found its most fervent expression. It is no historical accident that all the twelfth century Hospitaller grand masters after the Blessed Gerard were Frankish in origin, as their names attest. And despite the first centuries spent in Outremer, the Knights Hospitaller were always conscious of being Europeans in ethnicity, language and religion. But what was the Europe of the twelfth century, and how did its history and institutions determine who the Knights of Saint John were?

The institution of knighthood itself was in full flower. The knight, in short, was the smallest and most basic unit of the defence of homeland and law and order. Long before standing national armies and regular police forces, it was the knight and his retinue who were responsible for maintaining the order of feudal society where social class boundaries were strictly defined and rarely crossed. The ideals and practices of chivalry grew out of a mixture of Germanic military initiation customs, Saracen influences from Persia, Syria and Spain, and Christian devotion to duty. The details of knighthood varied in Europe, from Spain to Byzantium, but in England they attained their most precise structure.

A knight was almost invariably of aristocratic and landowning birth, and preferably an elder son who would inherit the family title and lands; younger sons, however, could become knights if they struck out on their own, for example, going to join the Hospitallers or Templars. Training for the knighthood took years. At age seven or eight a future knight would become a page; six or seven years later he would be promoted to squire. This involved being a servant to a lord, including being at the lord's side in battle, rather like an orderly. During that period the squire would receive rigorous military training, and at some point in his late teens he would undergo the coveted ritual: after a symbolic purification bath he would put on a white tunic (for moral purity), a red robe (for the blood he should not hesitate to shed in the fight for honour and God) and a black coat (for the death before which he must not flinch). This would be followed by a day-long fast and a night spent awake in church, praying and confessing his sins.

On the following day, after receiving communion and listening to a sermon on the sacred duties of a knight, he would walk to the altar with a sword hanging from his neck. The priest would take the sword, bless it, and put it back where it was. The young man would then turn to the lord he had so far been serving – a kind of sponsor – and the lord (perhaps with a deliberately stern expression) would ask the ceremonial question: 'For what purpose do you desire to enter the order? If to be rich, to take your ease, and be held in honour without doing honour to knighthood, you are unworthy of it, and would be to the knighthood what the simoniacal clerk is to the prelacy.'

It was a classic leading question, and of course the candidate must have carefully and painstakingly rehearsed his reply for days beforehand. The question, however, was a healthy reminder that a knight's privileges should not be abused, as a 'simoniacal' priest – that is, an insincere one who paid for his post – would do in the profession of the Church. The proper reply duly given, the candidate was dressed in a new suit of armour and given golden spurs. Then the sponsoring lord would deliver the accolade – three soft blows with the flat of the sword on the neck or shoulder. Sometimes the lord might slap the candidate on the cheek, as the last affront the younger man might receive without the right to hit back. 'In the name of God' (and whoever the relevant saints might be in France and England), the lord continued, 'I make (or dub) thee knight.' The newly-minted knight would receive a new lance, helmet and horse, and ride home through the congratulations of all present to throw a party.[1]

Whether these elaborate ceremonies, especially involving the golden spurs, took place as described in the spare and dusty Middle East is open to question. There was certainly plenty of chivalry and sense of honour on the Muslim side, and it could be argued that the knights in Outremer adopted some of that example and influenced their fellows back home in western Europe. Chivalry could, and often did, descend into barbarism; jousting, a favourite sport in which two knights on horseback would charge each other full tilt with lances levelled, often resulted in considerable fatalities – it was actually banned by the Church, but few took any notice. Christianity moderated the more savage instincts of the knight; women, too, had a civilizing effect on their men in armour, who found an added incentive to be valorous in battle in order to be admired by the ladies.

France, the physical and cultural origin of the Hospitallers, was reviving as a political power in the twelfth century after a long period of weakness. There were several major signs of this. The Frenchman Urban II became pope, reflecting the growing importance of the French nobles. These men had ruled aggressively independent regions, all but ignoring the weak kings of the Capetian house whose real authority was limited to the tiny area around Paris. It was Philip I (1060–1108) who broke out of that vice and brought more of France under royal control, followed by his corpulent but very energetic son Louis VI 'the Fat' (1108–1137). Despite his size, Louis personally saw to it that the bumptious nobles – little better than robber barons – toed his line at the point of his sword.

A king who took his duties seriously had no time for leisure in that violent age. Year after year this 'ironclad judge' heaved his great weight into the saddle and rode forth to defend the clergy, the weak, and the oppressed. His life was one long battle against feudal tyranny and rebellion, filled with sieges of castles and hand-to-hand fighting, in which the king himself, in his egg-shaped steel helmet and chain mail, swung as lusty a sword as any knight in his army.[2] We see at once in Louis the Fat the ideal of the Military Orders warrior (except perhaps for the appearance).

Louis also had his hands full with the English, who by mid-century owned more than three times as much French land as the French monarchy did. The growing English threat, ironically, drew the French nobles closer to the royal cause, yet after Louis VI's death they reverted to their independent ways under the mild and saintly Louis VII (1137–1180). After the abortive adventure of the Second Crusade (see below), Louis' remaining years were absorbed in fending off the English who had forged a marriage alliance with the French house of Anjou and through their new King Henry II vastly increased their holdings in France proper. But Louis' personal life was a shambles. 'I married a king only to find him a monk!' exclaimed his wife Eleanor of Aquitaine, acting on her disappointment by divorcing him and marrying Henry II, who had more power and territory.

If Louis VII lacked his father's raw and ruthless energy, he seems to have inherited his talent for defending the oppressed and dispensing justice. He didn't hesitate to call unruly nobles, even the most powerful, to his palace to answer for their misdeeds. All who favoured peace and order, including the Church, were on the king's side. He was a pillar of strength for Pope Alexander III, who was having his troubles with the Holy Roman Empire, raising the moral prestige of the French kings. In internal administration he leaned heavily on a senior clergyman, Abbot Suger of Saint Denis, who combined military judgement with sound theology. Yet in the end Louis VII was virtually a one-man show, though his example undoubtedly boosted the recruitment of men who would eventually become Knights Hospitaller.

The spiritual centre of western Europe was papal Rome, which by the early twelfth century had overcome a period of weakness and degradation and under a series of vigorous popes had reasserted its old authority. The process had begun with the German monk Hildebrand, who had become pope under the name Gregory VII in 1073. By sheer force of character Gregory had forced the Holy Roman Empire to recognize the principle that only he, the pope, had authority to appoint bishops and other clergy throughout the empire. His rationale was that since the divine authority is superior to the mere worldly, that principle ought to prevail as well in relationships among powers and leaders. In Gregory's view, pope outranked emperor.

The Holy Roman emperor, of course, chose to view this as a naked contest for power which, stripped of its religious window-dressing, it essentially was. And as such, no emperor worth his crown could take this challenge sitting down. Henry IV, who had become emperor at the age of six in 1056, had since grown up to be a character quite as strong-willed as Gregory and fully resolved to be the boss in Germany and Italy, the main territories of the empire. The pope, however, rather got the better of the struggle; in the winter of 1077 Henry was forced to display his penitence by standing barefoot in the snow for three days in front of the Italian castle where the pope was staying, as a confessed sinner against His Holiness.

But after that little tableau of drama Henry reverted to his old ways, which forced Gregory to depose him, triggering a sordid chapter in papal history where the empire appointed anti-popes as rivals to the official ones.

After some confusion Urban II took the throne of Saint Peter, attempting to unify Christendom, as we have seen, by sponsoring the First Crusade. In 1106 Henry IV died, to be succeeded by his son Henry V, who continued his father's hard line against Rome. It wasn't until 1122 that both sides could calm down enough for a clumsy compromise known as the Concordat of Worms that could satisfy both church and state. But the papacy had been the gainer by it all. It sponsored the great feudal family of the Guelfs who, battling their pro-imperial rivals, the Ghibellines, were to plunge Germany and Italy into many decades of civil and social strife. It's not hard to imagine a German or north Italian noble knight of an idealistic bent being turned off by such chronic squabbling within European Christendom and preferring to migrate to the East where the battle lines between good and evil seemed to be much more clearly drawn – in the Holy Land.

The Hospitallers were by no means confined to France and Outremer. In the twelfth century we find them going on the offensive in Spain against their Muslim mirror image, the Murabits, a religious military brotherhood founded in Senegal whose members wore veils over their lower faces. The Murabits, whose ranks were boosted by Tuaregs and black Africans, founded the city of Marrakesh in Tunisia and by the early twelfth century had become the masters of southern Spain with their capital at Seville. Relations with King Alfonso VIII of Leon and Castile seem to have been respectful enough and the cultural interaction vigorous, until a Christian adventurer named Rodrigo Diaz de Bivar dedicated his life to driving the Muslims out, in a long campaign known as the *reconquista*, or reconquest.

The name by which this warrior is known to history – El Cid, a corruption of the Arabic *sayid*, or noble lord – illustrates the respect in which he was held even by his foes. In fact, in the 1080s he had no hesitation in serving Muslim and Christian paymasters indiscriminately. He was also not above committing atrocities if it served his purpose; on capturing Valencia he had its chief justice burned alive and only with difficulty was persuaded to spare the judge's wife and daughters from the same fate. Yet at his death in 1099 he was revered as a wise and just administrator, a model for any aspiring Military Order knight and an enduring heroic legend for the Spaniards. The epic *Cantar de mio Cid* has been described as 'one of the grandest and oldest Spanish poems';[3] his bones at Burgos are still revered as those of a saint. By the time of El Cid's death the *reconquista* was well and truly underway, a promising field for the first Iberian Hospitaller knights.

There was one Europe-based power, however, that had already had 500 years' experience battling the Muslim tide. That was the Byzantine

Empire, a mighty Christian state that had grown and mutated out of the late Roman Empire and by the twelfth century controlled what are now Greece and the southern Balkans, parts of southern Italy and all of what is now Turkey. Its mighty capital of Constantinople, situated at the geographic meeting point of Europe and Asia, was the greatest metropolis of its time. Byzantium was now a Greek rather than a Roman empire, and fiercely committed to defending Orthodox Christianity against the Muslims to the east and south, and the Catholics to the west.

At the time of the First Crusade the emperor of Byzantium was the capable Alexios I Komnenos, who indeed had been the main inspiration for Pope Urban II's call for action. But when Alexios heard that the crusade was underway, he was appalled. Freeing Jerusalem and the Holy Land from the Muslims, he believed, was the job of Christian Byzantium, not the heretical Franks. In fact, he was on the point of trying it himself. Alexios had hopes of enlisting Frankish volunteers in the Byzantine forces, but once he personally caught sight of the first ragged crusaders led by Peter the Hermit on 1 August 1096, and heard of the rape and looting they were committing, he changed his mind and hastily shooed them on their way into Asia Minor, where they came to a tragic end at the hands of the Seljuk Turks. Alexios may well have smiled ruefully at the news; not for one moment did he believe the Frankish Crusaders to be as morally motivated as they claimed to be. With good reason, he suspected that several Crusader leaders eyed the Byzantine Empire itself. And they kept coming. Another wave – rather more organized – appeared before the great walls of Constantinople at Easter 1097 under Godfrey of Bouillon and his brother Baldwin of Boulogne with undoubted menacing intent. As we have seen, Alexios' daughter Anna Komnene, an eyewitness and historian, expressed a very common Greek view of the knights when she wrote that 'to all appearances they were on pilgrimage to Jerusalem; in reality they planned to dethrone the emperor and seize the capital'.[4] After a severe mauling by crack Byzantine units, both Frenchmen swore oaths of fealty to Alexios, who packed this lot, too, off to the East.

Were the Frankish knights who ostensibly had taken a sacred oath to fight for Christ against the infidel really as cynical and grasping as Anna Komnene relates? If unchanging human nature is any indication, many certainly must have been. As for the rest, they may have had holy motivation when they set out; but the rigours of the campaign would have had a hardening effect on character. Moreover, this was far from an age of comprehensive education, and even the best-disposed knight was at the mercy of Catholic priests who railed in their pulpits against the 'schismatic Greeks' who refused allegiance to the pope. In the blinkered eyes of many a knight or common soldier who had never in his life gone more than a few miles from his rural home, any non-Catholic was worse even than a Muslim (a sentiment, by the way, which the Greeks heartily returned).

At the time of Alexios I the Byzantine army had barely recovered from a stunning defeat at the hands of the Seljuks at Manzikert in 1071. But in the meantime it had been reinforced by Anglo-Saxons who had fled England after the Battle of Hastings in 1066 and enrolled themselves in the emperor's personal guard; the Englishmen's axe-wielding tactics proved very effective against Arab and Bulgarian adversaries. They and a corps of hardy Russian volunteers made up the Varangian Guard that was invariably in the forefront of Byzantium's battles, often plucking victory from seeming defeat. Moreover, there was a good deal of truth in the prevailing Greek opinion of the Crusaders, confirmed when the Frankish domains were set up in Outremer and proved to be quite as grasping and pleasure-loving as any other realm anywhere. For this reason – and Christian doctrinal differences were employed as an excuse – the knights in the Middle East paid little attention to the Byzantine power to the north-west, and therefore Greek aid to the Crusaders was minimal.

When the Military Orders were taking shape in Outremer the dominant Muslim dynasty was that of the Fatimids, who had appeared in Tunisia in 909 and, thanks to an aggressive promotion of Shia Islam, had taken over Egypt. In 969 the leader of the Fatimid forces, Jawhar al-Siqilli (a Sicilian Greek, as his name implies, who had been captured as a slave), laid out a new city on the site of al-Fustat on the Nile, renaming the place al-Qahirah – better known since as Cairo.[5] Jawhar founded a powerful dynasty whose fifth member, abu-Mansur Nizar al-Aziz, brought the Fatimids to the peak of their power.

As is often depressingly the case in history, a wise and capable ruler was succeeded by a cruel and deranged son. Among the atrocities committed by the mad al-Hakim, who succeeded al-Aziz, was the destruction of the Church of the Holy Sepulchre in Jerusalem in 1009 – an event duly noted in western Europe. When al-Hakim had himself proclaimed divine, his sister had him murdered on Muqattam Hill, now in the centre of Cairo. Fortunately, al-Hakim was the exception to the general rule that the Fatimids were tolerant rulers. His young son al-Zahir made a point of improving relations with Byzantine Emperor Constantine VIII whom he allowed to rebuild the Church of the Holy Sepulchre. Al-Zahir's son and successor Ma'dd al-Mustansir enjoyed the longest reign in Fatimid annals –

nearly sixty years – but by his death the writing was clearly on the wall for the dynasty. Syria was breaking away, while the new and worrisome power of the Seljuk Turks was at the gates. The Fatimids managed to hold on to Baghdad, but in Cairo the state mechanism was paralysed under a series of weak caliphs who sat helplessly on their thrones while army factions and ambitious viziers struggled for ascendancy.

The twelfth century opened with a 5-year-old child, al-Amir, on the Fatimid throne. He managed to hang on for twenty-nine years, but in the meantime his authority had shrunk to the area around the caliphal palace. The court itself was a dark maelstrom of intrigue and murder. The Egyptian state essentially withered away; the mass of people, prostrated by repeated famines and plagues, was also overtaxed to feed the legions of greedy soldiers and their puppet caliphs. So when Saladin's army loomed before Cairo in 1171 and swept away the fourteenth and last of the Fatimid caliphs, the 20-year-old al-Adid, it may well have been an act of mercy.

The Seljuks, of whom Saladin was the most accomplished example, were now the dominant ethnic and political group in the region. The first of several Turkish tribes to emerge from central Asia and make themselves at home in the Middle East and parts of south-east Europe, the Seljuks cemented their position by vigorously adopting and upholding Sunni Islam. Indeed, they were seen as the saviours of Islam when they appeared almost out of nowhere, defeating various foes of the Abbasid regime in Baghdad and appearing at the gates of that city in 1055. Their entry was made easy by the fact that the military governor of Baghdad was himself a Turk and Caliph al-Qaim a weakling. The Seljuk commander, Tughril, ensconced himself as sultan (i.e. he with authority), even though he couldn't speak Arabic and had to talk to the puppet caliph through an interpreter.

Tughril, his nephew Alp Arslan and his grand-nephew Malikshah presided over the Seljuks' greatest period. 'The fading glory of Muslim arms [was] revived.'[6] Alp Arslan seized Armenia from the Byzantines, following it up with the crushing victory at Manzikert. For the first time, Muslims gained a foothold in 'the land of the Romans', a foothold that was to expand hugely in coming centuries: Asia Minor has been Turkish ever since. The Seljuks appropriated the pleasant Byzantine city of Ikonion as their capital, renaming it Konieh. But they had not reckoned on the determination of the First Crusaders, who wrested Antioch from the Seljuks, annihilating a Turkish force under Karbuqa after the Christians claimed to have discovered the lance that pierced the crucified Jesus' side. When the Crusaders captured

Jerusalem and inaugurated the realm of Outremer, the Seljuks had their work cut out for them.

Baldwin I was crowned king of Jerusalem on Christmas Day 1100; the ceremony took place at Bethlehem, less for symbolic emotional reasons than the fact that the Latin clergy at first envisaged Jerusalem as a purely ecclesiastical domain untainted by politics.[7] A man of intense energy and strong will, Baldwin may have been gay, a possible explanation for the fact that he had no children.[8] His courage was beyond doubt; on several occasions he personally fought Famitid Egyptian raiders outside Ramallah. Once he saved himself by jumping on his horse and racing to the coast, where he boarded a passing English pirate ship, got off at Jaffa and raised a band of knights – possibly including Hospitallers – to defeat the Egyptians again. In 1104 Baldwin converted the al-Aqsa mosque into his royal palace. Six years later he welcomed the teenage king of Norway, Sigurd, who had landed with sixty ships at Acre, helped Baldwin eject the Muslims from Sidon, and spent the winter in 'Jorsalaborg'. After a reign of almost constant fighting, Baldwin I fell ill while fishing in the Nile and died in 1118.

His successor Baldwin II, five years into his reign, attempted to rescue Antioch from a Muslim threat and was captured, to be ransomed two years later. But his health was not of the best, and in 1131 he abdicated under the burden of illness. Succeeding him was his daughter Melisende, her veteran Crusader husband Fulk of Anjou (a descendant of the bride-burning Fulk) and their infant son Baldwin III. The marriage was doomed from the word go. The thickset, red-headed Fulk was somewhat dull when compared to the slim and clever Melisende, and no one was unduly surprised when word got around that she was having an affair with her good-looking cousin Count Hugh of Jaffa. One day the count was stabbed, though not fatally, while playing dice at a café in Jerusalem. His attacker, however, disclaimed any involvement by Fulk. The execution of the assailant helped defuse tensions, and Melisende's marriage veered back onto the rails. But beyond the confines of the Frankish kingdoms and their intrigues, the Muslims were regrouping.

Chapter 4

Gaining Experience

The Hospitallers in the early twelfth century – Krak des Chevaliers – organization and equipment – the fall of Edessa – the Second Crusade – Byzantine suspicions – Conrad III and Nur ed-Din – siege of Ascalon – the Hospitallers invade Egypt – rise of Saladin

In the reign of Baldwin I of Jerusalem the Knights Hospitaller had assumed their definitive form and had taken part in many of the king's incessant campaigns against the Muslim statelets that separated Jerusalem from the other Frankish principalities as well as the more powerful Seljuk Turks in the north and east. There was thus plenty of scope for action for the more aggressive of the knights who made the journey from western Europe. It was thus in the middle to late twelfth century that weapons and horses became part of the Military Orders' regular equipment, in France and Spain as well as the Middle East. These potential weapons of war could at first have been intended for the armed servants of the orders rather than the brother-knights themselves, though this point is disputed.[1]

Neither the Hospitallers nor the Templars were at any time very numerous. By the time of the Second Crusade they probably numbered no more than about 300 or 500 knights each, not including their larger retinues of brother-sergeants and turcopoles. This meant that strategy had to concentrate on conserving their strength. For this purpose they decided to rely on castles more than did knights in the West. These castles helped protect the local people as well as the knights, so they were not under any domestic threat.[2] They also gave an air of permanence to the Military Orders, a place where they could live, train, pray and play as if they were back home in Europe. The Hospitallers had the most formidable of the castles, the Krak des Chevaliers dominating the much-used Buqaiah Valley between Antioch and Tripoli. Built on the ruins of an earlier Arab fortification, Krak des Chevaliers astounds us even today with its sheer massiveness and sense of strength. More than 170m long from its northernmost battlement to the southern angle of the outer wall, and 100m wide, it stands on a sandy hill with precipitous drops on the west, north and east, being accessible only from the south; there a pathway leads to the small Outer Gate, through which it doubles back into a 150m ramped hairpin bend before finally debouching through the Inner Gate into the Upper Ward, the heart of the castle.

'The innermost ward,' writes Sidney Toy, an expert on fortifications, 'is on a much higher level than the [outer], its towers and battlements dominating the whole fortifications ... The curtains of the [Upper Ward] are strengthened by massive battered plinths, which soar up to a great height, engulfing the lower parts of the towers.'[3] Field Marshal Montgomery of Alamein, while a field officer serving in Palestine in the 1930s, noted that the Crusader castles were 'visible one from the next in a chain across the country; this inter-visibility was clearly considered important.'[4] The sheer sight of this miracle of military engineering must surely have had a deterrent effect on potential attackers; the most conspicuous feature of the Krak des Chevaliers are the great sloping plinths, built to discourage sapping as well as discourage any attempt at scaling. The Hospitallers in 1186 acquired the even more formidable Marqab Castle overlooking the coast, leased to them by the Mazoir family for 2,200 gold pieces a year.

Krak des Chevaliers and other great strategic redoubts helped the Knights of Saint John to become one of the biggest landowning concerns in Outremer. The chatelains lived, writes Runciman, 'more splendidly than any king in western Europe.'[5] Such economic independence buttressed the Knights' considerable military independence. By no means were they always at the beck and call of the king at Jerusalem, much less any of the lesser Frankish rulers. The popes had more authority over them than the kings had, and even then they could pick and choose their master according to the circumstances. They and the Templars were elites and acted like it.

By the time the Hospitallers had moved into the Krak des Chevaliers, their weapons and armour had become more sophisticated than they were a century before. The average knight's chain-mail tunic, the hauberk, was worn over a padded undergarment known as a gambeson; the former could be knee-length (though it must have been dreadfully uncomfortable in a hot climate), with separate chain segments protecting the neck, hands and legs. The helmet of choice was now the pot-helm seen so often in illustrations from the time; this was a simple flat-topped cylinder, rather like a saucepan, with slits for the eyes and for air. Its advantage over the previous conical helmet was probably that it was simpler to manufacture and sturdier (though again, in a hot climate the interior of a pot-helm must have been hellish). The knight's horse, too – a hulking, specially-bred destrier – was clad in either chain mail or a thick quilt. The main offensive weapons were the lance, broadsword and mace, with a shield providing added defence. Auxiliary units and turcopoles, given camp and siege duties, were armed with bows for when they, too, had to fight.[6]

Recruitment was a constant concern, as there was a steady attrition of the brethren from military action and disease. There was not much of a selection process; even former serfs could apply, as long as they found the means to pay their way. The French (a term which would include the Anglo-Norman aristocracy in England) constituted by far the largest contingent of the Hospitallers. A number of recruits came from Germany and Bohemia. There were those in their midst who dreamed of seeking martyrdom against Islam, but they were the exception to the general rule. Married men were accepted, though they were expected to leave their wives at home. And as we have seen, once a man was a Hospitaller knight, he was one for life.

The induction procedure was similar to that of a typical European knight, including the solemn injunction not to consider a knighthood as a ticket to status and good living, but rather the opposite. 'When you would like to eat, it will be necessary to fast,' the rookie was told, 'and when you want to sleep, it will be necessary to keep watch.' He would then pledge to be a servant of 'my lords the sick' and put on the coveted mantle with the cross 'in remembrance of Him who suffered death and passion on the Cross for you and for us other sinners'.[7] In the early years there was little distinction between brother-knights and brother-sergeants. On the fringes of the order were the donati, a waiting list of noble aspirants, and the confraters, high-ranking non-members who aided the Hospitaller cause as early as 1111, and often included kings, princes and counts. In-house priests appear in 1154, though there was often a shortage of such clergy. The vast bulk of manual and administrative work was done by the ordinary sergeants, distinguished from the brother-sergeants by their noncombatant duties. They included everyone from doctors and lawyers to cooks and scullery boys; especially important were the horse grooms and scutifers who kept the weapons and armour in good shape.

In the twelfth century the Hospitallers' policy was to keep weaponry and armour as simple as possible against the human temptation to show off. The standard items were a shield and sword and sometimes a dagger; this last was often known as a *misericord* and available for the nasty but practical purpose of putting a grievously wounded soldier out of his suffering, as its name – French for mercy – indicates. The knight was dressed in a chain-mail hauberk over a felt undergarment known as an *afeutreüre*, complemented by quilted leggings, a helmet and the distinctive Hospitaller surcoat with the white cross. In Outremer, however, the hauberk was doffed in hot weather, folded and put with the other personal baggage on a packhorse. This also aided in mobility when engaging enemy light cavalry.

The knight's warhorse, the destrier, was carefully chosen, as it would be his friend and companion in life and sometimes in death. 'Let the horse be well-tested and not a poor one,' wrote one authority at the time. 'Put on it a good saddle and a really fine breast-strap so that nothing is unsuitable.'[8] Austerity in dress and decoration extended to the Hospitaller horses. Three straps secured the saddle, which was a fairly basic affair, with extensions protecting the rider's lower hip area. A finely-woven *couverture*, or saddle-cloth, protected the horse's back from chafing. Very rarely a horse might be armoured in imitation of what was by now usual in the Muslim armies but virtually unknown in western Europe. A mounted knight was advised to hold his weapons high for maximum psychological effect and to keep his squires close by.

Not much is known about the Hospitallers' military training. Most of the brothers-in-arms had been trained soldiers before joining up, and book-learning even into adolescence was frowned on. It was commonly said that 'he who stays at school until the age of twelve is fit only to be a priest'. That was the age at which a healthy boy had to start being turned into a fighting man. The Hospitallers practised limited jousting – they didn't want to lose men in silly sporting accidents – and allowed the men to hunt lions. In the spiritual sphere a typical brother was expected to say 150 Latin paternosters every day and take communion at least three times a year. Sleep time was strictly set; sleeping naked in a scorching Middle East summer was banned, probably to discourage homosexuality. Only senior officials could have their own cells, and silence in the dormitories was rigorously enforced.

The experience of the First Crusade changed the policies somewhat. By the time Jerusalem was taken, the Crusaders' western horses were no more and the cavalry had to be raised from scratch. The Military Orders slowly gained battle experience as Baldwin I and Baldwin II of Jerusalem constantly fought off Muslim raiders and Frankish rivals alike. Outremer, the society they were defending, was becoming more sophisticated as the rough Frankish nobles settled down and sometimes intermarried, having children who regarded the ways and manners of the Middle East as natural. A vigorous culture grew up that drew on armed power from the West, the scholarship and refinement of the Byzantine Empire from the North, and the sophistication of the Arabs around them and from the East. 'He who was a Roman or Frank in this land,' wrote Baldwin I's chaplain Fulcher de Chartres, 'has been made into a Galilean or a Palestinian ... We have already forgotten the places of our birth.'[9]

Thomas Asbridge, a pre-eminent Crusades historian, cites the above quote as evidence that Outremer, particularly the kingdom of Jerusalem, aimed to attract more recruits from the West to restore the French identity. Despite the assimilation of cultures and customs, there were still strict rules against relationships between Christian men and Muslim women – a knight could end up being castrated if found guilty of having sex with such a woman, who would have her nose cut off by her own people. Such strict discrimination seems to have been accepted as normal by both sides, though the Arabs never did quite get to like the Westerners, however much the latter adopted local customs and dress. A knight might establish a close tie of respect and friendship with an individual ranking Muslim, though a subliminal sense of western superiority was always there. Usama ibn Munqidh, a Syrian noble who closely observed Crusader society, reports that one day a group of Templars willingly vacated a small mosque where he was going to pray.[10] Partly because of their familiarity with the peoples and customs of the Middle East, the Hospitallers were never considered Crusaders per se. Their task was to aid in the military defence of Outremer, though all too often the two roles became indistinguishable.[11]

Several decades into the Frankish rule of Outremer, it was perhaps inevitable that someone in the Muslim world would revive the defeated Arab-Turkish forces and forge them into a hammer of revenge. Such a one was Zengi, the son of a Turkish slave who had risen to the position of Atabeg of Mosul and Aleppo, a region comprising much of today's Iraq and Syria. Zengi's passionate jihadist calls united the fractured Muslim world. This self-styled 'tamer of atheists and destroyer of heretics', with the blessings of Fatimid caliph al-Amir, had the single-minded goal of expelling the Europeans and eliminating Outremer. Making his task rather easier was a dispute between Byzantine Emperor John II Komnenos and an ambitious Frank, Raymond of Poitiers, over the possession of Antioch. This dispute had the effect of weakening the Christian camp. In 1138 John at the head of a Byzantine army marched as far as Aleppo, found it occupied by Zengi, and veered away to besiege Shaizar, a small town controlling the Orontes River Valley.

At Shaizar the defending Muslims got their first glimpse of John II and had to admire his courage. 'Conspicuous in his gilded helmet, he seemed to be everywhere at once, encouraging the faint-hearted, berating the idle, consoling the wounded, instructing the siege engineers, infusing all his soldiers ... with his own indomitable spirit.'[12] John's army of Greeks, Scandinavians, Englishmen and Turks fought well, but was let down by Raymond's Franks, who had little stomach for battle and probably resented playing second fiddle to the 'heretic' Greeks. Raymond, in fact, spent his time in the rear playing dice. This was most likely before the Hospitallers had become a full military order, and if they had been at the siege of Aleppo it is unlikely that they would have shared or approved of Raymond's dishonourable conduct. John II Komnenos raised the siege after receiving tribute from the local emir, but inter-Christian distrust lingered, and its importance was not lost on Zengi.

Though he remains a hero of sorts in Turco-Arab tradition, Zengi has had, to put it mildly, a bad press. Contemporaries described him as more than usually cruel and bloody even by the standards of the age. We are told that captured enemies of rank were scalped and skinned alive, and that to preserve his boy lovers' beauty he had them castrated, a treatment he also meted out to the blameless sons of any general to whom he took a dislike to. A habitual drunkard and sex maniac, he might divert himself (we are told) by watching one of his ex-wives being gang-raped in the stables. His troops, of course, walked in terror of him. Any soldier who inadvertently trampled on a farm crop could expect to be crucified. If any soldier deserted, two of his comrades would be cut in half as deterrent to any would-be-imitators.[13]

Zengi's notoriety, of course, was well known to the Crusader states. But all attempts to bring him to heel were half-hearted and ineffectual until one of his main Muslim allies, Unur, the Atabeg of Damascus, turned coat and travelled to Jerusalem to join cause with King Fulk and Queen Melisende. In the palace visitor and hosts got on quite well, though one high-ranking Muslim in Unur's retinue sniffed at the Crusader knights, whom he considered good for nothing except fighting, apparently devoid of the finer points of character. Yet Jerusalem impressed this same observer, with its 30,000 people, waves of pilgrims, the public baths and Roman-era sewers, great churches, vast and bustling markets, the babble of half a dozen tongues, the hustlers, the noisy drinking bars, the prostitutes arriving by the boatload from the West and sure of a lucrative market by 'dedicating as a holy offering what they kept between their thighs', the proud demeanour of the Hospitallers and Templars, and the general sacred-profane mystic of that city.[14]

The pact with the Kingdom of Jerusalem kept Zengi at bay for a few years until King Fulk died after suffering a fractured skull in a fall from a horse. Six weeks later, on Christmas Day 1142, Fulk's 12-year-old son was crowned as Baldwin III, though his mother Melisende held real power as his regent. According to William of Tyre, she was a capable and wise queen, but she was not allowed to savour peace for long as Zengi saw his chance to strike, taking Edessa in 1144. The County of Edessa had been the very first Crusader state, established in 1098, taking up the north-east corner of Outremer and corresponding to the present Turkish-Syrian border area. Its fall, accompanied by a massacre of Europeans, shocked not only Jerusalem but also the whole of western Europe. Inevitably, calls for another crusade resounded from the pulpits and in the castle halls.

The crusading spirit in Europe, however misguided, was by no means dead. The Venetians, with the backing of Pope Calixtus II, had staged an ineffectual expedition in 1122, and Templar Grand Master Hugh de Payens had attempted a conquest of Arab Syria seven years later. These moves had soon petered out and amounted to nothing. There also had been assorted minor crusades in Spain and the Balearic Islands. Then Bernard of Clairvaux came on the scene with his inflammatory rhetoric and Pope Eugenius III and French King Louis VII, both for their own reasons, thought it right and just to speed to the defence of Outremer, seen to be under renewed threat from the enemies of Christ. Louis himself, just 27 years old, was fervently pious. Moreover, his conscience tormented him; during a recent outburst of civil unrest his soldiers had burned hundreds of people in a church, and he wanted to atone for that. On 1 December 1145 the Papal Curia issued a formal call to arms.

The Second Crusade, in contrast to the huge fanfare that preceded it, turned out to be a rather short and sad affair. At first Raymond of Antioch, correctly assuming that his city would be next on Zengi's list, reluctantly appealed to the new Byzantine emperor, Manuel I Komnenos, who promised him money but no troops. A rather more favourable development was Zengi's death at the hands of one of the men he had applied his castration hobby to. The new pope, Eugenius III, and Louis VII of France saw the way clear to redressing the balance in Outremer. However, there seems to have been a lack of coordination between pope and king, and it wasn't until late 1146 that the papal encyclical *Quantum praedecessores* sounded the starting gun for the new campaign, with the irrepressible Bernard of Clairvaux doing the cheerleading throughout western Europe via his popular Cistercian order. Bernard, in effect, was calling for Europe's nobles to follow the example of the Military Orders and provide backup for them. Nobles flocked to Vézelay in France to enrol in the new cause, including Louis and his vivacious young Queen Eleanor and his brother Robert, the Count of Dreux. Louis showed up at Vézelay resplendent in a new tunic featuring the cross, a present from the Pope. Everyone suddenly clamoured for this must-have fashion accessory, forcing Bernard to rip up his own cloak so that crosses could be made out of the fabric. In late December Conrad III of Germany entered the lists after being verbally pummelled by one of Bernard's emotional harangues. As the armies were assembled, the soldiers sang:

> Edessa is taken, as you know,
> And Christians troubled sore and long.
> The churches there are empty now,
> And masses are no longer sung.[15]

By June 1147 the Crusade was ready to start. Pope Eugenius fondly imagined that 'the whole of Christendom' had got involved, but the reality was quite different. The expedition got going on 11 June with an elaborate ceremony in the Church of St Denis near Paris; after kneeling, Louis VII received his symbolic pilgrim's staff and bag and raised the old French *Oriflame* standard. A hundred Templars accompanied him on the first leg of the march. A month later Conrad III's forces set out from Regensburg; both armies arrived before Constantinople, the first main stop, in the early autumn. But if the French and German kings counted on support from the Byzantine Empire, they were in for a shock. Remembering the chaos and insecurity of the arrival of the First Crusaders half a century before, the Greeks this time were staying out of this. Secure in their belief that their Orthodox Christianity was the correct dogma, they could not fathom why the Catholics were so intent on destroying themselves in a part of the world they knew little about. If anyone could consider themselves fighters for Christendom it was the Byzantines who had been doing it for hundreds of years, not these naive western come-latelies. And if anyone was going to retrieve the Holy Land, it was going to be a Byzantine emperor in his good time, whenever the proper strategic opportunity would present itself.

Emperor Manuel I has thus been blamed for putting the skids under the Second Crusade. But responsibility must lie primarily with the amateurishness of the campaign itself. The crusading troops were hardly models of good conduct, pillaging the Christian communities through which they passed. To Manuel, the marauders risked triggering a mass Muslim reaction that would endanger the Byzantine Empire itself, and the empire was engaged on other vital fronts. The saintly Louis VII, however, seems to have made a good impression on the Byzantine emperor, who during a lavish banquet advised him, if he was intent on traversing Asia Minor (modern Turkey), to take the safer long route around the western Asia Minor seaboard to lessen the risk of interception by Turkish forces in the treacherous mountain passes of Anatolia. Privately, however, Manuel shook his head at the sight of the naive Crusaders and feared they would come to grief. He turned out to be right. Conrad had gone ahead impatiently, contemptuous of the Greeks' sound advice, only to blunder into a brutal ambush at Dorylaion, south-east of Constantinople; Conrad himself was one of a tenth of his men who barely escaped with their lives.

Though wounded, Conrad did not give up hope, joining up with Louis' Frenchmen who were taking the safer coastal route. Winter had now set in, and the going was hard. At Ephesus Conrad became ill, to be doctored personally by Manuel, who was something of a medical man, and taken to Constantinople to recover with a promise of resuming the trek to Outremer in the spring. Louis, now in sole command of the French-German army and guarded by a contingent of Templars, struck east along the Meander Valley, there to run into a determined Seljuk attack that had Louis climbing a tree to save his life while his soldiers were slaughtered. The Templars were left to lead the shattered remnant of Louis' army to Attaleia (now Antalya) on the south coast – a distance of a few hundred miles. Almost daily, bands of Turks would come thundering out of the scrub to attack the flanks; the route of march was littered with corpses, but Louis grimly marched on and managed to reach Attaleia safely.

Thanks to a timely lift from the Byzantine Navy, the long-suffering Conrad finally set foot in the Holy Land in spring 1148, soon to be followed by Louis and his even longer-suffering queen, wishing she had never come along, and thoroughly tired of the ordeal. But after they had arrived at their destination, what then? Thousands of soldiers had already died. Had anything of worth actually been accomplished? William of Tyre, our leading authority for the period, thought not, confessing that the whole Second Crusade had turned out to be 'a joke'. It was a joke, though, that gave the Turks a present on a silver platter, as succeeding Zengi as chief Muslim champion was his son Nur ed-Din, who was to outshine his father in ability.

The new Muslim atabeg seems to have been an impressive man, tall and dark, with well-proportioned features and deceptively sensitive eyes. William of Tyre respected him as a God-fearing leader, a quality he would need in large measure as he tried to wrest some order out of the anarchy into which Syria was falling after Zengi's murder. Nur ed-Din's first urgent task was to seize the strategic citadel of Aleppo, before Joscelin II, the Frankish Count of Edessa, got there. In 1146 Nur ed-Din in a remarkable forced march reached Edessa before Joscelin could and proceeded to slaughter all its male Christian population – including those who had invited him in against the Franks. The city never quite recovered.

Only such savage resolve, it seemed, could shake Nur ed-Din's Muslim rivals into compliance. And once it was accomplished he could turn his attention to the Franks of Outremer, many of whom were still harbouring crusading ambitions. The Second Crusaders (what was left of them, reinforced by the Franks of Jerusalem) launched their drive on Damascus in July 1148; Nur ed-Din moved to meet them there, and after three days of bloody fighting under the fierce Levantine sun, the demoralized Franks withdrew. Conrad sailed for home two months later, with Louis following soon afterwards. In 1151 Nur ed-Din eradicated the Frankish County of Edessa, carrying off Joscelin II in chains.

For the next twenty or so years Nur ed-Din coexisted uneasily with the Kingdom of Jerusalem. This period probably saw the Hospitallers' first major action: the siege and capture of Ascalon by King Baldwin III in 1153. Ascalon, one of the few major ports on the Palestinian seaboard, was in the hands of the Egyptian Fatimids, a fact that stuck in the craw of Outremer. Baldwin and both the Military Orders moved against the city, but such were its massive fortifications that it defied the Frankish siege for months. During that time fresh volunteers joined the force from the pilgrim boats that regularly arrived. The campaign brought the Hospitallers new prestige and power. It wasn't long before they came into conflict with the ecclesiastical authorities in Jerusalem. In one particularly nasty dispute in 1154 some Hospitallers burst into a church where the Patriarch was conducting a service and fired arrows at his congregation. Grand Master Raymond du Puy and the Patriarch sailed to Rome to settle the issue; the pope confirmed the Hospitallers' privileges at the expense of the churchmen's power. In the struggle for power and influence in Jerusalem, the Hospitallers had won the first round.

The siege of Ascalon continued into the summer of 1154. Baldwin put a large wooden siege tower against the huge outer wall where the Templars were stationed. One night the defenders set fire to it, but the blistering heat shattered the masonry, opening a breach into which about forty or so Templars rushed. But in their short-sighted eagerness to take the credit for capturing Ascalon, they kept the other Frankish units out. The result was that the Muslim defenders had little trouble eliminating a mere forty knights; the next morning the Franks were treated to the sight of 'Templar corpses … hung out over the city walls'.

Before the king could get too discouraged, Hospitaller Grand Master Raymond du Puy urged a fresh offensive; a majority of the accompanying nobles, probably infuriated by the dishonour shown to the Templar dead, agreed with him. The bombardment was renewed; mangonels hurled boulders and flaming wood over the walls, until the defenders capitulated on 19 August. In a noble departure from the ruthless general practice of the time, Baldwin allowed the Muslim inhabitants a safe-conduct out of Ascalon. The 'Bride of Syria', as the westerners fondly called that vital port, was at last in Christian hands.

Barely had Baldwin III returned to Jerusalem than he was forced to face down Nur ed-Din, who had just taken Damascus largely thanks to the incompetence and arrogance of the Frankish lords who had managed to alienate local Muslim and Christian alike. Baldwin, perhaps badly advised, had sent troops to steal the flocks of some Turcoman shepherds, infuriating Nur ed-Din. A company of Hospitallers sent to raid Banyas south-west of Damascus was wiped out in a retaliatory action.

In February 1162 Baldwin III died of a fever at Tripoli, just 33 years old. As he had no children, and his Greek wife was still a mere teenager, the succession devolved on his brother Amalric, the Count of Jaffa and Ascalon. Tall and good-looking, in the first flush of strength at 25, he seized on the idea of conquering Egypt from the Fatimids as the cornerstone of his foreign policy. The Byzantines in the north were not averse to the idea, while the Sunni Muslim Nur ed-Din, for his part, wouldn't have minded getting rid of the Shia Fatimids. With those cards in his favour Amalric invaded Egypt in September 1163, but a flooded Nile stopped him short. At the same time, however, the wily Nur ed-Din made an attempt on the Hospitaller-held Krak des Chevaliers, but his Muslims were trounced in the valley below by a joint Frankish-Byzantine army that had rushed to the scene.

By now the kings of Jerusalem were relying heavily on their Hospitaller corps, which was given a leading role in a second invasion of Egypt in 1164. Egypt was the scene of a confusing power struggle between an ambitious general, Shirkuh, who tried to put some backbone into the declining Fatimid dynasty, and his rival Shawar, a former vizier. Shawar invited Amalric to help him, promising to pay the Hospitallers well for their trouble and defray the upkeep of their horses. The Franks appeared to be about to topple Shirkuh when trouble in Syria forced Amalric to break off the campaign. Two years later Amalric returned to the Egyptian theatre, bottling up Shirkuh and his able lieutenant Saladin in Alexandria; in August 1166 Shirkuh agreed to evacuate the city, leaving Amalric free to confront the ever-dangerous Nur ed-Din in Syria.

Such was the danger, in fact, that Amalric decided to reorganize the defence of Outremer by delegating more resources and power to the Military Orders. The Templars were given all the castles and surrounding lands in the County of Tripoli in the north, while the Hospitallers confirmed their existing ownership of the forts, including the Krak des Chevaliers, dotting the Buqaiah Valley; a new acquisition was Belvoir Castle dominating the Jordan River south of the Sea of Galilee. On the diplomatic front Amalric firmed up ties with the Byzantines whose emperor, the capable Manuel I Komnenos, was stoutly defending his realm.

Egypt was something of an obsession for King Amalric. Politically, he wanted to weaken, if not eliminate, a potential Muslim foe on his south-western flank, but he may not have thought out the strategic implications. Frankish military manpower, never very numerous compared to the Muslims, would find it hard to control or occupy Cairo and the Nile Delta for any length of time. The Hospitaller Grand Master, Gilbert d'Assailly, knew it all too well. In 1168 he urged a fresh attack on Egypt before the local Muslims could recoup their strength; besides, he wanted the fort at Pelusium. Amalric, reasonably, wished to wait until the Byzantines could help with their navy, but d'Assailly talked him into immediate action.

The invasion of Egypt of October 1168 showed the folly of Amalric's thinking. When the Franks approached the fort of Bilbeis the Muslims fell on them, inflicting heavy casualties on the Hospitallers, who numbered perhaps 500 knights and an equal number of turcopoles. In return, the Franks engaged in an indiscriminate slaughter of Muslims and Christians alike (though the initiative here probably did not lie with the Knights of Saint John). This act incurred the bitter hatred of all Egyptians. Within a month Amalric's army was at the gates of Cairo, but Shawar and the defenders had received plenty of warning. As the Franks dithered, Shawar sent word to Nur ed-Din in Syria, who sent Shirkuh and his nephew and chief lieutenant Salah ad-Din Yusuf south with 8,000 troops and a considerable war chest. This force slipped past the unwary Franks, forcing them to evacuate what Egyptian territory they had taken. In January 1169 Shirkuh entered Cairo and had Shawar beheaded; he may have celebrated a bit too vigorously, for two months later he died after a binge of overeating. The way was now clear for the more temperate and disciplined Salah ad-Din – better known to history as Saladin – to rise to prominence.

In Jerusalem the recriminations were bitter. Amalric was blamed for being too willing to bargain with the late Shawar, though the scapegoat turned out to be Gilbert d'Assailly, who had lost a lot of knights at Bilbeis; he was sacked as Hospitaller Grand Master and packed off home to France. The Hospitallers' appetite for Egypt had been extinguished, at least for a time. D'Assailly's temporary replacement, Guibert, the Preceptor of the Order, joined a mission that sailed to Rome and then moved on to France and England to appeal for a new crusade. But the western leaders didn't want to know; Henry II of England was preoccupied with his conflict with the French, while the popes and the Holy Roman emperors were at the height of their own diplomatic war.

The only Christian leader to respond was Manuel I of Byzantium, whose great-niece was Amalric's queen. The emperor despatched a large fleet under Grand Duke Andronikos Kontostephanos to Alexandria while Amalric marched by land. The Greek ships ferried his men across the Nile, but when the king came up against the great fortifications of Damietta, he hesitated. Kontostephanos, his own supplies dwindling, urged an immediate attack, but the fearful Amalric held back. Again, as in the first invasion of Egypt nearly a year before, he allowed the initiative to slip out of his hands. Day by day the Muslim garrison in Damietta became stronger until in December the Christians had to realize that the cause was lost. On its way back home Kontostephanos' fleet was decimated by a severe storm, while Amalric's army had to trudge back disconsolately after burning its siege engines.

By now Saladin was the undisputed master of Egypt, and when his mentor Nur ed-Din died in 1174 he was free to pursue his long game of crushing Outremer and driving the westerners out once and for all. Political developments in Europe were on his side. Within months of one another, Conrad III of Germany, Pope Eugenius III and his successor Anastasius IV all left this world. To the papacy and much of central Europe, the prime threats were the aggressive Norman realms of southern Italy, and potentially the Byzantine Empire. This left the Kingdom of Jerusalem and the Principality of Antioch alone against the growing power and determination of Saladin.

Chapter 5

The Horns of Blood

Cult of violence – Raymond of Tripoli – Reynald of Châtillon – Saladin loses patience – Battle of the Cresson Spring – the leper-king – a lady in distress – Guy of Lusignan – disaster at Hattin – the fall of Jerusalem – reaction in Europe

The Military Orders in their first century grew around an inner core of steel. It wasn't enough, as it had been in the early days, to simply defend Christendom against the attacks of the Muslims; the fight had to be carried actively right to the enemy. The old concept of martyrdom for the faith had now been elevated into almost a rule of tactics, lending an aura of glory to those who took the initiative in warfare and met death doing so. It has been well written that 'mediaeval Christianity had more in common with the violent and angry reaction of the Apostle Peter on the Mount of Olives than with the calm and stoic reaction of Christ on the night of His arrest'.[1] There was certainly no longer any question of turning the other cheek.

The Templars in particular drew their inspiration from the violent Old Testament: 'And ye shall chase your enemies, and they shall fall before you by the sword.'[2] To 'eat, drink and swear like a Templar' was a common saying. The Hospitallers of the late twelfth century were no less eager. Yet the enemy was by no means held in contempt. A mutual respect for one another's valour crossed the opposing lines. The fanatical Muslims ruefully complimented the Castellan of Krak des Chevaliers, who fell under their swords in 1170, as 'a bone stuck in [our] throat'. Saladin well knew the fighting qualities of the Military Orders and their imperviousness to any kind of canvassing or bribery. He feared them enough to suspend his usual clemency when he captured any of their members, almost invariably ordering their instant execution. 'Beware of the warrior monks,' the Arab al-Harawi advised the sultans. In contrast to civil clergy, they were incorruptible, 'paying no attention to the things of this world'.[3]

When Hospitaller knights were captured by Muslim potentates the experience was seen as extremely humiliating. But senior captured knights could generally raise a ransom out of their assets, as by now the Order owned the entire Buqaiah Valley. The Muslims, after long experience fighting the Byzantines, had evolved an elaborate prisoner-exchange and ransoming system that was soon copied by the Franks. The Hospitallers in particular made great efforts to have their men released by the enemy while at the same time gathering up Muslim captives of their own to use as labourers or slaves. In 1172 the Order had enough money to be able to buy the freedom of Raymond of Tripoli, the ruler of the county of the same name, who had been captured by Nur ed-Din after the disastrous battle of Artah eight years before.

Thanks perhaps to this gesture, Raymond of Tripoli and the Knights of Saint John forged a close relationship. He himself was well-read in Arabic history and culture and saw his mission – especially when he became regent for the infant-king Baldwin V – as forging a stable state in coexistence with the Muslims rather than trying to eliminate them. He was not the typical swashbuckling crusader in the western sense, all brawn and armour and little brain. Aloof and reserved, Count Raymond preferred peace to war, and carried the Hospitallers with him. Besides, the Hospitallers were the larger and wealthier order, with consequently more to lose.

The Templars, however, were another matter. Almost all the knightly new arrivals from France were attracted to the Templars, who had a reputation as the more aggressive of the Military Orders. Most of these men were naturally pugnacious and adventurous, knowing little and caring less for the peoples and cultures of the Middle East, eager to use a superficial Christianity to sate their violent appetites. They found a natural magnet in Reynald of Châtillon, the despotic master of Kerak, and a prime specimen of those who would give crusading a bad name. Relations between the Templars and the Hospitallers steadily deteriorated. We have seen how some Hospitallers were provoked into firing arrows inside the Church of the Holy Sepulchre as part of a vendetta they were waging against the Patriarch of Jerusalem. Though Durant may be guilty of a slight exaggeration when he writes that both the Military Orders 'hated each other religiously',[4] their fierce rivalry more often than not worked to the detriment of Outremer and the entire Christian cause. It was also directly responsible for perhaps the greatest military disaster of their careers.

Saladin waited patiently in Egypt for dissention among the Christian states to work to his advantage. He saw a chance in 1182 when Châtillon talked Baldwin IV into concentrating the Frankish army east of Jerusalem, clearing the way for Saladin to march to Damascus. The two armies clashed bloodily but inconclusively beneath the Hospitaller castle of Belvoir. A year later Saladin took Aleppo as a prelude to a major offensive against the Frankish states; Raymond of Tripoli doubted that the Franks could prevail against the offensive, but as much as Saladin tried, he was unable to draw his foes into battle. In 1185 the leper-king Baldwin IV died, to be succeeded by Queen Sibylla and their infant son Baldwin V. The boy, however, lived only for another year. Raymond of Tripoli's efforts to establish a legitimate succession were stymied by Sibylla, who enlisted the Templars to secure a hold on power in Jerusalem. Only the Hospitaller Grand Master, Roger de Moulins, sided with Raymond and the legitimist cause, and were duly outmanoeuvred by Sibylla and Châtillon. The end result was that Sibylla and her husband, Guy of Lusignan, were proclaimed queen and king. The coronation ceremony involved unlocking the royal insignia from a coffer with three locks; the keys were held by the Patriarch of Jerusalem and the grand masters of the two Military Orders. De Moulins at first had no intention of producing his own key, and under pressure, chose to hurl it out of the window rather than break his oaths. With King Guy of Lusignan in their camp, the Templars were in the ascendant.[5]

Saladin had frequent health problems, and during the Frankish succession in Jerusalem he had become seriously ill with what was probably malaria. It took him a long time to recover, but by early 1187 he was back in something resembling his old fighting form. Saladin's incapacitation had encouraged Reynald of Châtillon to raid Muslim caravans plying their peaceful routes up the valleys between Egypt and Syria. These caravans were extraordinary sights, with their miles of camels lumbering along, lit by a procession of torches by night. The great commercial wealth of these caravans was a constant temptation to any rapacious western knight, which is why the Crusader states and Saladin had firmed a truce protecting them from harm. One such caravan rested for a few days at Petra in what is now south Jordan, before continuing along what was known as the King's Highway, past the Crusader fortress of Shobak (also called Montreal) and into a desolate stretch of desert east of the Dead Sea. There, in the territory of Kerak, Châtillon unleashed a wave of Franks on the unsuspecting caravan, in clear violation of the treaty.[6]

This was just the latest of a series of outrages committed by Châtillon. This man's contribution to the Second Crusade had so far been the rather unedifying one of invading Cyprus, pillaging its towns and cutting off Greek priests' noses, only to cower abjectly when Byzantine Emperor Manuel I confronted him with overwhelming force and forced him to hold the emperor's horse's stirrups as Manuel rode into Antioch in triumph. In 1160 the Muslims had captured Reynald, but fourteen years in a dungeon had worsened his already questionable character. After being ransomed he set up an independent fief at Kerak notorious for its inhumanity even in that callous age. His method of executing an opponent was to hurl him off the castle walls after fastening his head inside a wooden box so that the victim would remain conscious after his body smashed into the rocks. His reckless callousness went as far as plotting to seize the holiest shrines of Islam, Mecca and Medina, exhume the remains of the Prophet Muhammad and destroy the Kaaba, the central monument of Mecca inside which lay the original black stone believed to have been sent down by the angel Gabriel and to this day the pre-eminent Muslim sacred object. With maniacal energy Châtillon built a pirate fleet that raided the Red Sea shores, spreading terror through the Arab communities. The pirates were eventually hunted down and beheaded, though their leader, with the perverse good luck that often aids the evil, escaped. Saladin, however, would not rest until this nasty Frenchman was in his hands and he could have the pleasure of decapitating him personally.

'Let your Muhammad come and rescue you,' Châtillon mocked his captives when they invoked the truce between the Frankish kingdom of Jerusalem and the Muslims. Saladin, encouraged of course by no lack of suitable passages in the Koran, was planning precisely that. Guy of Lusignan, now King Guy, joined Saladin in appealing for the prisoners to be freed and the caravan restored, but Châtillon paid not the slightest attention. So in March 1187, mere weeks after the capture of the caravan, Saladin formally issued his call of jihad against the Christian states. 'Fight and slay the infidels wherever you find them,' he fumed. 'Lie in wait for them in every stratagem of war.' Muslims from all over flocked to his banner. The gloves were off.

But who exactly would the 'infidels' be? Reynald of Châtillon was, of course, beyond the pale, but the Muslims had a potential friend in Raymond of Tripoli. It was his reputation that sowed a certain Muslim respect for the Hospitallers – the Isbatariyah, as they were called in Arabic.[7] Closer to Saladin's description of an infidel was the hawkish Grand Master of the Templars, Gerard de Ridefort, a supporter of Châtillon. King Guy was put on the spot when Saladin asked permission from Raymond to allow Muslim forces through his territory to strike at Châtillon. Raymond agreed, albeit reluctantly, while the Military Orders had been specifically asked not to intervene. But to Ridefort Raymond was a nothing less than a traitor. No Templar could tolerate any Muslim incursion, however innocent-seeming.

The Muslims marched in force into Lower Galilee on 1 May 1187. Saladin well knew the dilemma he had forced upon Raymond of Tripoli, and divined correctly that in a crunch Raymond would decide to stand by his fellow Christians. That evening about 130 knights including eighty Templars and ten Hospitallers, and their grand masters Roger de Moulins and Gerard de Ridefort, scouted Mount Tabor for a sight of the enemy. At noon the following day some 7,000 Muslims were spotted camping at the Cresson Spring, a couple of miles from Nazareth. At the sight, de Moulins thought it would be madness to attack, and carried the Templars' marshal, Brother James de Mailly, with him. But de Ridefort would have none of it and turned on de Mailly. 'You love your blond head too well to want to lose it,' he snapped. 'Our task is to overcome the enemy not by force of numbers but by faith and justice and observing God's mandates.' With that he spurred his horse forward and galloped downhill towards the Muslim camp, his Templars close behind. After the affront to his courage, de Moulins and the Hospitallers had no honourable choice but to follow.

De Mailly's blond head was a good deal sounder than that of his boss, but he wouldn't be using it any more. The few score Frankish knights came thundering down on the Muslims who coolly let the attackers sweep right into their formation, and once they had them encircled, proceeded to cut them to pieces. Roger de Moulins fell, along with at least sixty knights of both orders. James de Mailly was said to have dismissed Muslim calls for him to surrender; encircled on his white horse by an enemy horde, he perished heroically under a hail of projectiles as 'his soul fled triumphant, bearing the palm of martyrdom to a heavenly kingdom'.[8] Somehow de Ridefort escaped, riding grievously wounded to Nazareth where he collapsed, though he survived. The Muslim soldiers marched back across the Jordan River with the knights' heads decorating their pike tips. Some of the Christian prisoners were taken to Mecca and slaughtered in place of goats at the annual pilgrimage sacrifices.[9]

The disaster at the Cresson Spring came close to undoing the Military Orders. Perhaps one-tenth of their total manpower in Outremer had perished in one rash hour, along with more than a hundred precious combat horses. Naturally, the blame game went into top gear, with de Ridefort and the Templars blaming Raymond of Tripoli for his permission to let Saladin's forces enter Christian territory, and Raymond in turn slamming de Ridefort's foolhardiness. Some of Raymond's own soldiers turned against him, at one point unfairly accusing him to his face of having become a Muslim himself. The Archbishop of Tyre threatened to excommunicate him. Mortified, he agreed to cease all diplomatic and military contact with Saladin. In Rome Pope Urban III issued an appeal to the clergy and nobles in England to rebuild the battered Templars – no mention appears to have been made of the Hospitallers – 'so that, for God and for their salvation, they may, by their strong hand, succour Christianity' in the Holy Land.[10]

King Amalric had died of dysentery in Jerusalem in 1174, leaving the Latin throne to his clever young son Baldwin IV who, it was soon discovered to everyone's consternation, had contracted leprosy from his wet-nurse. There was little that even the best Arab doctors could do about Baldwin's malady, and as he got older it ravaged him mercilessly. Nonetheless, he managed to ride with his one good arm, and did not hesitate to take the field against Saladin's forces when he could. 'It is hard,' writes Montefiore, 'to find a case of nobler courage and grace under fire than this doomed young king.'[11]

This courage enabled the leper-king to win a tremendous victory against Saladin's troops at Montgisard, north of Jerusalem, in 1177, but leprosy was no respecter of personal qualities. As Baldwin gradually got sicker and less able to do any fighting, he finally had to acknowledge his disadvantage in a letter of appeal to Louis VII of France. 'It's not fitting that a hand so weak should hold power when Arab aggression presses upon the Holy City,' he admitted. It was a sad day in Outremer when Baldwin IV, blind and helpless and just 23 years old, passed away in 1185. The leper-king not having had any offspring, the succession passed to his 8-year-old nephew Baldwin V, who himself had barely a year to live, and was succeeded, as we have seen, by Queen Sibylla and her consort Guy de Lusignan.

After the disaster at the Cresson Spring, King Guy and Saladin were placed on a collision course. On 27 June 1187 a newly-heartened Saladin led 30,000 troops towards Tiberias on the shore of the Sea of Galilee, hoping to lure the Franks to what he hoped would be their decisive defeat. Guy had at his disposal about 1,200 knights, including Hospitallers and Templars, plus some 16,000 foot soldiers. Yet, as before the encounter at the Cresson Spring, dissent split the Christian camp. Hospitallers and Templars could not hide their distrust of each other. The bad blood between Raymond and Châtillon festered, poisoning politics. There was an atmosphere of foreboding among the troops. King Guy's chamberlain had dreamed that an eagle had overflown the army with arrows in its talons screeching, 'Woe to thee, O Jerusalem!'[12] At the time, this was a portent not to be taken lightly. King Guy, in the grip of a probable inferiority complex over his lack of royal blood, let himself be swayed by the hawks. Over the scorched scrub of Galilee, Raymond and the Hospitallers marched at the head of the formation; following was the central sector containing the king and the True Cross, with the Templars under Balian of Ibelin, a distinguished and gallant knight, in the rear. (The records show Armengaud d'Asp as succeeding Roger de Moulins as Hospitaller Grand Master, but he was probably appointed after the battle at Hattin.) They reached a well-watered village called Sephoria, and Guy was in favour of resting there, but he was talked into pressing on; Tiberias on the Sea of Galilee was just nine more miles distant and moreover, Raymond's wife, the Countess Eschiva, was cut off there. The mental picture of a lady in distress in a tower appealing for rescue was too much for the knights' gallant instincts to ignore.

Was Eschiva's predicament, rather than any cool-headed strategic consideration, the real reason for Guy's expedition into the hellish semi-desert? The evidence would suggest so. Saladin had captured Tiberias on 2 July with a picked detachment, but had left the countess and her personal guard in the citadel unharmed. 'Send help at once or we shall be taken and made captive,' Eschiva messaged the king. Châtillon and de Ridefort, characteristically, bayed to go and rescue the lady, but oddly enough, her own husband was cooler to the idea. Raymond suggested playing a waiting game, believing that the Tiberias citadel could hold out and that Eschiva could make her escape on the Sea of Galilee; besides – and this was the main point – the height of a Syrian summer was no season for armoured soldiers to exert themselves in a parched landscape – and with 30,000 Muslims dogging their steps.

At a meeting Châtillon accused Raymond of being coward, if not a crypto-Muslim himself, 'otherwise you would not speak this way'. The senior officers tended to agree, shouting at King Guy to let them 'rescue the ladies and maidens of Tiberias'. The clincher was the tearful appeal of Eschiva's two young sons who were in Guy's court. Torn between the impetuous Templars and the cautious Hospitallers, Guy could not come to any decision. After a day of tense debate the king appeared to have decided to wait on developments. But that night de Ridefort took the king aside to subtly remind him that as he had been accused of faint-heartedness before, here was a chance for him to erase that stain on his escutcheon. Besides, he added tellingly, the Templars as a military order were not formally bound by any royal allegiance and could take matters into their own hands if necessary. His manliness thus impugned, Guy ordered a move on Tiberias in the morning – to be then confronted by a frantic Raymond who cried that such a mission would be suicide. Angrily brushing off barbs that he didn't love his wife and was an imperfect Christian to boot, Raymond warned that the troops couldn't 'survive half a day without an abundance of water'. Of which there was very little, if any, between the king's camp near Nazareth and Tiberias. But the king had decided – advance!

Nine miles may not have been a long way for an ordinary day's ride or march, but in the extreme summer conditions of Galilee and with Saladin's deadly efficient light horse swarming around and behind, it was well-nigh impossible. Raymond, properly preoccupied with the water situation, talked Guy into authorizing a stop at the village of Hattin to take on supplies. To get there, however, Raymond and the Hospitallers had to pass over a ridge with two peaks on it, known as the Horns of Hattin. And a large Muslim force was blocking the way. Not knowing what else to do, the king decided to halt with the centre of the army and pitch camp at Maskana, near the southern horn, where there was no water at all. Tormented by heat and thirst, Raymond groaned, 'We're dead'.

Some of the Christian soldiers would probably have been told that Hattin was the site of Christ's Sermon on the Mount. But now it looked like a hill of death. Raymond's men tried to get some sleep that night, if the incessant cries of '*Allahu akbar!*' ('God is great') issuing from the darkness would let them. Muslim advance guards crept to within spitting distance of Christian lines. As dawn approached Saladin had his army ready – colourful contingents of fanatical Arabs, Turks, Kurds, Armenians and Sudanese, flashing their armour and deadly swords – to hit Guy's position as soon as it became light enough. They had been issued extra arrows to dispose of the Franks' horses, without which the knights would be powerless. At this point four of Raymond's knights could endure no more and defected to the enemy.

Stopped in front of Hattin, Raymond had little choice but to resume the march east to Tiberias, directly into the rising sun. But before he could start, before dawn on 4 July Saladin put into effect his secret weapon – fields of dry grass which he ordered set on fire. Rolling walls of flame and smoke smothered the Christian force trapped between the Horns of Hattin and the hill of Nimrin to the west. A hail of arrows whizzed through the smoke, striking down men and horses. Fighting ferociously, the Hospitallers pushed their way to the northern horn for a desperate glimpse of the glistening Sea of Galilee. Behind them they left their dead and wounded, swollen-mouthed with thirst, and many prisoners. 'Kill us all to end our suffering,' five captured Frankish knights begged the Muslim commanders, and in some cases the request was granted.

Saladin was the master of the encounter from the outset. His cavalry launched charge after charge against the tormented Christian soldiers, who nonetheless fought back so desperately that the Muslims couldn't keep the height. Guy got an order through to Raymond to pull the Hospitallers – or what remained of them – back to defend the king and the True Cross fragment that was with him. But they refused; the Sea of Galilee was tantalizingly visible, and all the orders in the world weren't going to keep them from water. With desperate all-or-nothing courage, Raymond threw his men against the Muslim lines on Taki ed-Din's front. It was the Cresson Spring all over again; the Muslims opened their lines to let the charge spend itself harmlessly, and closed around from behind. Raymond and his remaining men found themselves cut off from the main force, and after telling anyone with earshot to save himself as best as he could, galloped off westwards towards Tripoli, followed shortly afterwards by Balian of Ibelin.

With Raymond and the Hospitallers neutralized, Saladin sent divisions under Taki ed-Din and Kukburi to cut off the withdrawal routes for the Christians. While Guy dithered, more Muslim cavalry – highly mobile and protected only by their *kazaghand* (tunics of layered cotton) – thudded into the Templars at the rear. After a few futile countercharges, the thirsty Templars soon became dispirited and were pushed back towards the Horns of Hattin. These were fierce encounters, and more than once the watching Saladin turned pale with anxiety. His son al-Afdal, getting his first taste of serious battle, tried to encourage his father by pointing out the times the Franks retreated. But Saladin was not so easily swayed. 'See that tent there,' he told al-Afdal, pointing to Guy's red tent on the hillside. 'As long as that is still there, we haven't beaten them.' Moments later, the tent was seen to collapse. Saladin jumped off his horse and bowed to the ground, tears of joy rolling down his face.

Guy, not knowing what else to do, had ordered that the tents be quickly put up as some kind of barrier, but it was to no avail – the core of Christians with the True Cross found themselves marooned in a sea of attacking Muslims. Prayers were unavailing. In less than an hour almost all the horses were dead and their riders milling about on foot powerlessly. The king had tried to work his way up to the twin summits of the Horns where the ruins of some ancient walls could afford protection; somehow he accomplished it, pitching his tent again and brandishing the True Cross defiantly. Then, as Saladin watched from atop his horse, the red tent went down and the battle was over. Guy and Reynald of Châtillon, too exhausted to fight any more, were soon in Saladin's hands.

Saladin's secretary, Imad al-Din, viewed the carnage on the Horns of Hattin:

Limbs of the fallen cast naked on the field of combat, scattered in pieces … lacerated and disjointed, with heads cracked open, throats slit, spines broken, necks shattered, feet in pieces, noses mutilated, extremities torn off, members disjointed, parts shredded.[13]

Ultimate responsibility for this must in the end lie with Guy of Lusignan. In Montgomery's judgement he 'threw good sense and experience overboard'. So far the Frankish strategy had been the successful one of avoiding open combat with the quick-moving Muslims and staying close to protective fortifications, but Guy appeared to ignore what almost a century of warfare in the Middle East was supposed to have taught the Franks. When Saladin's tactical genius was brought onto the balance, the result was all too predictable.[14]

Saladin most likely had allowed Raymond, 'God curse him', to escape, but that's as far as his mercy extended. He had waited a long time to wreak his vengeance on Guy and in particular the unpleasant Châtillon, who had shown his villainous colours repeatedly. In Saladin's own words, 'the eyes of the Muslim spears sought out the diseased hearts and livers of the unbelievers' who 'drank the cup of fate'. It was a cup of water rather than fate that the parched and shattered Guy was now in dire need of when he was brought before Saladin seated comfortably on a divan. Guy as a king was graciously given a place by the Muslim leader's side, a gesture which elicited a sneer from Châtillon. Saladin personally handed a cup of sherbet-flavoured rose water to Guy, who gulped some of it down and then passed it to Châtillon, but Saladin stopped him. 'You didn't ask my permission to give him water,' he told Guy with a menacing calm, and, turning to Châtillon, gave him personal permission, adding that it would be the last drink he ever took.

Everyone present knew what that meant. But Saladin wanted to draw out the ordeal, accusing Châtillon of repeated acts of treachery. The Frenchman's arrogant reply was the cynical one that might makes right, especially against a Muslim. In reply to a question of what Châtillon would do if the roles were reversed and it was Saladin who was the captive, he replied that he'd behead Saladin in short order. Stung by the Frenchman's arrogance, Saladin rode out to meet his returning soldiers, and when his anger had subsided he had Châtillon brought back to him, offering to spare him if he would convert to Islam. When the expected contemptuous reply came, Saladin took careful aim with his flashing sword and sliced off one of Châtillon's arms at the shoulder. That was signal for armed retainers to remove the Frenchman's head as well.

King Guy was then brought in, fearing he would be next. But Saladin reassured him: 'Real kings do not kill each other,' he said. Châtillon, by contrast, had been pretty much a monster, and besides, he wasn't a king. Thus by a bitter round of justice, Guy of Lusignan and Raymond of Tripoli, who had argued against the campaign from the beginning, were safe, one in captivity and the other free. But a grim fate awaited the captured Templars and Hospitallers, numbering between 100 and 200, who had survived the massacre at Hattin. To Saladin they were bearers of 'impure cults', and he put aside his usual magnanimity to have them bound hand and foot and executed en masse. Muslim scholars and clerics were deputed for the task that ordinarily would have been left to specialists: some made a clean job, others proved clumsy. A few refused to kill on the grounds of conscience. The Templar Grand Master, Gerard de Ridefort, was spared as a potentially profitable hostage. A few knights saved their lives by accepting Islam. The bodies of the rest were left where they fell, their whited bones still visible to passers-by a year later.

Captured knights and other soldiers, who came cheap for anyone interested, flooded the slave markets of Damascus. Countess Eschiva, the putative cause of the whole mess, had to surrender Tiberias to Saladin, who allowed her to live in safety and comfort in Tripoli. Saladin was free now to roll up Outremer, which he proceeded to do systematically. Acre fell on 10 July and was given to al-Afdal to govern. One by one the Crusader castles of Galilee capitulated. Balian of Ibelin surrendered Nablus on honourable terms. Saladin's brother al-Adil marched up from Egypt and sacked Jaffa. Only Tyre held out, thanks to its robust fortifications and near-impregnable position on a promontory. In September it was Ascalon's turn to fall to Saladin, eliminating the only southern Outremer port of any consequence. The town held out for a while, ignoring the pleas of King Guy and the Templar Grand Master de Ridefort that it should surrender; but when the inevitable happened the Templar garrison in the town was treated leniently. Guy was held in various jails, still technically the king of Jerusalem, with the privilege of visits from Sibylla.

Jerusalem was now the great fruit waiting to be plucked, and Saladin politely asked to be allowed to pluck it. The Frankish nobles and Military Orders of course refused, and Saladin prepared to take the city by storm. Balian of Ibelin, the leading knight in the city, prepared for a desperate defence, knighting every noble boy over sixteen and thirteen wealthy non-nobles. A considerable sum of money that Henry II of England had donated to the Hospitallers was requisitioned to procure food and weapons.

Saladin's attack began on 20 September. For the first five days his troops could make little headway against the great north and north-west walls, so he moved his operations opposite the east wall on the Mount of Olives. Muslim sappers undermined the wall at that point, and on 29 September the first attackers broke through. The Frankish knights were all for dying in a blaze of glory, but Balian of Ibelin had more sense; whatever the fanatic knights might think, there were families and noncombatants to consider. Moreover, the local Orthodox Christians were no fans of the ruling Latins, and openly preferred what they saw to be a more tolerant Muslim rule. All of which made the Frankish position very weak. On the last day of September Balian rode to Saladin's tent to ask for terms.

The meeting in Saladin's tent was a tense one. As the sounds of battle raged in the city, the Muslim leader demanded nothing short of unconditional surrender. He pointedly reminded Balian of the butchery that had accompanied the First Crusaders' seizure of Jerusalem nearly a century before, and asked the Frenchman if that dubious favour ought to be returned in kind. As he spoke, Saladin pointed to the wall of Jerusalem, on top of which his yellow standard had just appeared. But that success turned out to be momentary; a sally by the Franks at that moment drove the attackers back. Balian, newly encouraged, remarked that the defenders, unless given honourable terms, would destroy everything in Jerusalem, even the Muslim holy places. That brought Saladin up short; his counter-proposal was that all the Christians in the city – perhaps 25,000 at a conservative estimate – be ransomed for an enormous sum. Balian, hardly knowing how the money could be raised, agreed, and on 2 October Saladin's army entered Jerusalem, ending nearly nine decades of Frankish rule. The contrast with 1099 could not be greater. Runciman writes: 'The victors were correct and humane. Where the Franks, eighty-eight years before, had waded through the blood of their victims, not a building now was looted, not a person injured.'[15]

The Latin Church, the Hospitallers and Templars had to cough up a great deal of their wealth to help ransom the poorer Christians, and they have been accused of doing it reluctantly; Henry II's donation to the Hospitallers is estimated to have secured the freedom of 7,000 people, though the Order was doubtless capable of more generosity. While leading churchmen made off bowed down with the gold in their bags, ignoring the plight of their poor, Saladin had to step in and personally ransom every old or infirm person who otherwise would have been dragged into slavery. Having thus displayed a nobility of the best Christian type to the shame of his enemies, Saladin carried the True Cross, pinned upside down to a spear, off to Damascus.

Personnel of the Military Orders joined the thousands of Christian refugees crowding the westbound roads out of Jerusalem. They moved in three main columns, with the Hospitallers in charge of the second. The port of Tyre, already overcrowded, would admit only the fighting men; the noncombatants, after several vicissitudes, ended up mostly in Antioch. The Crusader castles at Kerak and Montreal took longer to fall; the Hospitaller garrison at Belvoir Castle held out until January 1189. Raymond of Tripoli was dead; he never recovered from the shock of defeat at Hattin and had wasted away in depressive illness a few months later. The Hospitallers in Krak des Chevaliers were too strong to dislodge, and Saladin didn't even try. After an unsuccessful attempt on the Templar Castle at Tortosa, Saladin brushed with a Hospitaller detachment outside the castle of Marqab. But apart from those temporary setbacks, Saladin had rolled up all the Frankish lands by the end of September 1187, disbanding his army on the first day of the following year. The only holdouts were the Hospitallers at Krak and Marqab, the Templars at Tortosa, and most important of all, the city of Tyre. Barely three-quarters of a century after its official founding as a charitable protector of needy pilgrims in the Holy Land, the Order of Saint John came close to ending its career.

At the time of Hattin the Christian powers of Europe had issues to worry about closer to home. The Byzantine emperor, Isaac II Angelos, having already lost much of Asia Minor to the Turks, was preoccupied with a Norman advance across the Balkan peninsula. Frederick I Barbarossa of Germany was embroiled with the popes; Henry II of England, in the last years of his life, was fending off treacherous intrigues by his ambitious sons Richard and John; and Philip II Augustus of France, on the throne for seven years, was disturbing the rest of Europe with his multiple marriages and openly envying Saladin 'who had no pope above him'.[16] Into this maelstrom of European problems came the double blow of the news of Hattin and the fall of Jerusalem. The ailing Pope Urban III collapsed and died of the shock. Crusading fervour in Europe had declined considerably, thanks to the catastrophic results of the Second Crusade, attributed by many to divine punishment for the sin of arrogance. But a new generation of Europeans had since grown up and, having no direct memory of the tribulations of the 1140s, required only a fresh spark to reignite the old fervour. Fanning that spark into a flame was Urban III's successor, Pope Gregory VIII, who promptly issued an encyclical entitled *Audita Tremendi* (Shocking News) in which he lamented the 'severe and terrible judgement' that had befallen Outremer at the hands of 'savage barbarians thirsting after Christian blood'. The twelfth century equivalent of a cartoonist contributed to the incendiary mood by circulating a picture of Christ with blood pouring down His face. 'This is the Messiah,' read the caption, 'struck by Muhammad, the Prophet of the Muslims, who has wounded and killed Him.'[17] The Hospitallers and Templars publicized their own appeals for more recruits.

Interestingly, the publication of the *Audita Tremendi*, about four weeks after the fall of Jerusalem, focused its lament on the loss of the True Cross at Hattin rather than on the fall of Jerusalem. It may well have been written after news of the first event arrived at Rome, but not the second.[18] What was about to become the Third Crusade, then, had a clear and galvanizing symbolic object – to recapture the True Cross. Anyone who volunteered for this most vital of crusades, the pope assured his hearers and readers, would have all their sins remitted and immunity from being taken to court for anything – a clear and cynical appeal to recruit anyone on the fringes of the law. Their families meanwhile would be under Church protection and those who died on service were assured of a place in Heaven. One of those hearers was Prince Richard of England, the most ambitious son of Henry II whose most convenient death two years later elevated the son to the English throne as Richard I.

Chapter 6

'In Vi Sancti Spiritus'

Richard I's dilemma – dissention in the Military Orders – negotiations with Saladin – skirmishes at Beit Nuba – the vision at Emmaus – Battle of Jaffa – treaty with Saladin – Richard departs – the Assassins – Saladin's death – 'legalized anarchy' – the 'Fourth Crusade' – the Hospitallers in Syria – battles on the Nile – the Fifth Crusade

After the battle at Arsuf, which was Richard I's finest hour (and one of the Hospitallers' finest as well), the English king faced a strategic conundrum. He was in control of the Palestinian seaboard but to strike inland to well-fortified Jerusalem would be no easy task. What was he to do first – build up his strength on the coast waiting for ships to arrive with reinforcements, or strike while the iron was hot and the Muslims were exhausted and disorganized? Before he could decide, bad news came from Ascalon, which he had intended to keep as the main resupply port; the Muslims had just razed it to the ground, a decision that Saladin took with a heavy heart but with strategic good sense. All right, then, Richard decided, Jerusalem can wait – Ascalon must be recovered first. But to his surprise and chagrin, not everyone agreed with him.

Richard I is popularly known as the Lionheart, but the sobriquet has tended to cast an unrealistic sheen over his actual historical record. Admiring contemporaries of a classical Greek bent described him as possessing 'the valour of Hector, the heroism of Achilles, Nestor's tongue and Ulysses' wisdom'.[1] English schools until recently held up his example as that of the quintessential English king. In fact, there was almost nothing English about Richard, the Count of Anjou and Duke of Aquitaine. He never learned to speak English, preferring the courtly French in which he was brought up and educated. Richard was the clear favourite of his mother, Eleanor of Aquitaine, and with some justification; his looks – a fair complexion and strawberry-blond hair – and personality skills elevated him head and shoulders above his less prepossessing brothers. On the negative side, he actively fought and undermined his father. His first foreign conquest was of the Christian island of Cyprus, hardly a blow against the infidel. Controversy surrounds his character, especially in the area of sexuality. His repeated failure to consummate marriage is cited as an indication that he was gay, though by no means all authorities are agreed on that point.[2]

Yet against these shortcomings Richard had one overriding virtue that counted for much: he was a born soldier.

He excelled at the basic military skills: horsemanship, fighting with spear and shield, mace and war-axe, shooting with the bow, scouting, analyzing terrain and choosing optimum sites for defence and points to attack. Tall and long-limbed, muscular and agile, Richard was made for warfare, able to withstand the punishing shock of encounter when an opponent's lance struck his armour and able to deal deadly blows with deadly accuracy.[3]

If anyone was qualified to do any serious crusading with the required abilities, Richard was the man. On one of his precious few visits to England he had quipped that he was prepared to sell London itself if it could raise him enough money for the campaign.[4] Setting out for the Holy Land, his soldiers sang: '*Lignum Crucis, signum ducis, sequitur exercitus, quod non cessit, sed praecessit, in vi Sancti Spiritus.*' ('Behind the wooden Cross and duke's banner follows the army which never yields but marches in the power of the Holy Spirit.')[5] If the Knights Hospitaller sang anything, it would have been very much along those lines, as it encapsulated the Order's perceived mission.

With Ascalon destroyed and the Crusaders' position in Outremer more precarious that he had expected, Richard began to think seriously about what he could realistically do. His position was made more difficult by outbursts of protest among his commanders and soldiers: what were they doing marching towards Ascalon while Jerusalem – the entire object of this whole campaign – was left untouched? Had they come thousands of miles and lost hundreds of men to enemy action and disease only to be within striking distance of the supreme prize and then march away? The Hospitallers wanted their old headquarters back. Richard had to confront the angry voices at Jaffa, and perhaps unused to being opposed, gave in. But something else may have been germinating at the back of his mind. If a direct military attack on Jerusalem was inadvisable, could not the object of the Crusade – the freedom of Christians to worship in the City of Christ – be attained by more peaceful means? He sat down and wrote a letter to his Muslim adversary.

'The land is ruined,' the king wrote to Saladin. 'Muslims and Franks are finished. Jerusalem is the centre of our worship which we will never renounce.' He suggested a meeting with Saladin to talk specifically about the True Cross, lost at Hattin, and the city itself. As a reasonable man, Saladin could be expected to value such sincere religious sentiment, and replied in kind: 'Al-Quds [the Muslim name for Jerusalem] is as much ours as yours, [as] it is where Our Prophet came on his Night Journey and the gathering place of the angels.'[6] Both sides began protracted negotiations, including what we would now call summits, where the wine and the honeyed words flowed, but agreement did not.

For the next few months, as uncomfortable cold weather descended on Palestine, both leaders conducted a diplomatic and military game of chicken, each hoping the other would give up. Saladin strengthened the walls of Jerusalem, rolling up his sleeves and applying himself personally to the task alongside 2,000 Frankish prisoners, while Richard advanced slowly until the new year of 1192 found him at Beit Nuba, twelve miles from the city. As the men shivered in the rain and mud, trying to chew their basic rations of soaked biscuit and pork, and horses perished of cold and malnutrition, Richard saw that with his army in such a condition a prolonged siege of Jerusalem would frankly not be possible. On 13 January he withdrew to Ascalon. The military barons from the West, and probably some of the Templars as well, were close to mutiny. Through the pressure the king insisted on trying to work out an agreement with Saladin through negotiations 'comparable in complexity to those between Israelis and Palestinians in the twenty-first century'.[7] But then, as now, emotions ran too high and the contacts came to nothing.

When warm weather returned Richard led the army back to Beit Nuba. The militant barons were on his back the whole time, clamouring for Jerusalem. The Hospitallers, and those of the Templars and native-born Franks who knew the local realities, argued against it, but several individual knights itched for action. One of them was the Flemish Hospitaller Robert of Bruges, who challenged a couple of hundred Saracens who had charged out of the hills onto a convoy. He escaped only by taking the horse of a brother-sergeant, who was killed. A countercharge by both the Military Orders failed to dent the Muslims, and Hubert Walter, the Bishop of Salisbury, had to intervene to stop the fight in order to save the French. Robert of Bruges was promptly court martialled for indiscipline, but a majority of knights of the Order pardoned him.[8]

When Richard got word of a Saracen force lurking at Emmaus, where Christ had appeared to His disciples after His resurrection, he felt he could not tolerate the sacrilege and rode out at night at the head of a detachment to dislodge the enemy. As dawn broke he surprised them and killed twenty of them. Thus encouraged, Richard and his men rode into the hills looking for more of the enemy; he ran down one Arab and as he pulled his sword from the bloody body he looked up to see a large sunlit city on the horizon a few miles away. Jerusalem! At once he raised his shield in front of his face, unable to bear the sight of the city that he 'could not deliver from [God's] enemies'.

Soon after his tantalizing glimpse of the Holy City, a ragged old man with a long white beard came to his camp and introduced himself as the abbot of a nearby Cistercian abbey. The visitor claimed to know where the True Cross was hidden, but when he led Richard to the place, all that could be found was a small crucifix said to be made of the same wood as the actual cross. This crucifix was set up in the middle of the camp. The abbot then forecast that Richard would never take Jerusalem. While the king was digesting this, an Arab spy came in and reported that a large and wealthy caravan was on its way up from Cairo. Forgetting Jerusalem, Richard got together 700 knights and 1,000 turcopoles and fell on the caravan in the hills of Hebron. Few of the Egyptian military guard survived. The Crusaders marched triumphantly back, bearing in their train 3,000 camels and about the same number of horses and pack mules, and an incredible hoard of gold, silver, weapons, silks, medicines, grain and spices. Richard's military budget was replenished. And camel meat, the soldiers said, had a most exquisite taste.

But more was on Richard's mind than mere booty. First and foremost, he had to make a decision about Jerusalem, and he was finding it difficult. Did he want war or not? His reaction when inadvertently glimpsing Jerusalem reveals his confused state of mind. Had he already given up the Third Crusade as a bad job? Had the old abbot's dire prediction that he would never achieve his goal unnerved him with the fear that he might be killed before Jerusalem? The whole Crusading army, especially the Military Orders, clamoured for an advance, now that reinforcements in personnel and supplies had arrived. But, he told his barons gloomily, a siege of Jerusalem would prove costly. Even if the army managed to breach the city's immense walls, Saladin could easily snap the Crusaders' supply line from the coast and trap them in a vice. Moreover, the Muslim leader had poisoned all the wells in the vicinity of the city.

'If I should lead the host to besiege Jerusalem,' he said, 'and the endeavour should come to defeat, all my life long I should be blamed … I am aware that there are many people here and in France who would love to see me make such a mistake."[9] Here, then, could be the key to his change of heart. His long absence from home had enabled his brother John to usurp more and more power in England. In April the Prior of Hereford had arrived at the camp with an urgent request that he return to England. He then and there offered to resign his command if it would break the impasse in the army.

If there was one moment in the Crusades where sound military judgement prevailed over hotheaded impetuousness, this was it. Richard the Lionheart has been roundly criticized for his so-called failure of nerve before Jerusalem, but in common-sense terms he really had no choice. He handed the command of the army to a committee of twenty senior officials including five Hospitallers and five Templars. This committee held its first meeting and, probably influenced by the Military Orders' cautious majority, the immediate military objective was changed from Jerusalem to Egypt.

The decision prompted a storm of protest from the newly-arrived French, who had set their hearts on recapturing the Holy City of Christ. Some of them were so overcome by emotion that they rolled in the dust in self-punishment. Others heaped abuse on Richard, calling his manhood as well as his spirituality into question. But the king, undaunted, opened negotiations with Saladin. When they broke down on 20 July over the Muslim demand to disarm Ascalon, Saladin's army appeared before Jaffa, defended by about 5,000 tired and weakened troops, among whom were many sick and wounded. But the garrison commander, Alberi of Rheims, initially did a good job of defending the port against Saladin's big siege engines, until at one point his spirit inexplicably broke and he tried to flee in a boat; he was brought back in chains and replaced by a senior clergyman whose courage was rather more robust. He was also cleverer than Alberi, sending a mission to Saladin with an offer to surrender Jaffa in return for the defenders being allowed to go free after being ransomed.

After at first rejecting the proposal, Saladin accepted after realizing that his own troops, too, were battle-weary. But Richard, having been absent in Beirut, had hurried south, and six days after the start of the siege, sailed into Jaffa on his red-painted royal ship, the *Trenchemere*, at the head of a flotilla of thirty-five galleys manned partly by Hospitallers and Templars. The voyage had been a frustrating one, with contrary winds holding him up at Haifa. There the king is said to have gazed at the sky and cried, 'Mercy, O Lord! Why do You hold me and retard me when I go upon Your quest?' The biblical tenor of the words, if they are not chroniclers' exaggerations, indicate the religiosity that may have pervaded even ordinary speech at the time. We can well imagine that the members of the Military Orders, at least, would be prone to speaking in spiritual terms that would lend an air of magnificence to their duties.

Richard's appearance gave new heart to the defenders, who halted the ransoming process and prepared to renew the fight. The senior clergyman was negotiating with Saladin in the latter's tent when the trumpet gave out the news of the royal arrival. Saladin knew what it meant and dismissed his visitor. He already had the advantage, as the Muslims had already broken through the walls, were thronging through the city and were now ordered to form on the beach to stop the Crusaders from landing. Yelling Muslim archers, one foot in the water, fired volleys at the Christian ships. The spectacle from the ships was a daunting one; Richard could not be sure if the citadel of Jaffa was still in Frankish hands. While he was pondering what to do, a figure was seen jumping down from a perilous height on the citadel, racing for the water's edge and swimming out to the ships. It was a priest who gasped out the news that the citadel was indeed in Christian hands but the garrison itself was gradually being slaughtered like sheep.

'A curse on him who hesitates,' shouted Richard, stripping off his leg and body armour and jumping into the sea first. He waded through nearly chest-high water, followed by his troops, 'like Saul's men at Gibeah'.[10] We are told that the very sight of Richard unnerved the Saracens, who pulled back, allowing the king and the Military Orders to penetrate to the Templars' house after killing a good many of the enemy. Saladin fumed, but could do little to reinstate courage into his fleeing soldiers.

The recapture of Jaffa was the chief fact on the ground that led to a resumption of the peace talks. But one more incident remained; during the negotiations Saladin approved a plot to kidnap Richard, but the king awoke just as the plotters were outside his tent. In a matter of minutes the whole Crusader army outside Jaffa was in formation to repel a furious attack by several thousand Saracen cavalry. The horsemen shattered against a solid wall of Crusader spearmen kneeling in tight order, their spears pointing outwards. Behind them were the crossbowmen in pairs, one firing while the other loaded. Behind these stood eighty knights, having to share just a dozen destriers. Richard ran along the line encouraging the men and when the wave of Muslim cavalry faltered Richard, on foot, led the furious countercharge.

Saladin, watching, marvelled how a king's dignity could allow him to join his foot-soldiers. We may imagine him shaking his head in admiration as he turned to his brother al-Adil and told him to take two thoroughbred horses through the lines to Richard so that he would not be without a mount. Somehow al-Adil got through and delivered his present. But Richard had little time for thanks, as arrow after arrow thudded into his armour and padded breastplate, luckily not penetrating to flesh. He was seen to emerge from a pile of bodies, and when a Muslim emir charged him, he sliced off the emir's head and right arm. Such conspicuous deeds might impress Saladin but struck terror into the ordinary Saracen soldier. 'The King of England, a lance in his hand, rode down the whole length of our army,' wrote Saladin's secretary Beha al-Din, 'and none of our men did come forth to challenge him.'[11] By nightfall the battle was over. The body count, we are informed, was 700 Saracens to just two Crusaders.

After the battle Richard fell grievously ill, probably infected by the masses of unburied bodies. Saladin was generous in sending him fresh fruit and ice to cool his fever. By now both Richard and the Muslim emirs were weary of constant warfare that had ravaged the land. In September 1192, from his sickbed Richard agreed to the terms of a five-year peace treaty. The king claimed to be too weak to sign the document himself, so Henry of Champagne, who had succeeded Conrad of Montferrat as titular king of Jerusalem, signed on his behalf, with Hospitaller Grand Master Garnier de Nablus adding his own signature. Al-Adil signed for his brother. The Franks would retain the Palestinian coast as far south as Jaffa, while the Muslims would keep Jerusalem. Christians would have unhindered access to the city and the holy places; several touring parties of knights made the trip, and Bishop Walter of Salisbury had a long and cordial meeting with Saladin. This was probably the supreme moment of the Muslim leader's career, the culmination of a brilliant military and diplomatic whirlwind.

While Richard was slowly recovering at Acre, the remnants of his disconsolate Crusaders mustered at the port to sail home, leaving behind the bodies of thousands of their comrades dead from enemy action and disease, crowding onto the transports to take their chances in the unpredictable autumn winds of the Mediterranean. The king was tormented by a sense of failure powerful enough to solemnly warn Saladin that he would return to complete his unfinished business. Saladin aristocratically remarked that if it were God's will, he wouldn't mind losing his domains to such an all-round excellent king. On the ship that bore him away, Richard looked back at the coastline of the Holy Land and prayed that God might allow him to return. God did not so allow. After daunting adventures on sea and land, including a spell as the prisoner of Holy Roman Emperor Henry VI, he returned to a host of problems in England and France, to be felled by a French arrow in 1199.

And what of Outremer? For five years, while the hapless ex-king Guy had been loitering at Acre, Richard entertained hopes that he might still be of some use. But a grand council of knights and barons had called for Conrad of Montferrat, a capable marquis who had saved Tyre from Saladin, to be named titular king of Jerusalem in place of Guy, who was given Cyprus to rule in compensation. The news of his royal election by acclamation unnerved Conrad who, we are told, fell to his knees and asked God not to make him king if he was unworthy of it. The prayer was fulfilled in a gruesome manner: a few nights later, as he was walking home from the Bishop of Beauvais' house in Tyre a couple of fanatic Muslims pounced on him and stabbed him to death. The killers were members of the sinister sect known as the Assassins, headquartered in the mountains of Syria and under the absolute control of Sheikh Rashid al-Din Sinan, known to the Crusaders as the Old Man of the Mountain (*Le Vieux de la Montagne*). The Assassins (from *hashishin*, or hashish-smokers, the method by which they could attain stupefaction and absolute obedience to the master) had taken no part in the Crusades and had used the decades of turmoil to amass great wealth. The sect had evolved into a highly efficient murder network that for about 170 years struck terror into every regime, Christian or Muslim. Even Saladin had lost his nerve when he found a dagger under his pillow – a chilling calling card of the invisible and undetectable Assassins. Conrad of Montferrat's offence, it turned out, was to have confiscated a ship full of goods that the sect had bought.

Saladin's health had been failing under the strain of five years of active campaigning while trying to run an extensive and often unruly Muslim state. He collapsed in Damascus on 1 March 1193, and passed away two days later, smiling as the Koran was read over him. Runciman's judgement is a fitting epitaph:

> Of all the great figures of the Crusading era Saladin is the most attractive … [H]e respected [the Christians'] ways and thought of them as fellow-men. Unlike the Crusader potentates, he never broke his word when it was pledged to anyone, whatever his religion. For all his fervour, he was always courteous and generous, merciful as a conqueror and a judge, as a master considerate and tolerant.[12]

Saladin's eldest son al-Afdal became sultan, but he proved nowhere near the calibre of his father. His Ayyubid dynasty soon broke down in a series of quarrels which could have been advantageous to Outremer if it had itself been united. Though Guy of Lusignan hankered after his old kingdom, his putative successor Henry of Champagne couldn't secure the agreement of the barons for his own elevation to what had by now become a pseudo-throne (though his wife Isabella remained the official queen). There was now no Richard to impose his organizing talents on the Franks of the East, whose days were now numbered.

During this confused period the Hospitaller and Templar Grand Masters were often called upon to have a say in who should wield the sceptres of power. Their Knights were sent marching to and fro, following the wealthiest or strongest bidder, in a period that has been aptly described as 'legalized anarchy'.[13] They were constantly in demand because they were simply the most professional military forces that Outremer possessed, and could generally be trusted to do the job assigned to them. They also retained a religious sanction (albeit sometimes superficial) through the popes, which underpinned their credibility and legitimacy, regardless of whether their leaders displayed any strategic talents or not. Perhaps just as important, the Military Orders were by far the wealthiest organizations in the East, and had no budgetary worries when it came to paying for campaigns.

When Guy de Lusignan died in 1194 his brother Amalric angled for the throne of Jerusalem with Military Order backing. Three years later Holy Roman Emperor Henry VI launched a German crusade that buttressed Amalric's claim. Henry of Champagne reluctantly agreed to help the Germans. When al-Adil made a diversionary move on Jaffa, Henry began pulling reinforcements together, and he would very probably have put the German Crusade on an organized footing had he not accidentally stepped backwards out of a palace window in Acre while reviewing his troops. His dwarf tried to grab him, but both plunged to their deaths.

The unfortunate Henry had been the third of Queen Isabella's husbands, and for the royal concern to keep going a fourth had to be quickly found. Amalric seemed to many, including the new and strong-willed Pope Innocent III, to be the man for the job. Supported by the Military Orders, Amalric II was capable enough but managed to alienate a few barons who made an unsuccessful attempt on his life in March 1198. Meanwhile, the German Crusade had collapsed under the weight of a determined counter-offensive by al-Adil. But before they fled for home, the Germans had set up their own version of the Hospitallers in the form of the Teutonic Knights. The Teutonic Knights' origins had been similar to those of the Knights of Saint John. During the Third Crusade some merchants of Bremen and Lübeck had established a hospice for German pilgrims at Acre; the German Crusade had boosted the numbers of knights who chose to stay and be warrior monks, and in 1198 they were recognized an a Military Order by Pope Innocent III. The Teutonic Knights were given Saint Nicholas' Tower in Acre, and later they bought Montfort Castle, whose name they Germanized into Starkenberg.

At the turn of the thirteenth century an old power in the region showed signs of revived strength. This was Armenia, a Christian nation yet opposed to the Byzantine Empire, taking up much of what is today eastern Turkey with a bit of Syria thrown in. All political boundaries were very flexible in those days, altering year to year and even month to month. The new ruler of Armenia, King Leo II, engineered a family claim on the Frankish Principality of Antioch, triggering a succession conflict that would last more than two decades and drag the Hospitallers into its morass. The Order reluctantly joined the Templars in propping up the Antiochean leader, Bohemond IV. Meanwhile, potential knightly recruits continued to flow in from France, eager to wade straight in and kill Muslims. In 1202 Amalric II advised them to be patient, only to be openly reviled by one of them, Reynald de Dampierre, as a coward. The consequence was not unexpected; when Dampierre and a team of aggressive knights rode into the Muslim territory of Latakieh without asking permission, they were ambushed and massacred.

If this was the kind of help the West would be sending, Amalric was right to be wary. Fortunately he had in al-Adil, an Egypt-based ruler who was rather weaker than his redoubtable late brother Saladin, and had no intention of rocking the political boat more than absolutely necessary; trade along the Syrian coast was beginning to boom, benefiting everyone. Al-Adil chose to overlook a Hospitaller raid from Krak des Chevaliers and Marqab into Muslim territory near Hama, and in September 1204 signed a six-year pact with Amalric. The following year, however, Amalric died unexpectedly after (we are told) consuming a rather large amount of fish, and Isabella was tragically widowed yet again.

Farther north, momentous events were unfolding. Pope Innocent III, who was calling for a fresh crusade, had his wish granted in a way far from what he intended when the Venetians, ever resentful of Byzantine control of eastern Mediterranean trade, hatched a plot to capture Constantinople. The plot was dressed up as a campaign to bring the 'schismatic' Greek Orthodox Church under the Latin thumb; to delude the initial volunteers, they were told that Egypt was the destination. The Venetians took great pride in their sea power, valuing themselves as far more capable than the landlubber Franks who were good for little more than 'charging around on horseback'.[14] 'There was never a greater crime against humanity than the Fourth Crusade,' writes Runciman sternly, and with ample reason.[15] The Venetian sack of Constantinople in April 1204 was horrifying in the number of its victims and sheer destruction of a cultural treasure going back to classical Greece. Any supposedly Christian motive was totally vitiated as we are told that a prostitute sat herself on the patriarch's throne in the great cathedral of Sancta Sophia and sang indecent French songs while drunken Frenchmen and Italians looted the church and the blood of innocent civilians ran in the streets.

The Military Orders, fortunately, had no part in this outrage, which would place the Latin boot on Constantinople for the next fifty-seven years. In fact the Hospitallers, even though Catholic, ended up cultivating good relations with the Greek emperors-in-exile, who were conducting a vigorous resistance out of Nicaea. After Amalric II's binge-eating death the succession to the exiled throne of Jerusalem passed to his teenaged stepdaughter Maria. John of Ibelin, son of the distinguished Balian, served as the regent. When Maria turned seventeen she was betrothed to a 60-year-old knight from Champagne called John of Brienne; they were married in Tyre in September 1210 and crowned king and queen the following month. John of Brienne's age and knowledge spoke in favour of stability; he had earned the respect of the Military Orders and the Muslims alike, and accepted an extension of the truce with al-Adil. But he, too, itched for some crusading fame. The unexpected death from a fever of Maria at just 21 demoted him from king to regent, as their young daughter Isabella II (better known as Yolanda) automatically assumed the throne.

At this time the Hospitallers were preoccupied with events in north Syria. Bohemond IV was engaged in a tussle for Antioch with Leo II of Armenia. But the keen and often bitter rivalry between the Military Orders had never subsided, and almost automatically when Bohemond recruited the Templars to his cause, the Hospitallers sided with Leo. This was only one complication in a whole web of them, which the Teutonic Knights wisely decided to stay out of. Enter at this point the Assassins, who assassinated Bohemond's teenage son Raymond in church in Tortosa in 1213. The Hospitallers, now led by Grand Master Garin de Montaigu, were widely suspected of being in league with the terrorist sect, a suspicion that deepened after Patriarch Albert of Jerusalem, an opponent of the Order, was done away with the following year. Were the Knights of Saint John really in league with the Assassins? There seems to be no firm evidence either way, though the authoritative Runciman, citing earlier serious studies, appears to take it for granted. If so, it would indicate that the Hospitallers' (and the Templars') original pure aim of defending Christendom had been considerably diluted by time and power.

Apart from the reported flirtation with the Assassins, in the early thirteenth century the Hospitallers retained a high reputation. Around 1203 Grand Master Alfonso de Portugal, who succeeded Geoffrey de Donjon in that year, drew up new statutes for the order; these statutes distinguished the professed knights, who had taken perpetual vows of poverty, chastity and obedience on joining, from the secular knights who agreed to serve for a specific time and were not required to take the ultimate vows. Alfonso's rules also divided the brethren into three functional classes; the military brothers whose duty was to fight, the infirmarian brothers who looked after the sick, and the brother chaplains who could devote themselves fully to priestly duties. It was a division of labour that solved what may have been a tendency to organizational confusion in times of conflict. Their formal insignia of a white cross on a black surcoat was kept.

More internal reorganization followed in 1206, when the Marshal of the order, who until now had limited military authority, was given field command over all the brethren-in-arms, knights and sergeants. As a leading bailli, or official, he was second to the Grand Commander, who served as a chief of staff to the Grand Master and deputized for him when necessary. The Marshal, whose insignia consisted of the order's emblem, a purse and a seal, also was in charge of maintaining and distributing weapons, horses and provisions. He outranked officers of the next lowest rung, such as the Gonfalonier (standard-bearer), Master Esquire and Commander of Knights. Later the order's Castellans (castle commanders) and turcopole forces would also come under the Marshal's authority. The Marshal usually had the best knowledge of political and military conditions in the Middle East, but this advantage was often offset by a periodic tug-of-war with the Treasury – a bane of all military organizations in all ages.

The office of Constable appeared very early in the Hospitallers' history as a kind of executive officer for the Marshal. But by about 1180 it seems to have been somewhat eclipsed. The Master Esquire, a brother-sergeant rank established in 1206, was the senior officer responsible for the horses and stables and the staff of squires; below him was the Crie (or Acrie) who was in charge of the stables themselves. The Master Esquire was allowed three horses and his own household (though the Grand Master had his own Master Esquire, who later, to avoid confusion, was named the Grand Esquire). The reform of 1206 raised the Gonfalonier's status to one rung below the Marshal; as the standard-bearer, he had to be a knight of noble (and legitimate) birth, a rule that was codified in later years. The rank of Gonfalonier was probably a promotion for valour in the field, as he had to be the steadiest officer to keep the banner high in the tumult of combat. If the Grand Master or Marshal were incapacitated or absent, the Gonfalonier would assume temporary command.

In the Hospitallers' campaigns of the thirteenth century the Grand Master and Marshal had to be prepared to be killed in action or captured. To fill a gap in command that such an eventuality might create, the rank of Commander of the Knights was created about 1220, but seems not to have been very important. Middle ranks included the Commander of the Vault, responsible for stores, the Sub-Marshal and the Turcopolier, a brother-sergeant who commanded the turcopole auxiliaries. The Castellans, though nominally under the Marshal, were afforded considerable freedom of policy; each was assigned three horses, two squires and a turcopole batman. The Castellans of the major fortifications of Krak des Chevaliers, Belvoir and Marqab, for example, had the status of baillis. Non-military staff of the Hospitallers included the Drapier, another creation of the 1206 makeover, who ran the Parmentarie, or clothing store; this official also gave the clothes of those killed in action or captured to the poor. The Treasurer had his hand on the purse-strings, while the Conventual Prior headed the sacerdotal personnel. On the lowest non-commissioned rung were the Master Crossbowman and Master Sergeant who had to eat separately from the knights and brother-sergeants.[16]

The launch of the Fifth Crusade in 1217 gave the Military Orders a fresh chance to prove their mettle in a cause wider than their own. For some years the West had been in the grip of one of its periodic crusading fervours, and Pope Honorius III, who had succeeded Innocent III, tried to make the most of it. Among the luminaries leading the Fifth Crusade were Duke Leopold VI of Austria, King Andrew II of Hungary and King Hugh of Cyprus, though Andrew soon backed out. John of Brienne defined the Crusaders' target as Egypt, the wealthiest Muslim province and a constant strategic threat on the southern flank of the Frankish domains. Al-Adil was worried, but believed that his good relations with the Venetians and many Franks would help him weather this latest threat – until in May 1218 John and the Crusader army appeared in a fleet of Frisian ships and landed off Damietta in the eastern Egyptian Delta. Among those first ashore was the Hospitallers' Grand Master, Garin de Montaigu.

Two miles inshore the Muslims protected Damietta by a chain backed by a bridge of boats across the main eastern branch of the Nile and an island on the west bank. On the island was a tower that controlled the surrounding district. When he heard the Crusaders had landed, al-Adil sent his son al-Kamil and the main Egyptian army to al-Adiliyah to take up a position south of Damietta and reinforce the garrison at the tower. The Crusaders' first attacks concentrated on the tower, which held out, so someone had the idea of tying two boats together and building a siege tower on them; this device gave the Crusaders the ability to attack by water as well as land. The decisive push took place on 24 August, after the hottest part of the day had passed. Twenty-four hours later the tower was captured and the river chain broken. The Crusaders were at the walls of Damietta, but somehow they didn't storm the town. The most likely explanation is that John was waiting for promised reinforcements in the form of a papal army under Cardinal Pelagius of Saint Lucia that was reportedly sailing over from Italy. News of the battle at Damietta made its way to Cairo, probably in exaggerated form, which could explain why al-Adil, now an old man, did not survive the shock. Succeeding him as sultan was al-Kamil, who would prove to have some of the stamina and talents of his late Uncle Saladin.

Cardinal Pelagius was by most accounts a haughty and disagreeable man who considered himself, as a cleric, the real boss of the campaign, outranking John of Brienne who, it was unkindly pointed out, wasn't a 'real' king as he had been the consort of Queen Yolanda, and she was dead. Clashes with the Muslims around Damietta continued, with John in the forefront and al-Kamil at a distinct disadvantage. In the autumn more French and English reinforcements arrived, to be almost swept away by a flood, with the loss of many horses. As soon as that hazard had passed an epidemic – perhaps caused by rotting horseflesh getting into the water supply – carried off one-sixth of the troops. The winter was a bad one, but by February 1219 Cardinal Pelagius got enough men of spirit together to plan a decisive assault. They were on the point of starting when al-Kamil suddenly pulled back, unnerved by news of a conspiracy being hatched against him. Pelagius took al-Adiliyah with no difficulty, encircling Damietta.

Al-Kamil, having seen off his domestic foes, returned to the field in the spring. Pelagius hesitated to attack Damietta, knowing it would be fanatically defended. Another hot summer came around; John argued that Damietta, if besieged long enough, would eventually capitulate, while the cardinal urged an assault. On 20 July the Muslims surged out to hit the Crusader camp, and retired only after heavy and bloody fighting. The Muslims also had the advantage of a Byzantine invention called Greek Fire – a wildly flammable concoction of pitch, oil and resin that was blown through the precursors of flame-throwers to incinerate everything in its path. Water was useless against it. Many Frankish siege engines were burned to crisps. As casualties mounted without any concrete result, the soldiers began to desert and direct testy sentiments against John and Pelagius. Leopold of Austria had long ago gone home; the Templars' Grand Master, William of Chartres, and many other noble knights, were dead. To end the ordeal, the troops took matters into their own hands on 29 August and threw themselves against the Muslim lines. The result would have been a complete disaster had it not been for the steadiness of the Hospitallers and Templars who just managed to hold the camp. A witness to that chaotic affair had been none other than Saint Francis of Assisi, who crossed the lines to al-Kamil to urge a peace. The sultan kindly heard out this holy man and just as kindly rejected the proposal, loading the saint with gifts and sending him back.[17] In fact, the saint may well have had his influence on al-Kamil, as the sultan's next move was the most startling development in a long time: he offered the Crusaders nothing less than Jerusalem, plus central Palestine and Galilee, in return for control of the castles east of the River Jordan and the Franks' evacuation of Egypt. And the Franks could have the True Cross as well.

The proposal at first glance seemed too good to be true. John and the English, French and German senior Crusaders, many of them probably homesick, urged immediate acceptance. But Cardinal Pelagius set his face against it, refusing to parley with Muslims. The Military Orders agreed with him, but for more cogent reasons; without control of the castles east of the Jordan they would be unable to defend Jerusalem. Pelagius, the stubborn visionary who hoped that he could crush Islam once and for all, carried the day. In support of his view he had heard of a vigorous new power surging out of central Asia and about to fall on the Muslim states from the east, led by a man named Jenghiz Khan. From the West new reinforcements were expected, headed by Europe's most powerful king, Frederick II Hohenstaufen of Germany.

The waiting in Egypt, however, frayed nerves. The Hospitallers, frustrated at the inaction, raided the town of Burlos, twenty miles west of Damietta, but they seem to have been careless, as on the way out they were ambushed and their Marshal captured. Then al-Kamil sent his navy all the way to Cyprus to destroy a Crusader fleet and take thousands of prisoners. On 4 July 1221, the thirty-fourth anniversary of the slaughter at Hattin, Pelagius ordered a three-day fast and then moved the dispirited Crusader army to meet the Muslims at Fariskur, a few miles up the Nile branch from al-Adiliyah. The Military Order contingents were among the cardinal's 5,000 knights, 4,000 archers and 40,000 infantrymen, followed by a host of noncombatant pilgrims. More than 600 ships plied the river in support. The Muslims were waiting south of Sharimshah, about twenty miles upriver, in a strong position behind a tributary, Bahr as-Saghir, that connected the river with Lake Manzaleh immediately to the east.

When the Frankish army reached Sharimshah, John of Brienne wanted to stay put; the time for the annual Nile floods was approaching and a Syrian force was reportedly on its way down to help al-Kamil. However, Pelagius, buoyed by the common soldiers who were glad to be advancing, gave the order to press on and by 24 July the army was in position along the Bahr as-Saghir. But the Crusaders had overlooked a small canal that was swollen by the Nile floods, and the Muslims' ships surged into it to cut off the Frankish ships' retreat downriver. As Pelagius realized that his line of retreat to Damietta was blocked, he found that the only thing he could do was withdraw as hurriedly as he could, before the encirclement was complete. Much of the soldiery, however, was in a poor state to follow orders, having guzzled the stores of wine they had seized in Damietta. The chaotic retreat turned into a nightmare when al-Kamil opened the sluices on the right bank of the river, flooding the Franks' course. As the men floundered through the mud, Turkish cavalry and Nubian infantry sniped at them. The Hospitallers helped the Templars and Teutonic Knights deal with the Nubians, but only after taking heavy casualties. Pelagius himself escaped on his ship which managed to elude the Muslim navy.

Al-Kamil had the Crusaders over a barrel, and Pelagius knew it. A few days of negotiating ended in a deal by which the Franks would give back Damietta in exchange for the True Cross. To buttress the eight-year truce that was agreed, Hospitaller Grand Master Montaigu was one of a number of high-level hostages, including the grand masters of the other orders, transferred to al-Kamil's court. They actually didn't remain more than about a week, as early in September John and al-Kamil exchanged their hostages after a sumptuous banquet, whereupon the sultan entered Damietta, the Franks boarded their ships for home, and Cardinal Pelagius' hotheaded Fifth Crusade was over. And the True Cross? Despite al-Kamil's promise, the holy relic was never found, and has never been seen since. (It is believed to have vanished sometime during Saladin's rule in Jerusalem.)

Chapter 7

Exodus

Frederick the 'Stupor Mundi' – massacre among the dunes – clashes with the Templars – Jerusalem destroyed – Battle of La Forbie – the Mongols appear – Louis IX – Baybars' victories at al-Mansurah – collapse of the Sixth Crusade – War of Saint Sabas – fall of Jaffa and Antioch – fall of Krak des Chevaliers – Prince Edward at Acre – fall of Acre

Frederick II Hohenstaufen was one of the most remarkable monarchs in European history. Born in 1194 to Holy Roman Emperor Henry VI and Constance, a Norman heiress of Sicily, Frederick was three years old when he could technically have inherited the German throne, but was beaten to it by Otto IV. He spent his youth, paid for by Pope Innocent III, in bustling, polyglot Palermo, where he learned the ways of the street as well as of the mind. Short of stature but good-looking and with red curly hair, by the age of twelve he was clever and confident enough to set in motion his claim to the imperial crown. Wrong moves against the Pope by Otto IV gave Frederick – already 'as old in wisdom as he [was] young in years' – his chance.[1] With the Pope's help Frederick was crowned emperor at Aachen in 1215, in return for a pledge to take up the cause of the Cross in a crusade.

Frederick was more than willing to flex his considerable abilities overseas. To his admiring subjects, the 21-year-old emperor seemed 'a God-sent David who would free David's Jerusalem from the heirs of Saladin'.[2] He himself, having been brought up in a warm climate and Mediterranean culture, wished naturally to return to them. The new pope, Honorius III, arranged his marriage to Yolanda, heiress to the ex-Kingdom of Jerusalem, which added the title of King of Jerusalem to his qualifications. The Fifth Crusade was running into trouble in Egypt, but Frederick could do little about it, having his hands full with revolts in Italy and Sicily, during which Honorius III died, to be succeeded by the sterner Gregory IX. In 1227 the new pope told Frederick that he had dithered long enough and that he should sail right away. But before he could do so, a plague ravaged his army of 40,000 would-be-Crusaders mustered at Brindisi; Frederick himself sickened, but recovered, to find himself excommunicated by the impatient pope.

But that little bothered Frederick, who in 1228 sailed for the Holy Land and entered Jerusalem with no trouble at all and crowned himself, still technically an excommunicate, in the Church of the Holy Sepulchre. That did not mean he was popular; word had already got around that in spite of (or maybe because of) his extraordinary abilities he was not a likeable man. The Templars, in fact, were so incautious as to suggest to al-Kamil that he kidnap the newly-arrived German. But the sultan, who appreciated someone who spoke Arabic and understood the Arab culture as well as Frederick did, did not rise to the bait. Both rulers negotiated the sharing of Jerusalem, exchanging Aristotelian philosophy and dancing girls, while Frederick enjoyed the flower of Middle Eastern womanhood, earning the bitter censure of the Church.

In February 1229 Frederick got his act together and marched on Jaffa, signalling a subsequent move on Jerusalem. Al-Kamil relented and granted the Christians the Holy City and Bethlehem, plus access to the sea, for ten years. In this aura of glory Frederick made his grand entrance into Jerusalem by the Jaffa Gate along with about 500 Teutonic Knights. He spent the night in the old Hospitaller Grand Master's palace, and the following day – still under excommunication – crowned himself in the Church of the Holy Sepulchre surrounded by German knights, convinced that he at last was 'high among the princes of the world in the house of [God's] servant David'. He also made a point of alleviating the suspicions of the Muslims and respecting their religion, which didn't help his relations with Rome or with the Military Orders, to whom he was still something of an interloper. But so that he wouldn't overstay his welcome, after three days he moved to Acre, where the local Christians threw butchers' refuse and excrement at him as he walked to his ship to return to Italy to deal with domestic problems.

Though he longed to return to Jerusalem, Frederick never managed it. He was in fact the absentee king for ten years until the city fell anew to the Muslims in 1239. Too widely experienced to believe in democracy, he ruled his empire with an arm of steel. He fully believed himself the equal, nay the successor, of the *augusti* of ancient Rome. His mind ranged with equal competence through any subject under the sun, and may well have eroded his original keen Christianity. Admiring subjects called him *Stupor Mundi*, a wonder of the world. But as far as the Holy Land was concerned, he gave up too soon. He never seemed to understand the nature of the Military Orders, or indeed of the states of Outremer in general. The Hospitallers' attitude toward him softened somewhat when he made his peace with Rome in 1230, though they still held aloof when a year later Frederick announced that he would send a new seaborne army to the Holy Land under an Italian marshal, Riccardo Filangieri. After several adventures the fleet arrived at Tyre, where Filangieri defeated a Frankish force led by John of Ibelin.

There followed a period of great confusion in Outremer, where Frankish factions fought one another, and there wasn't too much unity on the Muslim side, either. The kingdom of Armenia was also intriguing for influence in the region through dynastic connections. Within this complex of events the Hospitallers, as we have seen, saw fit to ally themselves with the Assassins as an insurance policy against the Muslims who were a constant threat to Krak des Chevaliers and other centres of the order; they also earned regular tribute from the murderous sect. There seems to have been no coherent military policy under Grand Master Bertrand de Thessy, who held the office from 1228 to 1230, or his successors Guerin (other names unknown) and Bertrand de Comps from 1236. They staged two ill-advised attacks on Barin and Hama, the later along with the Templars, which were repulsed, and a raid on Jabala succeeded at first but was reversed after a few weeks.

When the treaty between al-Kamil and Frederick II expired in 1239, the pulpits of the West again resounded to calls for a new crusade. The champion this time was Pope Gregory IX, who influenced a high French noble named Tibald of Champagne (a nephew of the late Henry of Champagne) to lead it. Senior officers of the Military Orders greeted Tibald when he set foot in Acre on the first day of September, and agreed to lend their forces to him. Like all newcomers from the West, Tibald and his knights were single-mindedly intent on rushing into combat, contemptuous of the advice that long-timers such as the Military Order knights might give him. Tibald's first objective was Egypt. On 12 November his army of 500 cavalry and twice that number of infantry was approaching Gaza when the Grand Masters of the three Military Orders received news that a large Egyptian army was on its way up from the Nile Delta and urged Tibald to withdraw to a safer position. But one of Tibald's senior knights, Henry of Bar, flung the now-familiar charges of cowardice at them and went on. Tibald had little choice but to go along. Henry of Bar realized his foolish mistake soon enough when he found his detachment surrounded by the Egyptians in an indefensible hollow in the sand dunes. Henry's chief associates fled as best they could, but Henry himself stayed to face the fatal music. He and about 1,000 of his soldiers were cut down as they and their horses floundered in the sand. Six hundred others were marched off to Muslim captivity. Tibald retreated to Tripoli, giving up his crusade and returning home a year later.

The failure of Tibald of Champagne's crusade left the Hospitallers and Templars free to continue their cold war, which at any moment threatened to turn hot. The streets of Acre regularly resounded with the sounds of brawling between the two sets of knights. The situation appalled a distinguished pilgrim, Richard of Cornwall, the brother of King Henry III of England, who exercised some subtle diplomacy to secure the release of Frankish prisoners taken at Gaza. Richard failed to reconcile the two Orders; the Hospitallers, by now the disadvantaged of the two, began to seek alliances with Filangieri and Emperor Frederick. They wanted to preserve a truce signed with the new Egyptian sultan, al-Ayyub, who was also on cordial terms with the Holy Roman Empire. Grand Master Pierre de Vieille Bride, skirmishing with the Muslims outside Marqab Castle, finally made his peace with Balian of Ibelin (the grandson of the Balian who handed over Jerusalem to Saladin), but the knights remained restless, a virtual state within a state, owing allegiance to no Frankish temporal leader yet unsure of what they were to do most of the time.

Throughout this confused period the Kingdom of Jerusalem continued to exist on paper, but was actually run from Acre. John of Brienne had given up the throne in 1212 to make way for Yolanda and incidentally carve out an extraordinary late-life career as Latin Emperor of Byzantium, even fighting bravely in the front line against the Bulgarians, until his death in 1237. Frederick II, the *Stupor Mundi*, held the titular throne for a few years after which royal power was exercised by the descendants of the four-times-widowed Queen Isabella headquartered in Cyprus. During this time the Templars built up a formidable banking and influence-peddling business, outclassing the Hospitallers in business acumen. When the Templars allied themselves with the Venetians in their attempt to monopolize the lucrative eastern Mediterranean trade, the Hospitallers naturally gravitated towards the Venetians' rivals, the Genoese. The Hospitallers also were more amenable to diplomacy with moderate Muslim regimes and the Byzantine Greeks.

But new threats were on their way from the East. The first of them was a tribe displaced from central Asia by Jenghiz Khan's sweeping invasions – the Khwarizmian Turks. In June 1244 some 10,000 Khwarizmian horsemen ravaged the region of Damascus, captured Tiberias and entered Nablus. The Frankish establishment, caught by surprise, attempted to reinforce the ramparts of Jerusalem with the help of the Hospitallers and Templars, but the wild Khwarizmians under Barka Khan burst into the city on 11 June, murdering any monks and nuns they could find. The Hospitaller Preceptor (area commander) fell in the defence of the citadel. Thanks to an intercession by a friendly Muslim potentate, some 6,000 Christians were allowed to leave Jerusalem. As they trudged off, most to be slaughtered by Arab bandits, the Khwarizmians torched the Church of the Holy Sepulchre, decapitated and disembowelled the few priests that had stayed there and unearthed and burned the bones of the Frankish kings. The venerated stone that had been placed at the entrance to Jesus' tomb was smashed. Such was the devastation that Jerusalem was not to fully recover for 600 years.

As the Khwarizmians continued their campaign south, intending to join up with Ayyub's Egyptians, the Franks gathered their forces outside Acre to attack them; with them was a Muslim force under al-Nasir of Kerak plus al-Mansur Ibrahim of Homs. The cream of this force were 300 Hospitaller knights under Grand Master Guillaume de Châteauneuf, and 300 more Templars under their Grand Master, Armand de Périgord. The Teutonic Knights sent a contingent. It's not certain who was in overall command; probably Philip of Montfort, the Lord of Tyre and Walter of Brienne, the Count of Jaffa, held the senior posts. They did not have far to march, as on 17 October they encountered the Egyptians and Khwarizmians in position north-east of Gaza at the village of La Forbie (called Herbiya by the Arabs). Al-Mansur Ibrahim counselled caution, expecting the Khwarizmians to lose patience and withdraw. But Walter of Brienne, the reports of the atrocities of Jerusalem fresh in his mind, and believing that the Frankish army outnumbered the enemy, wanted an immediate assault. His argument prevailed.

What neither Walter nor any of his soldiers suspected, however, was the calibre of the man who commanded the other side. Rukn ad-Din Baybars was a young emir who had begun life in central Asia as a child-slave sold to a Syrian potentate. Of Turkish stock, fair-haired and blue-eyed, with a formidable physique and rough-and-ready manner, Baybars by sheer ability had risen in the Ayyubid ranks thanks to a scheme which took promising slave-boys for intensive military training and indoctrination into Islam. These men were called Mamluks, a Turkish term for slave-soldiers. One of Baybars' eyes was clouded milky-white by a cataract, which gave him a suitably sinister and intimidating appearance. As he rose through the ranks, Baybars earned the title of *Bundukdari*, or Arbalestier, a master of the steel crossbow. He was assigned to the crack Bahriyya regiment that considered itself a Muslim version of the Christian Military Orders. Sultan Ayyub was a great fan of the well-drilled Mamluk regiments, convinced that a single slave could prove more loyal than all of his own sons put together. Little could he imagine that this able blue-eyed Mamluk would prove a greater leader than any of his own dynasty combined.

The Frankish army advanced in a line, the Military Orders on the right and the Muslim allies in the centre and on the left. The clash was more or less simultaneous all along the line; the Franks and al-Mansur Ibrahim held firm, but the Khwarizmians charged the Damascus troops with al-Nasir in the centre, sending them reeling. Having split the Frankish line, the Khwarizmians wheeled to entrap the Christian units against the Egyptian army; the Military Orders fought bravely but were outnumbered. Templar Grand Master Armand de Périgord and his Marshal were killed and Châteauneuf was taken prisoner, one of some 800. At La Forbie Baybars had scored a stunning victory within a matter of hours. At a conservative estimate, 5,000 of the Frankish-led army lay dead on the field. Of the Hospitallers, 325 brothers-in-arms and some 200 turcopoles fell, leaving just twenty-six knights, plus thirty-three Templars and three Teutonic Knights who escaped to Ascalon, whose Hospitaller garrison was being squeezed by an Egyptian naval blockade.

La Forbie was the worst military defeat for Outremer since Hattin, once more coming close to extirpating the Order of Saint John altogether. But this time the Frankish domains gained a reprieve as Ayyub turned to settle accounts with his rival Muslim potentates in Syria and eliminated the Khwarizmians when they turned against him. In 1247 Ayyub seized Belvoir Castle from the Hospitallers before making a determined move against Hospitaller-held Ascalon. In the autumn of that year, as bad weather disrupted Christian attempts to supply the city by sea, Ayyub's engineers built a great battering-ram made from the timbers of storm-wrecked ships and breached the walls of Ascalon with it on 15 October. The garrison was slaughtered for the most part, with some being taken prisoner. The Egyptian Sultan Ayyub appeared to be on a roll, but already the far eastern horizon was being darkened by a new and frightening phenomenon.

For some time now reports had been reaching Outremer, the Muslim states and the West about an aggressive and highly effective military nation surging out of the steppes of central Asia, annihilating anything and anyone in its path – the Mongols. The name of Jenghiz Khan was already known to the Crusaders in 1220, along with the myth of 'Prester John', a supposedly Christian ruler somewhere in Persia who was believed to be preparing to hit the Muslims from the East in conjunction with the Crusaders. When it became apparent that the myth was probably just that, a myth, Jenghiz

Khan was substituted for Prester John and papal hopes revived. But when Jenghiz Khan showed his true colours by defeating Christian King George IV of Georgia and apparently showing little regard for anyone's religion, the Christian and Muslim powers of the Middle East, until now consumed with their own quarrels, had to begin taking notice.

The Mongols originated along the Upper Amur River running off the Himalayan massif, to the north-west of China. By the time of Jenghiz Khan, who was born in 1167, a series of strong tribal rulers had made the Mongols independent of Chinese suzerainty. They gradually extended their influence over their Tatar and Kerait neighbours. Jenghiz Khan was the key player in this often-ruthless process; in 1206 he imposed his will on all the related tribes, which he united as the Mongols. Jenghiz Khan's first major campaign, with the huge and efficient army which he had at his command, was against the Chin emperors of China, who submitted after a series of heavy defeats. Next on the warlord's list was the Khwarizmian Turkic Empire that stretched from the Persian Gulf to the Indus River. Like all Mongol rulers, he assumed that every other nation on earth was waiting to fall under Mongol domination; the idea that there existed foreign countries and kingdoms with an innate right to independence never occurred to him or any Mongol. Conquest was the normal state of affairs, and anyone irrational enough to resist deserved to be wiped out. Faced with this kind of policy, even the half a million men that the Khwarizmians could put into the field could do little; after massacring every living thing in the towns that fell to him, Jenghiz Khan destroyed the Khwarizmians in a desperate battle on the banks of the Indus in November 1221.

What made Jenghiz Khan fascinating to the Christians in Outremer, besides the grisly accounts of his doings, was the fact that his victims were all either pagans or Muslims, and that he was well-disposed towards Christians. Though a shamanist pagan himself, he liked to consult Christian priests in his entourage, and his daughters-in-law were Christians. Naturally the rulers of Outremer, as well as the popes and monarchs of western Europe, hoped that Jenghiz Khan could be brought 'on side', as it were. Those hopes persisted even after the warlord demonstrated the grim reality of his policies by leaving mountains of ash and corpses in the Caucasus and Georgia and vanquishing a Russian army near the Sea of Azov in late May 1222. When Jenghiz Khan died in 1227, he had built up the greatest empire the world had ever seen, stretching from Korea to Persia and from the Indian Ocean to Siberia. No wonder the Muslims were anxious.

Jenghiz Khan's sons, though less capable as the sons of the illustrious usually are, were preoccupied with domestic matters including the suppression of a revolt in northern China. The Mongols returned to the West with a vengeance: in 1236 their general Batu smashed the Russian armies, penetrating as far as Moscow and putting the inhabitants of Kiev, among other unfortunate cities, to death wholesale. From Ukraine a Mongol detachment under Baidar broke into Poland, defeating a force sent to stop them under Duke Henry of Silesia, who had the Teutonic Knights under his command, at Wahlstadt. The invaders then veered south, reaching Croatia and the Adriatic Sea. At that point Great Khan Ogodai died, halting Batu's European campaign; another general, Baichu, invaded Anatolia (modern Turkey) to deal with the Seljuk Turks. Next on the Mongols' list was the Assassins' mountain redoubt in Syria; the sect appealed to Europe for help, and Pope Gregory IX was all for complying with the request. But the pope found few willing ears, except those of the French king, who took the idea very seriously indeed.

Louis IX of France, who assumed the throne in 1223 at the age of twelve, had always been conspicuous for his deep piety and good nature. In this he took after his mother Blanche, *la bonne mère* (the good mother). He is described as tall, good-looking and blond, and an admirer of the ladies until he married and settled down, gradually abjuring luxury and privilege for a life of work and prayer. Early in his reign Louis sternly upheld justice and humanized its processes. For twenty-seven years after 1243, France was at peace with its neighbours. The contemporary writer Jean de Joinville vowed that never, at any time, did he 'hear the king speak evil of anyone'.[3] His devoted subjects called him Brother Louis. In December 1244 he had fallen desperately ill from malaria, recovering after promising God that he would go on a crusade in thanks at his survival.

However, the great trap that the very good person is prone to falling into is intolerance. When four years after his illness Louis IX donned his simple pilgrim's apparel, and took up his staff for the crusade that he believed, unlike the previous five, would be blessed with triumph, there was a troubling element of excess zeal about it. To pay for the campaign he taxed his tolerant subjects heavily. His good nature, so evident at home, evaporated when he thought or spoke of the Muslim infidels. The air was one of great celebration when Louis' fleet set sail for what was to become the Sixth Crusade on 12 August 1248, containing a galaxy of noble luminaries. A little more than a month later the fleet touched at Limassol, Cyprus, where the king conferred with officials from Outremer, including the Hospitallers' Deputy Grand

Master, Jean de Ronay. All present unhesitatingly agreed that Egypt should once more be the target for two reasons: it was the richest Muslim land, and the Ayyubid sultans might well be talked into handing back Jerusalem in return for Damietta. The heads of the Military Orders advised the king to wait out the winter until better campaigning weather arrived. At about this time the Hospitallers, by order of Pope Innocent IV in 1248, changed their dress and insignia from the black cape to a red surcoat, keeping the eight-pointed white cross on the breast. The continued wearing of the traditional black, however, seems to have been optional. The surcoat was easier to wear over the armour than the restrictive cape had been.

Louis in his stubborn certainty brushed aside the Orders' sound advice. Like all the previous newcomers to the Middle East, and several who were to come after, he burned with impatience to measure his sword against the infidel. No sound military or diplomatic reasoning could penetrate the carapace of his simplistic faith; he ordered the Templars, who had already begun exploratory talks with the sultan, to break them off. But he had to remain in Cyprus anyway to see what he could do about a possible alliance with the Mongols; there is something surreal in the saintliest of kings reaching out to the bloodthirstiest of warlords. But those contacts broke down, finally enabling Louis and his Crusaders to sail for Egypt in May 1249. The Mediterranean storms were not yet over, and one of them scattered the first wave of ships. Somehow, most of the fleet was able to join Louis off Damietta on 4 June.

Without waiting for reinforcements, Louis threw himself into battle on the beach, with the Outremer knights under John of Ibelin in the front line. The initial push drove back the Egyptians under Vizier Fakhr ad-Din (Ayyub was seriously ill with tuberculosis) who retreated past Damietta, pulling out the garrison and Muslim population. On 6 June the Crusaders walked into Damietta, where the king decided to await his reinforcements. But, as so often happened in Egypt, the Nile took a hand in the proceedings; it was the season of high water, and little more could be done militarily until the river level went down, by which time it would be high summer and campaigning impracticable. Thus Louis and the army languished, as boredom, heat and disease whittled away at morale.

Sultan Ayyub had himself carried in a litter to Mansurah, about fifty miles upriver from Damietta, and turned it into a base for raids on the Frankish positions. In October, when the water level went down, Louis pondered his options: either attack Mansurah, where the sultan was, or make a surprise move on Alexandria to the west. Peter of Brittany, with the probable agreement of the Military Orders, urged the former course, carrying the king with them. At this point the ailing Ayyub died, throwing the Muslim camp into temporary confusion through which Louis saw his way clear to Cairo. There was, however, constant Egyptian resistance, which goaded the Orders into occasional action; the king, in fact, had to restrain the Templars in particular from pursuing the enemy too far. The Crusaders finally came upon the massed Egyptians on the far side of the Bagr as-Saghir, a tributary of the Nile.

There followed a six-week standoff over the new year. On 8 February 1250 Louis' army, with the king's brother Robert of Artois in the van with the Templars, brushed off the Greek Fire raining on their siege engines and painstakingly forded the Bahr as-Saghir – the scene of a past defeat under Cardinal Pelagius. Against orders they stormed the Muslim camp which was taken wholly by surprise. Among the many casualties was Fakhr ad-Din, who at the time was having his beard dyed. Leaping onto his horse without his armour, he was cut down by the Templars. Robert of Artois, flushed with success and deaf to pleas that he wait for Louis and the main body of the army, wanted to press on to Mansurah at once and destroy the Egyptian army. When even the Templars protested that he was being foolhardy, he denounced them as fainthearts and spurred on his horse.

It was the last order Robert of Artois ever gave. For with Fakhr ad-Din gone, he was now up against a far abler commander, the man who had smashed the Franks at La Forbie – Baybars the Bundukdari, who was in charge of the garrison and who knew exactly what to do. When Robert, with his Templar knights close behind, thundered through Mansurah and up to the citadel, Baybars coolly let them through and then fell on them in the narrow streets. The Frankish cavalry, unable to manoeuvre in the restricted space, fell into confusion and were butchered. Of 290 Templar knights, just five survived. Robert was slain along with his staff after trying to barricade himself in a house. The commander of the English contingent, William of Salisbury, and his troops perished almost to a man. Some knights who escaped the slaughter drowned trying to swim across the swollen Nile. Yet again had the Crusaders paid the price for a lack of sound military sense. What followed was a series of fierce charges and countercharges that ended with Louis managing to get his archers across the Bahr as-Saghir and into a tenable camping position. There the acting Hospitaller Grand Master informed the king of his brother Robert's death.

Rumours of an imminent Egyptian revolution helped assuage Louis' grief, but those hopes were dashed when the late Ayyub's son Turanshah arrived in Cairo from northern Syria after proclaiming himself sultan. While the Crusaders lingered indecisively before Mansurah, Turanshah ordered the construction of a fleet of light river boats and had them sent on camelback to where the Frankish vessels plied the Nile to and from Damietta with supplies for Louis' army. These attack craft were devastatingly effective; well over 100 Frankish vessels were seized in short order, and soon famine and disease wracked the Crusader camp. By early April the king realized that to stay where he was would be a recipe for disaster, and that the only route open to him was to negotiate with the sultan for an ordered retreat. Turanshah turned down the initial overtures, as he had the Crusaders where he wanted them. On 5 April the Crusaders decided to make the best of a bad situation and make as orderly a retreat as possible back towards Damietta, the sick and wounded being put on boats. Louis remained with the rear echelons in the march, but the Egyptians swarmed over the abandoned pontoon bridge on the Saghir Canal and hounded the army on all sides. At nightfall Louis himself, after fighting all day, collapsed exhausted, while the knights of Outremer under Philip of Montfort proposed surrendering Damietta in return for being allowed to retreat in peace. Then something odd occurred; a sergeant named Marcel rode up, relaying what he said were royal orders to the commanders to surrender to the Egyptians unconditionally. As Louis had not issued any such order, and as despite his weariness was unlikely to do so, the most probable explanation is that Marcel could have been bribed by the enemy to do this. Whatever the truth, the dispirited and broken Crusader army needed little prompting, and capitulated en masse.

The Muslims found themselves burdened with so many Frankish prisoners they didn't know what to do with them. Turanshah ordered that the sick ones be executed at once, followed by 300 others every evening for a week. Louis was kept in chains in a house in Mansurah. The barons and senior knights were kept alive in case they could raise good ransoms. Turanshah demanded all of Outremer, to which Louis replied that he wasn't qualified to cede any of that territory, which was nominally under the rule of Conrad II Hohenstaufen. The sultan conceded the point, and was on the point of finalizing negotiations for an immense ransom for Louis and his knights when during a banquet he drunkenly insulted the Mamluk military establishment and was promptly murdered. The killer was none other than the chief Mamluk himself – Baybars.

After payment of the first instalment of the ransom, and a very uncomfortable voyage, Louis found himself in Acre. The wounded men he left behind were all put to death. At Acre he sank into depression over his debacle in Egypt, where he believed his lack of humility before God had cost thousands of his soldiers' lives. Back in France, trouble was brewing with England, but Louis elected to stay in the Holy Land. High-level prisoners remained languishing in Egypt, such as Hospitaller Grand Master Guillaume de Châteauneuf who remained in Muslim custody for six years, which made him rather more amenable to the advice of the more experienced Franks. There followed a prisoner exchange that restored Châteauneuf to his post and was completed in 1252.

Surprisingly, in view of his holy reputation, Louis maintained excellent relations with the Assassins, who for several years had been paying tribute to the Order of the Hospital. There was, of course, no religious bond; the Shia Assassins simply viewed the Christians as a useful counterweight to their Sunni Muslim rivals in Syria. Louis also was well aware of the Mongols, one of whose princes, it was reported, had become a Christian, and sought their friendship. But growing troubles with England forced the king to sail for France in April 1254, thus ending what history knows as the Sixth Crusade. On his hazardous voyage home, Louis may well have reflected on whether his pious activism had done more harm than good. 'He had been a good and God-fearing man, and yet God had led him into disaster.'[4] And in the Outremer he left behind, the dispirited Franks, and the Italians who controlled trade and shipping, fell to quarrelling.

The Military Orders, for lack of anything better to do, were inevitably drawn into these fights, one of which was bizarrely known as the War of Saint Sabas. The name was that of an old monastery atop a height in Acre that separated the Venetian and Genoese quarters and was claimed by both. In 1256 the Genoese took it by storm, sending an armed force of thugs into the Venetian district. After some street fighting there was a standoff, but then Philip of Montfort, the Lord of Tyre, who had a long-standing grudge against the Venetians, threw in his lot with the Genoese. This in turn brought the Ibelin clan, as backers of the Venetians, into the fray. Completing the face-off were the Templars and Teutonic Knights, who supported the Venetians, and the Hospitallers, who by default took the Genoese side. When the Genoese in Acre took over the port, a Venetian fleet under Admiral Lorenzo Tiepolo sailed up and landed a force of marines who fought their way up to the Hospitallers' quarter, occupying Saint Sabas in the process but failing to dislodge the Hospitallers.

An intermittent civil conflict simmered for the next year and a half until Queen Plaisance of Cyprus – a member of the Lusignan clan that still clung to the illusion of sovereignty over Jerusalem – sailed to Palestine to see if her royal authority could settle it. The titular king of Jerusalem was the 5-year-old Conradin Hohenstaufen, away in Germany, and it was to his authority that the Hospitallers – despite their past hostility to the Hohenstaufens – now appealed. Queen Plaisance's efforts came to nought, however, and in June 1258 Tiepolo won a resounding naval victory over the Genoese off Acre. Shortly afterwards the Genoese abandoned Acre, but thanks to Plaisance's renewed diplomatic effort the Military Orders were reconciled in 1261. Which was just as well, because momentous developments were occurring in the wider region.

In August 1261 the Byzantine Greeks, thanks to six decades of effective resistance by the Greek emperors-in-exile of Nicaea, re-took their great capital, Constantinople, from the despised Latins, literally chasing the last Latin puppet-emperor, Baldwin II, through the streets. The Greek Orthodox element in the Middle East, never comfortable with the Catholics, took new heart, as did the Muslim Turks, who now hovered like a vulture over the dying Frankish realm of Outremer. Three years earlier the Mongol Prince Hulagu, a brother of the fabled Kublai Khan who subdued China, had smashed his way across Persia and into Baghdad, eliminating the old Abbasid dynasty of caliphs and wiping the city off the face of the earth in one of the most fearful massacres of history. Two years later, however, Baybars won one of the pivotal battles of history by trouncing the Mongols under Kitbugha, one of Hulagu's (Christian) generals, in the great and terrible battle of Ayn Jalut. That encounter paved the way for the unified Muslim control of Egypt and Greater Syria that lasts to this day. Baybars of the sinister white eye was now the master of Egypt under the Mamluk dynasty, 'unimpeded by any scruple of honour, gratitude or mercy'. In this he was unlike Saladin, whose reputation he vainly hoped to emulate.

The attempts of the rulers of Outremer to ally with the Mongols determined Baybars to stamp them out. For eight years, starting in 1263, Baybars made annual raids into Frankish territory. When the Military Orders refused his demand to hand over the Muslim prisoners in their possession, he seized Kerak Castle and destroyed the Church of the Virgin in Nazareth. Acre held out against him, while the Templars and Hospitallers joined forces for a raid on Ascalon that accomplished little, as the Mamluks were now virtual masters of the surrounding areas. Next on Baybars' list was the Hospitaller stronghold at Arsuf. For six weeks the 270 defending knights held off the siege with superb courage, losing one-third of their number. But after a part of the walls had been battered down, the commander surrendered after securing a promise that the surviving knights would go free. But Baybars was no Saladin, and placed no value on honour; all the Hospitallers were taken prisoner. Yet that was a mild fate compared to that of the Templars, 2,000 of whom surrendered the fort of Safad in July 1263. After promising them their lives, Baybars had them all executed on a hilltop. Both Jaffa and Antioch fell to Baybars in 1268: at least 16,000 men of the defending garrison of Antioch are reported to have been slaughtered and 100,000 civilians carried off to the Egyptian slave markets.

Besides having to fight the Muslims, the Knights of Saint John were caught up in the unseemly petty power struggles that were the outstanding feature of Outremer in its final decline. A bizarre episode occurred in 1269, with the so-called Crusade of the Infants of Aragon. The 'Infants' were in fact the Spanish king's two grown sons, Fernando and Pedro (Infantes in official Spanish usage). Setting off from Barcelona, the Infantes, like all the newcomers to the crusading practice, wanted to go straight into battle, swords flashing. On arrival at Acre it took a lot of persuading by the Military Orders to restrain them, and they eventually returned to Spain a little wiser. To complicate matters in the saintly sphere, Louis IX of France, old and ill as he was, had never been able to get over his bitter defeat in the Sixth Crusade, so he boarded his ship for yet another one in 1270. Duped by his villainous brother, Charles of Anjou, into believing that the Emir of Tunis was about to convert to Christianity, Louis landed at Carthage with high hopes. But the full force of a North African summer proved a worse foe than the Muslims. Disease felled knight and soldier alike, with Louis among the first victims. Legend has it that with his last breath he murmured, 'Jerusalem, Jerusalem.'

In 1271 it was the turn of the Hospitallers in Krak des Chevaliers. Baybars brought up his army and siege engines along the ridge from the south, the only route by which the castle could be approached. Of course, this was where the fortification was at its sturdiest, and where the surrounding glacis (sloping stone wall) deterred attempts at sapping. With Baybars was a contingent of Assassins, hoping no doubt to be rid of their tribute-masters. After some days of heavy rain, the Mamluks' relentless battering brought down a section of the southern wall. The defending Hospitallers withdrew into the near-impregnable citadel in the inner ward, where they held out for two weeks until the Mamluks burst in and killed a number of knights. There was another centre of resistance in the south tower, and for ten days fighting raged around it. Baybars knew he couldn't take that position without severe casualties and possible damage to the castle itself, which he wanted to preserve. A bit of tactical disinformation came in handy here; the sultan arranged for a forged letter purporting to be from Grand Master Hugh de

Revel advising the knights to surrender. Whether the letter was believed or not is a moot point; probably the surviving knights realized their position was hopeless and capitulated on 8 April 1271. They were granted a safe-conduct to Tripoli. The loss of Krak des Chevaliers was a serious blow to the Hospitallers' strength. Hugh de Revel could count just some 300 knights in the Order, compared to thousands in the great days of Outremer. Without the trading facilities and banking functions of the Templars, they found it hard to attract new recruits.

At this point a new actor entered the scene. On 9 May a ship sailed into Acre bearing a distinguished passenger. He was Prince Edward of England, the son of Henry III and heir to the throne. As Henry was old and tired, he encouraged his vigorous and strong-minded son, now just over 30 years old, to take over the crusading duties of the English royal family. But he didn't manage to raise much support in England (where crusading had rather fallen out of vogue), with the result that a mere 1,000 men sailed with him. Like all naive newcomers, Edward was stunned to find the local Franks and Italians doing good peacetime business with the Muslims. His attempts to get the Mongols on side met with some success, but a Mongol force coming from the east was stopped by Baybars. Edward's own military probes across Mount Carmel turned out to be mere pinpricks. After a year in Outremer, Edward became discouraged, and Baybars, to rid himself of another troublesome Crusader, hired an assassin to stab him with a poisoned dagger. Edward survived, but was seriously ill for a long time; moreover, Henry III was dying, and Edward had no choice but to return to England to reign as Edward I, the Hammer not of the Muslims but of the Scots.

In 1277 the ruthless Baybars died unexpectedly. The generally accepted version of his demise is that he inadvertently drank from a cup of poisoned fermented mare's milk, called kumiss, that he had prepared for a marked-down rival. His Mamluk successor, the able Qalawun, fixed up a truce with the Templars and went after the Hospitallers. The Order, perhaps unwisely, had joined forces with the Mongol Ilkhan Abaga and Leo III of Armenia for yet another crusade; moral support came from Byzantium and from Edward I of England, but without material aid it was useless. There followed a confused period of conflict as the new Hospitaller Grand Master, Nicholas Lorgne, tried unsuccessfully to settle a nasty quarrel between Bohemond VII of Tripoli and the Templars. In 1281 some Hospitaller knights, defying orders, rode out from Marqab Castle to join the Mongols and Armenian King Leo who were bracing for a stiff fight with the Mamluks near Homs in Syria. When battle was joined the Mongol commander Mangu Timur fell back, leaving Leo and the Hospitallers' isolated; they managed to fight their way out of their predicament at the cost of heavy losses, witnessed by the Prior of the English Hospitallers, Joseph of Chauncy, who wrote an account of the Battle of Homs to King Edward trying to present the Order in a favourable light.[5]

Homs turned Qalawun's attention to Marqab Castle, which he attacked with great force in April 1285. The number of mangonels and other siege engines employed on both sides was considerable, while those of the Hospitallers had the advantage of height. For five weeks the Mamluks pounded at the massive walls without effect, until Muslim sappers dug a tunnel under the north tower and filled it with firewood. When the mine was set alight, the resulting blaze felled the tower; the crash, ironically, stalled the Mamluk attack momentarily, and the defenders could have continued to hold out. But it turned out that the attackers' mine had penetrated farther than expected. With the inner castle thus in danger, the Hospitallers had to give up. The twenty-five brother-knights remaining were allowed to go free with their horses and weapons; the brother-sergeants and others were also allowed to go free but without their possessions. All made their way to Tripoli.

The fall of Marqab jolted the Franks of Outremer into considering whom they could follow as a leader on the Mamluk model. The Hospitallers suggested (with support from the Teutons and to a lesser extent the Templars) that King Henry II of Cyprus, the latest in the Lusignan line with pretensions to the 'Kingdom of Jerusalem', come to Outremer to exercise a more hands-on leadership. Henry, young and good-looking, arrived at Acre in June 1286 to general enthusiasm. The Hall of the Hospital at Tyre was the scene of festivities as elaborate as anything in a mediaeval romance. Believing that he had the situation well in hand, Henry returned to Cyprus, leaving the administration of Outremer to his two competent uncles.

That party in Tyre was the Franks' last hurrah. Hardly had Henry sailed off to Cyprus than the Venetians and Genoese fell to bickering again. For a while the coast of Palestine rang with clashes between the rival Italian navies. The Genoese backed down only after mediation by the Military Orders. This gave Qalawun the opportunity to seize the port of Lattakieh (now Latakia) from Bohemond VII in 1287. Later that year Bohemond died, to be replaced by Countess Lucia, who made her headquarters at Tripoli along with the Military Orders. Lucia, who displayed certain leadership qualities, had strong support from the Hospitallers in particular, and when Qalawun brought his whole force before Tripoli in March 1289, Lucia took general command. Heading the Hospitaller force was the Marshal, Matthew de Clermont; the Templars at Tripoli were commanded by their Marshal, Geoffrey de Vendac. In support were a French regiment from Acre under Jean de Grailly, plus King Henry's younger brother Amalric with a small force of knights. A few Italian galleys cruised offshore.

Qalawun launched his assault with a bombardment of the Tower of the Bishop in the south-eastern portion of the land walls. When the tower collapsed, the Venetians offshore decided the game was up and pulled out, closely followed by the Genoese. Within a matter of hours the Muslims were through the walls and swarming into the city, killing every civilian male unfortunate enough to be in their path and seizing women and children as slaves. Some civilians who had sought refuge on the small islet of Saint Thomas were slaughtered by Mamluk cavalry who had ridden through the shallow water; the stench of their bodies pervaded the area for days. Countess Lucia, Clermont and Vendac managed to escape to Cyprus.

The fall of Tripoli triggered a now-familiar reaction in the West: Jean de Grailly bore the sad news to Pope Nicholas IV, who tried to mobilize yet another crusade. The results were meagre apart from several shiploads of Italian peasants whose only way of fighting for the Cross was to murder any Muslim found in the streets of Acre. The incident, which the Military Orders had tried to halt, enraged Qalawun who vowed not to 'leave a single Christian alive' in Acre. But while he was on the way to carry out his threat he died and was succeeded by his son al-Ashraf Khalil. As it was late in the year 1290, al-Ashraf postponed the campaign.

But if the people and authorities of Acre had any illusions they would be spared, those illusions evaporated when an unnamed Hospitaller knight travelled with a Templar and a secretary to Cairo hoping to forestall a Muslim attack; they were promptly thrown into jail without a hearing and died later. In March 1291 al-Ashraf was ready. He gathered together about a hundred of the biggest and newest siege engines he could find, along with his forces from Syria. One of the bigger catapults, dubbed the Victorious, had been built at Krak des Chevaliers and took nearly a month to trundle down to Acre; of about equal size was the Furious, supplemented by mangonels of a new and more efficient design called Black Oxen. On 5 April the great host, numbering perhaps 100,000 altogether, arrived before Acre whose defenders numbered a mere 1,000 or so mounted brother-knights and brother-sergeants plus some 14,000 turcopoles and other infantry and an undetermined number of armed civilians and pilgrims.

Thanks to the care lavished on Acre by distinguished Crusaders over the years, its fortifications were formidable. The double walls girdled the city from the Patriarch's Tower by the sea in the south to the Templars' Ward by the sea in the northern suburb of Montmusart. About a third of the way along, going from north to south, the walls made an acute angle at the Tower of Henry II, the most vulnerable point, and here is where the toughest defence was mounted under Amalric, King Henry's brother. To the right, covering the Tower of Saint Nicholas, the Tower of the Legate and the Patriarch's Tower, were French and English knights under Jean de Grailly and Otto de Grandson, with Venetians and Pisans completing the line. To Amalric's left stood the Hospitallers guarding the Hospitallers' Ward, and then the Templars along the rest of the wall. The Teutonic Knights stood behind Amalric's men in the centre around a structure known sinisterly as the Accursed Tower. Sultan al-Ashraf's tent stood opposite the right of the Frankish line, while the Syrian regiments faced the Templars and Hospitallers.

Around this time, some of the noncombatants, accompanied probably by several Italian merchants, decided it was time to get smartly out; the Venetians and Pisans, however, bravely elected to stay and fight. Al-Ashraf opened his offensive on 6 April with a bombardment of explosive chemicals from the catapults combined with a fearsome rain of arrows from his archers. One of the Frankish vessels had its own catapult, which it fired back against the Mamluks to great effect. On the moonlit night of 15 April the Templars and Otto de Grandson launched a foolhardly attack on the Muslim camp on their front; in their clumsiness many of the raiders tripped over the enemy's tent-ropes and were captured, the rest fleeing after heavy losses. A similar Hospitaller attack a few nights later, when the moonlight was less bright, was a total fiasco. That particular tactic was abandoned.

On 4 May the beleaguered Franks received reinforcements in the form of forty ships containing about 100 horsemen and 2,000 infantry under the ailing yet determined King Henry of Cyprus. But they were too few to really offset the Mamluks' heavy preponderance and soon Henry felt compelled to put out peace feelers. The sultan insisted on the surrender of Acre. During the talks a heavy stone from an injudiciously-fired Frankish catapult landed nearby – the envoys were lucky to escape al-Ashraf's fury with their lives. Four days later the defenders burned the outer barbican of Acre as no longer useful. Then Muslim sappers undermined the English Tower near the acute angle of the walls, and the Tower of the Countess of Blois next to it. The Tower of Saint Nicholas to the south became very shaky. A new tower built by King Henry – probably not very strongly – at the point of the acute angle began to collapse. On 16 May the yelling Mamluks stormed Saint Anthony's Gate in the Hospitallers' sector, and would have broken through were it not for the gallantry of the two Military Orders fighting side by side, the Hospitaller Marshal Matthew de Clermont distinguishing himself in particular.

Two days later the sultan unleashed a general charge against the walls from Saint Anthony's Gate to the Patriarch's Tower by the sea, focusing on the Accursed Tower inside the angle, while his siege engines gave it all they had. Primitive grenades of Greek Fire flew into the defenders' ranks. The scene has been painted by Runciman:

> The arrows of [the sultan's] archers fell almost in a solid mass into the city; and regiment after regiment rushed at the defences, led by white-turbaned emirs. The noise was appalling. The assailants shouted their battle-cries, and trumpets and cymbals and the drums of three hundred drummers on camel-back urged them on.[6]

When the Accursed Tower fell, its Syrian and Cypriot defenders fell back to the Hospitallers' position at Saint Anthony's Gate where, again to quote Runciman, the two orders fought together 'as if there had never been two centuries of rivalry between them'. Matthew de Clermont made a move to retake the Accursed Tower, followed by Grand Master Jean de Villiers and his Templar counterpart, Guillaume de Beaujeu, but could make no progress against what seemed like 'a stone wall'.[7] Beaujeu was mortally wounded and died soon after being carried to the rear by Clermont, who returned to the fray and his own death soon afterwards. Villiers was wounded, but wanted to stay and fight on; his men, though, put him protesting onto a ship for Cyprus, following King Henry who had already quit the struggle.

By this time the whole angle had crumbled and the Muslims were surging into Acre through the ruins of the Gate of Saint Nicholas by the tower of the same name. The defenders of that sector under Otto de Grandson fled to the port along with the wounded Jean de Grailly and joined a mad rush to the Venetian galleys waiting offshore. Mothers dropped and trampled their infants in their haste. The elderly Latin Patriarch of Acre, Nicholas of Hanape, drowned when his overburdened boat capsized; in the goodness of his heart he had tried to rescue too many people. A group of Dominican Friars chanting 'Veni, Creator Spiritus' in their cloister were all cut down. Those civilians and soldiers who could not escape by sea met a grim fate under the

Muslim scimitars. An estimated 60,000 Christians were either enslaved or murdered. Some captured knights were to end their days miserably in hovels in Cairo or as labourers in the wastes around the Dead Sea; a very few, after many years, made it back to Europe. A whole population of Frankish women of all ages disappeared into the harems of the emirs.

A remnant of the Templars still held out in their quarter of Acre, and for about a week there seemed to be hope that they might be allowed a safe-conduct out. But such was the brutality and unreliability of al-Ashraf and many Muslim troops that the end was tragic; on 28 May the undermined Templar fortifications crashed down on attacker and defender alike, eliminating almost all of them. Al-Ashraf's revenge was characteristically thorough – he razed Acre so completely that it never thereafter recovered. Today, as Akko, it has revived to become a pleasant town in northern Israel, though overshadowed by its larger and more commercial neighbour Haifa.

One by one the remaining Frankish towns fell like dominoes. While Acre had not yet fallen the sultan invested Tyre, but the small garrison of that city, which had beaten even the efforts of Saladin, this time gave up without a fight. The Templars under their new Grand Master Tibald Gaudin held off a large Mamluk force at Sidon but after Gaudin inexplicably lost his nerve, the rest had to quit before the Mamluks could seize the city on 14 July. Two weeks later it was the turn of Beirut, and then Haifa, and by the end of August 1291 the great Templar Castle of Atlith, on the coast south of Haifa, was razed. The tumbling masonry was the sound of the death of Outremer.[8]

Chapter 8

Back to Square One

Gloom in Cyprus – Templars crushed – creating a Hospitaller Navy – raids on Syria and Egypt – Fulk de Villaret – landing on Rhodes – chivalry waning in western Europe – papacy in trouble, Byzantine decline – rise of the Ottoman Turks

The moment that the wounded Jean de Villiers was put on board a ship at Acre marked the end of the career of the Knights of Saint John in Outremer. The only conceivable place where they could start anew was Cyprus, where the Lusignan line still ruled and could provide the suitable political and religious environment. The Teutonic Knights at this point gave up the Middle East as a bad job and moved their activities to northern Europe and the Baltic with their headquarters at Marienburg. But there was scarcely a Hospitaller or Templar who at the close of 1291 did not hope and expect that someday the balance would shift again and Christian soldiers once more would march and sail to the rescue of the Holy Land. The orders were still under the authority of the popes of Rome and controlled vast assets, and after the fall of Acre there was a fresh outburst of crusading fever among some monastic writers. But for now more immediate matters had to be dealt with.

Morale, naturally, was at a low point. A mere seventy brother-knights and ten brother-sergeants were all that could muster at Limassol. Safe in Cyprus, but in pain from his wound, Grand Master Jean de Villiers described how he felt in a letter:

Most of [us are] wounded and battered without hope of cure … On the day that this letter was written we are still [in Cyprus], in great sadness of heart, prisoners of sorrow.[1]

The letter betrayed more than just depression over a military defeat. The remaining knights may well instinctively have felt that the bedrock that informed their whole way of life, the early mediaeval notions of chivalry and knighthood which had sought their supreme *raison d'être* in two centuries of attempts to recover the Holy Land, had singularly failed. The Crusades had also cost an enormous amount of money; to raise it, countless knights had to sell or mortgage their properties, while countless more serfs abandoned their farms to go crusading, many of them never to return. The kingdoms and fiefs of western Europe suffered a corresponding loss of prestige which many blamed on the irresponsibility of the knightly class; as a result royal houses such as those of France and England were strengthened at the expense of the nobles, while the very concept of the Military Order came under growing distrust. If they could no longer protect pilgrims in the Holy Land, what were they good for?

The Templars were the first to feel the changing attitudes, and hard. After being expelled from the East they settled in France to enjoy a tax-free good life financed by their considerable holdings and banking businesses. 'Unlike the Hospitallers, they maintained no hospitals, established no schools, succoured no poor.'[2] They became a virtual state within a state, and that was their downfall. On 13 October 1310 King Philip IV (the Fair) of France ordered the arrest of every Templar in the land. A host of knights and others were hauled before hostile tribunals and accused of the grossest crimes, sins and heresies. Many suffered fearful tortures; fifty-nine were burned at the stake. Philip himself was gleefully present at the burning of Templar Grand Master Jacques de Molay. Pope Clement V, controlled by the French throne, abolished the Order in 1312, transferring all its property to the Hospitallers.

But all that was in the future as the Knights of Saint John settled into their new headquarters at Limassol, on the south coast of Cyprus, to try and reorganize themselves. The surroundings were not unfamiliar; there had been a Hospitaller presence on the island since Richard I's conquest as part of the military establishment of the Lusignan kings. In the thirteenth century the Order had also acted as bankers, notaries and legal advisers, operating out of the main Commandery at Kolossi, amassing considerable wealth. Thanks to its elite position, however, it often came into conflict with the local Greek population and the Orthodox Church. Those tensions lessened somewhat after the last of the Hospitallers from Acre came to settle in and live among the population. The various language groups among them began to separate into distinct tongues, or communities, that resembled expat colonies.[3]

Apart from local business, there was little to do. We may safely assume that training continued along the familiar and established lines, as the handful of knights and sergeants who had survived the fall of Acre were gradually replenished by fresh recruits from the West who brought also horses and weapons and moreover had the benefit of prior training in their homelands. Tactics, meanwhile, had undergone alterations along with advances in military technology. The crossbow was by now coming into wider use, while horsemen were being taught how to stay in cavalry formation with the lance tucked tight under the right arm and the shield hanging from the neck – an innovation almost certainly learned from the Byzantines and Muslims.[4] In a warm climate such as Cyprus, armour (*guarnement*) was donned only when battle was imminent (not surprising when a full-mail hauberk weighed some 25kg), but there was by no means uniformity in what a knight or sergeant would wear; the helmets, in particular, came in all shapes and sizes, from the crude, open-faced barbute to the intricate salet and bascinet that protected the neck as well as the head.

As armour plating became stronger, so was the weapon required to penetrate it. From the late thirteenth century onwards, the thrusting sword became heavier and more pointed; the ideal tactic worked out for this was the foyne, the straight-ahead thrust with maximum strength, to complement the more established moves of thrust and parry. A hand–held dagger completed the small-arms equipment. All of these items, especially the guarnement, were expensive and time-consuming to manufacture, and mostly had to be imported from Italy. Grand Master Villiers ordered that every Hospitaller arriving from Europe should bring his own kit plus three horses, and leave it all behind for the use of others when his tour of duty was up.

Once he had recovered somewhat from his wounds, Villiers called together a Chapter General, or members' meeting, to assess the situation. As Cyprus was an island, and a Christian one at that, there was little scope for the kind of military activity the Order had been used to in Outremer. However, there existed powerful fortifications built in earlier years, mainly for defence against invasion. There were at least a dozen of these, mostly around the coast, dominated by the dramatic mountain-top Saint Hilarion ringed with cliffs, that served as the knights' bases and living quarters.[5] But with the Holy Land beckoning as always over the eastern horizon, and the ever-present danger of a seaborne invasion from Egypt, strategic thinking inevitably turned in a naval direction. The Order had a papal directive to employ a flotilla of galleys to defend Armenian Cilicia, the only other Christian state in the vicinity (corresponding to south-east Turkey), but the order proved impracticable as the naval bickering between the bitter Italian rivals of Venice and Genoa forbade any serious naval activity by the

Knights of Saint John. Nonetheless, to take account of the naval realities the office of Admiral was set up about 1300 to command all the Order's galleys and smaller vessels, including the crews and marines on board. The new Hospitaller Navy would prove useful very soon.

In 1294 the new Grand Master, Guillaume de Villaret, fed up and frustrated, made plans to relocate the Order to Provence in France. But the majority of Knights, though inactive, seem to have liked the Cypriot climate and their status as the ruling elite, and refused to consider a move. There was talk in the great halls of attacking Egypt and Syria once more, or of relocating to Cilicia or Byzantium. As the Templars were then still around, some Knights wanted to unite the Military Orders for a grand crusade. To test their naval skills, the Hospitallers took part in sporadic raids against Egypt and Syria, and sent small fleets to support Armenian Cilicia. In fact, a Hospitaller base was established in Cilicia, but it proved vulnerable to the neighbouring Turks as well as the Italian merchants who didn't want anyone else elbowing in on their trade. It was all very unsatisfying to the majority of brother-knights in Cyprus, who in the first decade of the fourteenth century didn't know what to do with themselves. Instances of drunkenness and indiscipline multiplied; King Henry II was deeply suspicious of the Hospitallers' power and limited it wherever he could, especially in supplies of weaponry and ownership of land.

The idea of a joint Hospitaller-Templar crusade was given fresh vigour by Fulk de Villaret, elected Grand Master in 1305 and backed by Pope Clement V. The pope asked for written opinions by both grand masters, and no two opinions could have been more different. The Templar proposal, typically, overstated the ease with which a crusade could be carried out, while Villaret's report was more thoughtful and detailed, 'a bureaucrat's report rather than one written by a military leader.'[6] Villaret, in short, argued for a series of effective, professionally-managed jabs at the centres of Mamluk power in Egypt that would wear down the Egyptians while diplomatic and possibly military support should be sought from Cilician Armenia and the Mongols. Assuming, of course, that enough money could be raised in the first place.

While Villaret's argument was cogent and well-reasoned, there were two basic flaws in it. The first was his apparent lack of knowledge about what was happening with the Mongols, who in fact at this period were converting to Islam and hence could be of no further use to the West. The second, more basic, flaw was his assumption that the crusading spirit that had once fired Urban II and Richard I and many thousands of ordinary Europeans in the name of Christ was still a strong policy-driving force. Sadly, it had long ceased to be so. The popes themselves were far more concerned with retaining their power and privileges against the kings in France, Germany and England, for example, than in sponsoring crusades, seven of which had come and gone, with nothing in the end to show for the massive wastes of lives and money. In the end, the plan to attack Egypt was shelved, and as disaster was beginning to hover over the Templars and the Teutonic Knights had already gone from the region, Villaret began to cast about for a more secure base from which the Order could more effectively fight the Muslims. He found one in the ethnically-Greek island of Rhodes.

At the time Rhodes was technically an outpost of the Byzantine Empire, though the Ottoman Turks – a new and vigorous tribe that had supplanted the old Seljuks in Anatolia – had established footholds on several places in the island. Rhodes also had an overwhelmingly Greek Orthodox population not too well disposed to the popes or anyone serving them. As the largest island of the Dodecanese (the 'Twelve Islands') of the south-east Aegean, it already had a long and rich history behind it. The island had succeeded Athens in the fourth century BC as the centre of ancient Greek trade and then had become a prosperous Roman, and later Byzantine, province. By the late thirteenth century, with the decline of Byzantine power, Rhodes saw the arrival of Italian trader colonies, with the Genoese in the ascendant. The island was also subject to periodic Muslim raids. Enough of Rhodes' old glory had remained to impress Richard I when he landed there in 1191, but that glory was fading fast. Gradually the Byzantine governors were supplanted by feudal Genoese lords who paid mere lip service to Byzantine suzerainty. Emperor Andronikos II came under pressure to sell the island to save it from Turkish conquest. He was reluctant to do so, as the island was a key source of wine as well as a key trading station, but in 1306 the Genoese feudal lord on Rhodes, Vignolo de' Vignoli, sold it to the Hospitallers, ignoring the emperor, who was unable to enforce his writ anyway.

But taking possession by purchase was not the same as taking control physically, and it took three years for the Knights of Saint John to finally consolidate their hold on the main city and port. The mechanics of this three-year campaign remain vague. So are the motives and methods of Villaret, who intrigued with popes and other European leaders and may even have abetted the destruction of the rival Templars.[7] He needed just two galleys, in fact, to land the Knights. We are told of a Trojan Horse-type operation in which several Knights entered the town of Rhodes one night in August 1309, hidden among a flock of sheep; once inside, they opened the gates to the rest of the force. Thus began another colourful chapter in the history of the Knights Hospitaller.

Meanwhile in western Europe, what had happened to the original political and social culture that had nurtured the ideal of the warrior-monk Military Orders? In France, the fountainhead of the crusading movement and origin of the dominant ethnic group in the Knights of Saint John, the Crusades had drained the power and resources of the once-powerful nobility, allowing the crown to arrogate more and more central power, as we have seen. Louis IX's son Philip III (1270–1285) expanded the realm, giving his son Philip IV the Fair (1285–1314) the chance to build up the French monarchy into a well-administered power that brought him into direct conflict with Edward I of England, who held a large part of south-west France and was unwilling to give it up.

For his wars with England and Flanders, Philip IV needed money, which is one reason why he crushed the Templars and seized much of their wealth. The king then sought wider support by setting up the States General, a rudimentary national assembly of the nobler and wealthier elements in society who were thus roped into paying tax. By the second decade of the fourteenth century, then, France was well on the way to becoming a centralized national state where policy and warfare were decided by the king and his advisers rather by the independent and aggressive nobles under the disappearing feudal system. In such an environment the Knights Hospitaller were always in danger of becoming an irrelevance. That they survived in France is a testimony to their internal honour system and dedication to Christian principles under the papacy, which took precedence over any aggressive instincts.

Much the same was occurring in England, where Edward I (1272–1307) was consolidating the royal power. His brief and disappointing foray into the Crusades in the year before his accession could have turned him off such faraway foreign adventures and helped him concentrate on reforming his homeland, which he did to an extraordinarily efficient degree. Besides, constant wars with France and Scotland, and the conquest of Wales, ensured that English military manpower was kept fully occupied closer to home. But under the inadequate Edward II (1307–1327) the English barons reasserted their old authority, deposing Edward and elevating his son Edward III (1327–1377). Soon afterwards, England and France became consumed in the Hundred Years' War that finally put paid to any lingering ideas of recovering the Holy Land.

The Holy Roman Empire at the turn of the fourteenth century has been described by mainstream historians as 'a shattered wreck'.[8] The long-standing feud with the popes and their accompanying bitter political rivalries had drained Germany of energy. After Emperor Conrad IV's death in 1254 there was no emperor for nearly twenty years, an interval in which independent German princes pretty well did what they liked. But enough national feeling and desire for order prevailed to ensure the election of the noble and strong-willed Rudolf of Habsburg as emperor in 1273. Rudolf's son Albert (1298–1308) tried to consolidate royal power on the French and English model, but was assassinated for his pains. There followed an uncertain period where successive emperors from different families tried, and failed, to recapture lost territory such as northern Italy. The Teutonic Knights in north-east Germany and the Baltic area had become a state unto themselves. The great weakness of the Holy Roman Empire was its elective system, which unlike a hereditary system weakened royal authority at a time when the popes in Rome were at the peak of their power.

The pope in 1300 was the elderly Boniface VIII. Despite his advanced age, he was competent and energetic, but at the same time utterly ruthless, dedicated exclusively to enhancing his personal and family power. Naturally, Boniface considered himself the superior of all the kings of Europe, pressing home the point with the First Jubilee in which millions of pilgrims flocked to Rome in what was probably the Eternal City's first tourism boom, pouring money into the papal coffers. Two years later he went further; in the papal encyclical *Unam sanctam* he laid down the law that 'for every human creature it is absolutely necessary for salvation to be subject to the Roman Pontiff', and that was to be as true for the most exalted king as for the poorest serf.[9]

In fact, that was Boniface's undoing. Philip IV of France, enraged by the *Unam sanctam*, sent a noble to arrest him, joined by an armed squad raised by the Colonna family of Rome who were the pope's bitterest foes. He was seized at his summer retreat south of Rome, only to be rescued by a local mob; but the shock proved too much for him and he died within a month. For two years the papal seat was vacant until Philip IV forced the election of his fellow-Frenchman Clement V. But by now Rome and most of Italy had become insecure, and Clement moved the papal residence to Avignon, where it was to stay for nearly seventy years. It was from Avignon that Clement oversaw the Hospitallers' conquest of Rhodes and the crushing of the Templars, both of which events solidified French control over papal and Military Order policy.

At the other end of the Mediterranean, the 1,000-year-old Byzantine Empire was a mere shadow of its former self and fading fast. First the Seljuk Turks, and then the Ottomans, had devoured almost all of the empire's territory in Asia Minor, leaving just Constantinople and its environs plus what is now central and north-east Greece. But the Catholic Venetians had never ceased to be hostile and were ever looking for ways to subvert the empire and bring the Greeks into the Latin fold. Catalan pirates regularly attacked points on the coast, torching monasteries and pillaging towns, and creating Balkan vacuums into which the Muslim Turks would penetrate. The Ottomans, originally known as Osmanlis after their founder Osman, were one of the Turkic tribes of central Asia driven westwards by the Mongol conquests. Testifying to their early ambitiousness is the title that Osman's son Orkhan gave himself – 'Hero of the World', after his father had dubbed himself Ghazi, or 'Warrior of the Faith'. As other Turkish tribes jumped on the Ottoman bandwagon, Orkhan established his capital at Brusa, just 100 or so kilometres south of Constantinople, following it up with the conquest of Nicomedia, even closer to the Byzantine capital.

Orkhan's great contribution to the Ottoman state was his reorganization of the army, which he transformed from a loose agglomeration of steppe-trained horsemen to a standing army paid by the state. There was plenty of manpower available from the conquered territories, but most of it was Christian manpower, and Muslim doctrine forbade anyone but a Muslim from bearing arms. Orkhan's solution therefore was to convert promising young Christian boys; the first thousand of these were snatched from their grieving families and brought up as fanatical warriors, the Muslim equivalent of the Christian Military Orders. These young men made up an elite force called the *Yeni Cheri* (New Force), known more commonly by the corrupt form, Janissaries. They were to form the core of a feared corps that would eventually number more than 16,000 and take the credit for the great majority of Turkish triumphs in the decades and centuries to come.

Chapter 9

Rhodes: The Good Years

Settling in – the Tongues – the typical Knight – ouster of Villaret – seizure of Smyrna – naval tactics – Ottoman advances – effects of the papal schism – Juan Fernandez of Heredia – debacle at Nikopolis – Rhodes fortified

Once established in Rhodes, the Knights of Saint John probably did not regard that island as a permanent settlement. Just as when they had fled from Acre to Cyprus nearly twenty years before, they saw their new home as a base from which to harass Muslims in the Mediterranean and plan a hoped-for return to some sort of crusading action. But, especially in the first ten or so years, the need to settle in and reorganize took precedence over everything else. Villaret and the Knights:

> gave thanks to God and the Virgin Mary for the wealth and abundance that had come to them. They built a great castle and conquered all around, collecting many fine men who wished to come to Rhodes to reconnoitre and to colonize the island.[1]

There was plenty to do. As well as with the incessant raids by the Turks, the Knights as papal subjects had to contend with the mistrust of the local Greek Orthodox people and clergy. Always conscious that they were a foreign body in an ethnically-Greek island, the Hospitallers were compelled to maintain a tightly-stratified military organization that from the outset formed a feudal elite whose object was self-preservation through self-perpetuation. The Knights of Rhodes have often been described as a state within a state, but that is not quite correct; there was no wider Rhodian state to speak of, as Byzantine power was all but eclipsed and the Turks were making bold inroads into an island that until 1309 was essentially without a government. Theoretically, the Knights were warrior-monks still, though the steady stream of recruits arriving from the West included all manner of men, many very far from saintly. Theoretically, the main policy continued to be the fight against the infidel Saracen and Turk; as late as 1378 Saint Catherine of Siena could honestly adjure the Hospitaller Prior of Pisa to 'bathe yourself in the blood of Christ crucified'.[2] But all too often, the advantages of life as a colonial power in a pleasant climate became ends in themselves.

The Grand Master continued to be the head of state, as it were, and in the first decade of the Order's sojourn in Rhodes the office under Fulk de Villaret arrogated greater powers to itself. The Grand Master, who had of course to be a Knight, was answerable only to the pope, and like him, theoretically held office for life. He was chosen by thirteen electors in the last stage of an election after the lesser offices were filled. Theoretically he ruled in consultation with his Council, though there was a check on his power in the form of the Chapter General which met every few years. The rest of the hierarchy remained essentially unchanged since the Outremer era, with the ranks of Grand Commander, Grand Marshal and Grand Hospitaller, except for the recent addition of Admiral; the Draper, Grand Bailli (or Treasurer), Grand Turcopolier and Grand Chancellor continued the basically administrative functions implied by their titles.

However, the outstanding organizational innovation of the Knights of Rhodes was their division into Tongues (*linguae*), or divisions reflecting the varied ethnic origin of the brother-knights and brother-sergeants. Though this had been the practice in Cyprus, in Rhodes it became formally stratified. There were seven such Tongues, each commanded by one of the office-holders (known as *piliers*, or 'pillars' of the establishment, so to speak) mentioned in the previous paragraph. The Provençal tongue, probably numerically the most important, was commanded by the Grand Commander, one rung beneath the Grand Master. The Grand Marshal led the Auvergne tongue, the Grand Hospitaller the French, the Admiral the Italian (probably reflecting the Italians' naval expertise), the Draper the Aragonese, the Grand Turcopolier the English and the Grand Bailli the German.

Though the ordinary Rhodian native would not have thought so, given the magnificence on display, Hospitaller finances were anything but robust. The European Priories were required to send roughly one-third of their revenues to the headquarters in Rhodes, though this proportion varied with the level of revenue in each Priory. Other sources of revenue were scattered properties on the islands, sugar plantations in Cyprus, banking (though not on the scale of what the Templars had practised) and booty from the periodic campaigns against the Turks on the Asia Minor mainland – though it could be argued that the material and human cost of those campaigns made them a questionable economic proposition.

To understand the nature of the Knights of Saint John during their Rhodes years, as nothing in our time quite parallels what they were, Anthony Luttrell offers the analogy of 'a late mediaeval NATO-cum-Red Cross'.[3] Eastern Europe and the eastern Mediterranean were in the grip of a cold war that would often turn hot; the ideological component of this war was the irreconcilable conflict between Christianity and Islam, the classic zero-sum game where a gain for one side meant a loss for the other. At the same time, the old charitable Hospitaller philosophy 'humanized', as it were, the Order's essentially coldly strategic purpose.

The Order began its new life in Rhodes with an estimated 100 or fewer Knights, and not many more auxiliary infantry. Yet this number grew rapidly in the first decade, as volunteers from the West arrived in response to offers of land and pensions. As we have seen, they were a mixed bag. Luttrell, a leading authority on the Hospitallers, describes them largely as 'moral men who had chosen a marginally unusual life'.[4] Many, if not most, were functionally illiterate, but considering the job they were recruited to do, that didn't matter much. We don't know how many fulfilled the 'monk' side of the warrior-monk duties, or how sincerely they did so. Nonetheless, the process of their induction into the Order was a solemn one, as evidenced by the example of Prince Jaime of Aragon, who joined up in 1319.

Father Arnau de Soler, the Preceptor of Barcelona and Aliaga, sat before the altar holding the Gospels and a cross. Jaime, dressed as a Hospitaller but without the characteristic mantle, knelt before him, placing his hands on the book and the cross. Father Arnau gave the normal explanation and said that the new entrant would have a probationary year. After making his vows of obedience Jaime rose, and placed the book and cross on Arnau's knees. The preceptor then received him as a brother, placing the black mantle with its white cross across his shoulders, whereupon all the brethren present knelt to pray for their new Hospitaller brother.[5]

Too much may perhaps be read into this sonorous account. Prince Jaime, in fact, was fleeing from an unwanted marriage, and it would have cost him nothing to pay mere lip service to the spiritual requirements of induction into the Order, as many others undoubtedly did. Whatever their personal qualities or flaws, the Knights of Saint John in the early fourteenth century constituted 'a permanent, disciplined, experienced, even brutal corps of trained military men whose value in action went far beyond their numbers'.[6]

From their base in Rhodes, what did such action consist of? For the first two years, the main task was to stave off constant Turkish attacks. To widen the defensive perimeter the Hospitallers seized the neighbouring islands of Karpathos and Kasos in 1313 and Kos the following year, only to have to give them up under pressure from the Venetians, who wanted to keep as many Aegean islands as possible for themselves to support their regional trading near-monopoly. Every spring the Turks would launch raids on Rhodes, burning farms, destroying vineyards and carrying off cattle and any unlucky peasant who happened to be in their way. These serious disruptions of the island's economy could be met only by turning Rhodes into an impregnable fortress, and almost at once an ambitious castle-building programme was started.

The Order had plenty of accumulated experience in building fortifications, going back to the fabled Krak des Chevaliers in Syria. There were also existing Byzantine structures to build on. Over the next few decades at least twenty formidable fortifications went up, the largest being those in the port of Rhodes and the eastern town of Lindos. Each castle was designed for a garrison of 500 horsemen and 1,000 infantry, though this ideal complement was rarely, if ever, attained. Even as late as 1340 the main Rhodes garrison did not number more than 200 brother-knights and about fifty brother-sergeants and 1,000 or so turcopoles, beefed up by a few dozen non-Order cavalry and Greek volunteer foot-soldiers.[7]

In building up and administering the Hospitaller state of Rhodes, Grand Master Fulk de Villaret may have become overambitious. As the Turks continued their annual jabs at the east coast of the island, there were growing complaints about Villaret's sumptuous lifestyle and despotic manner. The discontent erupted into open rebellion in 1317, when the leading Knights declared Villaret deposed and elevated Gerard de Pins as Lieutenant *pro tempore* until a new Grand Master could be elected.[8] To escape arrest, Villaret fled to the castle of Lindos. At this point Pope John XXII suggested a compromise candidate in the person of Hélion de Villeneuve; in 1319 the proposal was accepted and the internal crisis was over.

Gradually, as confidence was restored under Villeneuve, the Hospitallers put together a military strategy aimed at maintaining their naval influence in the eastern Aegean and rolling back Turkish expansionism in the region, including the Asia Minor mainland. It could be described as defensive crusading, maintaining the pope's foreign policy not by aggression but by parrying the Islamic thrusts. Yet as there were not many opportunities to gird the sword and don the armour, the Villeneuve administration was noted for the first real long period of peace in the Order's history. A formal alliance among the Hospitallers, the papacy, France, Venice and Cyprus, signed in 1334 helped maintain the status quo while Ottoman Sultan Orkhan was busy isolating what was left of Byzantium.

Ten years later the Order was strong enough to claw back Smyrna (now Izmir), a wealthy former Byzantine city, from Ottoman occupation. The attack was made in conjunction with papal forces, employing thirty galleys packed with armour-clad knights that made a formidable impression on the Turkish defenders. 'Their horse-armour and cuirasses were amazing,' a Turkish chronicler wrote. 'Innumerable Franks [were] dressed in iron from head to foot ... their gauntlets ... their helmets, all shone and glittered in the light.' The flotilla approached Smyrna in tight formation, turning and backing water in a coordinated movement so that the troops could surge out of the sterns and hit the beach around the same time. The light crossbowmen led the assault, followed by the heavier crossbows and archers, to the deafening sound of drums, cymbals and trumpets. The majority of troops carried swords, daggers and shields; there were specialist units whose job was to burn the enemy siege engines and smash the palisades in the defensive ditch before the Turkish positions with battle-axes. Within a short time the attackers had seized Smyrna Castle, which they were to keep for more than half a century.[9]

With Smyrna in their hands the Hospitallers could more confidently flex their naval muscles in the Aegean. In the intervening fifty or so years since the fall of Acre, Hospitaller naval expertise had made great strides. Constant corsair tactics against the Ottomans had helped build up a valuable store of experience, while the shipyards of Genoa and Marseilles supplied Rhodes with plenty of war galleys. The galley was developing in propulsive capacity, from single oarsmen to multiple rowers pulling on one oar, a method that more efficiently distributed muscle-power. It also was larger than the average merchant galley, to enable it to better withstand rough weather. Though Rhodes was not especially rich in timber, it could grow enough to take care of repairs at the Tersenal, the naval arsenal of Rhodes.

Ship complements varied, though as a general rule a Hospitaller galley would carry some 150 men including a squad of specialist crossbowmen, some of whom could double as rowers. Each ship would have its weapons and armour store. The strongest part of the vessel was its forecastle, where most of the troops were stationed; sometimes the forecastle would carry a small stone-throwing mangonel for use against a land fortification. In view of the overriding importance of the Navy for the Knights of Rhodes, sea service (called 'caravan') was compulsory for every brother-knight and brother-sergeant. They were almost always assigned officer positions, commanding the bulk of the ordinary soldiers and sailors who were mostly local Rhodian Greeks, other Mediterranean ethnic groups, Russians and some Muslim captives.

Naval tactics fell into a fairly efficient pattern. The two main aims of a Hospitaller fleet were to attack enemy coastal positions, as at Smyrna, or prey on his merchant shipping. The convoluted Asia Minor coastline and its many islands in the eastern Aegean were perfect for such action. Here a smaller and more manoeuvrable warship, the galiote, with about 100 or so oarsmen, could hide behind an island or headland while another would lure an enemy vessel into the trap. The enemy ship could then be boarded via the calcar, a raised beak over which the marines could attack. To prevent the enemy from boarding one's own galley, the deck might be covered with netting that would also offer some protection against large projectiles. Fighting also would be desperate, as there was little provision for taking prisoners, and the seriously wounded would simply be dumped into the sea along with the dead.

The early fourteenth century saw the introduction of firearms, which from then on would revolutionize the nature of warfare. Gunpowder had been known at least since 1260, though no one knows who first thought of using it to force a projectile out of a tube at great speed. The earliest known cannon, a *pot-de-feu*, literally 'firepot', appears in an illustrated manuscript in 1326, two years after the first gun was reportedly fired in anger at Metz in France. From then on, the use of cannon spread quickly. In 1345 King Edward III of England ordered a hundred ribauldequins, primitive rocket batteries with multiple firing tubes mounted on wheeled frames, for use against the French.[10] Turkish sources mention handguns used in the Hospitaller attack on Smyrna, and the 'shat-shat' sound they made, though it's not certain whether the reference is to the 1344 campaign or later ones. War galleys developed defences against seaborne cannon fire, such as heavy protective padding around the forecastle and along the sides.[11]

Thanks to their naval prowess the Knights of Saint John were able to defeat an Ottoman fleet off the island of Imbros in 1347, while another force of Knights sailed to the Christian kingdom of Armenia (which unlike present-day Armenia lay in the south-east corner of what is now Turkey, north of Cyprus) that was under threat from the Egyptian Mamluks. Meanwhile, however, the Ottomans were making steady and inexorable headway against Byzantium. Pope Innocent IV strongly advised Grand Master Pierre de

Corneillan to transfer the Hospitaller headquarters from Rhodes to Smyrna to be closer to the real enemy. But the strategic folly of moving to such a position exposed to attacks from the Asia Minor hinterland, plus, one suspects, the easy life in Rhodes, prevailed with Corneillan over the papal advice. His predecessor as Grand Master, Dieudonné de Gozon, had just given the port a ring of fortifications. Rhodes, at the crossroads of the main naval and commercial shipping routes in the eastern Mediterranean, could not be equalled as a naval base, and few wished to relocate to what could become another Acre.

Yet the crusading spirit was by no means eclipsed. In 1365 the Knights of Rhodes gathered to hear a hortatory address by a papal legate who flattered them as the 'chosen knights of Christ'. In ringing tones he urged them (in case they had forgotten how) to 'fight manfully in God's war, fearing not your enemy and hoping for victory from God, for today the gates of Paradise are open'.[12] It is hard to assess how literally these words would have been taken by hardened and practical men of action. Was there truly 'a mystique of martyrdom' inculcated among the Knights, as one modern authority claims, or did the papal legate resort to spiritual language in order to motivate them and prevent them sinking into a life of ease and privilege?[13] Whatever the truth, the immediate result of this exhortation was a raid on the Mamluk stronghold of Alexandria, 400 miles to the south-east. The hit-and-run raid, carried out with allies from the pope and Cyprus, was a stunning success, leaving the Egyptian fleet in flames but destroying a large part of the city as well. Among those in the attacking force was an English priest, Father Robert Hales, who seems to have been rewarded with the Priory of England. Two years later the stunt was repeated against Egyptian naval bases at Alexandria and along the Syrian coast.

Smyrna, meanwhile, was being ably defended by its garrison commander, Niccoló Benedetti, who repulsed a Turkish attack in 1359. The Hospitallers could have done more, had not King Edward III of England defaulted on his debts to Italian banking houses, wiping out a credit of 360,000 florins that the Order had as a reserve. Smyrna and its environs thus came deeper under the looming Turkish shadow. The vigorous Ottoman Sultan Murad I, who had succeeded his father Orkhan in 1362, captured Adrianople (now Edirne) in Thrace and made it his capital. This move more than any other secured the Turkish presence in Europe and sealed the fate of Byzantium, whose capital of Constantinople was a mere 100 or so miles away. With Constantinople in deadly danger Pope Urban V called for a crusade, but few heeded him. Murad, meanwhile, subjugated the disunited Balkan states and kingdoms one by one; the culmination came on 15 June 1389, when Tsar Lazar of Serbia confronted Murad and the Turks on the infamous Field of Blackbirds (Kosovo Polye) and sustained a crushing defeat that still reverberates bitterly in the collective memory of the Orthodox Serbs. (And underpins their present-day reluctance to allow the independence of Kosovo.) Both Tsar Lazar and Sultan Murad I fell on the field, though Prince Bayezid carried the day rallying the Ottoman left flank.

At this moment of supreme danger for Europe and Christendom, the papacy was at its weakest and least effective. For in 1309 it had split, amoeba-like, into two rival papacies, one in Rome and the other in Avignon. The proximate cause of this disheartening state of affairs was an ethnic dispute over whether the Italians (specifically the Romans) or the French should control the Roman Catholic Church. 'The rival popes thundered against one another, each denying the other any claim to authority, so that conscientious men did not know which way to turn.'[14] The schism did not heal until 1377, by which time it had penetrated into the pope's own battalions, the Knights Hospitaller, whose Grand Master at the time, the vigorous Juan Fernandez de Heredia, hewed strictly to the Roman pope's camp, even though the majority of Knights might have been expected to support the French side.[15]

There is evidence, though inconclusive, that the papal schism was a factor in a breakdown of discipline on at least one occasion. The Knights were, of course, no saints and misconduct was common at all times, but the due penalties were generally applied. Fist fights, for example, were punished by a seven-day or forty-day suspension from the Order (the *quarantaine*, from which our word quarantine) during which the offender was not allowed to wear his monk's habit, a visible sign of disgrace. A rather more serious case was recorded in 1381, when the Hospitaller Father Bertrin de Gagnac was accused of complicity in the murder of the Spanish Draper. A trial found him guilty as charged, but as Grand Master Juan Fernandez de Heredia was ceremonially removing the disgraced brother's cloak, Gagnac turned on him with a knife. Luckily Heredia was only slightly wounded but Gagnac was slain at once by the guards. The incident brought out severe tensions between the French majority and the Spaniards, possibly reflecting the recent rift within the Church. Heredia presently packed fifty-one French knights off to Europe.[16]

Heredia, who took office in 1377 and held it for six years, was one of the Order's more active Grand Masters, a Spanish noble by birth and a man of unique talents in the spheres of soldiering, diplomacy, culture, amassing riches and fathering illegitimate children. Pope Innocent VI had appointed him as mediator between the English and French embroiled in the Hundred

Years' War, a task at which he dismally failed, after which he elected to fight on the French side in the Battle of Poitiers in 1356. It was probably for such a perceived breach of neutrality that England's Black Prince wanted to execute him when he was captured, but he escaped that fate by putting his considerable personal wealth to good use, ransoming himself for a huge sum.[17] Heredia then oversaw the fortifications of the new papal seat at Avignon, which earned him the gratitude of Pope Gregory XI who rewarded him with the Grand Master's office. The Hospitaller Knights appear to have had little say in the matter, contrary to their established election process, yet we can gauge his general popularity from the fact that when in 1383 Pope Urban VI tried to sack Heredia and appoint Riccardo Caracciolo in his place, the latter was never formally accepted and during his twelve-year administration was referred to as the 'Anti-Master'.[18]

The year after his election Heredia personally led a Hospitaller expedition (a *passagium*, or minor crusade) to Epiros in north-west Greece to try and gain some possessions along the coast; at Arta he was ambushed by the local Albanians and captured, being freed only after payment of (another) ransom. The Order's other possessions in Greece, such as Karystos on the Aegean coast and the fortifications of Corinth, were constantly under threat from Turkish encroachments, as the Byzantine authority was now too weak, and moreover busy fending off aggressive Venetian and Genoese commercial interests. The Balkans, especially the Greek mainland, were a chronically unstable ethnic patchwork of Greek imperial, Italian, Turkish and Albanian possessions, each warring against the others. The Hospitallers' strategy in this interlude seems to have been to preserve their way-stations on the sea-route to Rhodes from western Europe, though Ottoman power, growing by the year, made this task increasingly difficult, while the Venetians were never cooperative.

The 1370s saw a drop in revenues and recruitment for the Knights of Saint John as the prestige of the papacy weakened in Europe and the attractions of a faux-crusading life as a military monk lost some of its appeal. The majority of long-term knights were getting older and less eager to go on arduous campaigns. The papal schism, as we have seen, triggered turmoil in the senior ranks and can be expected to have diminished some of the fighting fervour. A survey of all Hospitaller assets and personnel, drawn up in 1373, makes for 'dismal reading'.[19] It noted falling revenues, abandoned churches and an ageing priesthood, not only in Rhodes but all over the European Priories. Yet two decades later enough of the fighting spirit remained to propel the Hospitallers into the last of all the Crusades, the last futile attempt to halt the relentlessly driving Ottomans in their tracks.

For the Turks had already made alarming inroads into south-east Europe and, as in centuries past, fear fastened upon the hearts of pope and king alike, as well as the knighthood of the West. Sultan Bayezid I – known as *Yildirim*, or Thunderbolt) had seized the Bulgarian capital in 1393, plus central Greece and the Peloponnese within two years. In May 1395 Prince Mircea of the Wallachians and King Sigismund of Hungary met the advancing Turks at Rovine but fell back, abandoning all of what are now Serbia and Romania to the sultan. The ghosts of Peter the Hermit, Urban II and Bernard of Clairvaux again haunted the pulpits, and this time the Muslim had come a whole lot closer than Palestine. Pope Boniface IX, the knighthood of France and central Europe, and many in Spain and England, responded enthusiastically to this fresh call to arms reminiscent of the great days of Richard the Lionheart. The Knights Hospitaller, of course, could not be left out.

More than 100,000 men, a huge force for the time, assembled in August 1396 at the Hungarian city of Buda (half of what would later become Budapest) for a grand crusading expedition down the Danube. King Sigismund of Hungary led the largest contingent of some 60,000, and is presumed to have thus been the senior commander. With him were 10,000 French knights, 10,000 Wallachians under Prince Mircea, 6,000 Germans and probably another 15,000 or so men from Spain, England, Italy, Poland and Bohemia. A promise of ten galleys had come from Byzantine Emperor Manuel II, but Turkish naval power prevented them from sailing; Genoese ships based in the eastern Aegean took up the duty of sailing through the Black Sea and into the Danube, carrying the Hospitaller contingent commanded by Grand Master-elect Philibert de Naillac. Even the truculent Venetians agreed to patrol the Hellespont to keep open that vital waterway.

On paper everything seemed very promising. The stirring spirit of the Crusades was everywhere evident. Yet that was precisely to prove the expedition's undoing. King Sigismund had the best of intentions, but the Crusaders soon displayed the faults of their predecessors. As a leading mediaevalist has written:

> By definition, Crusades are hampered from the outset by an excess of religious enthusiasm: the ardent young knights saw themselves as heroes of an earlier age of chivalry, driving all before them to the very doors of the Holy Sepulchre. Were heaven itself to fall, they boasted, they could support it on the points of their lances.[20]

The western knights were nothing if not aggressively independent, resisting Sigismund's efforts to keep them on a common course. Blood-lust often takes hold in such circumstances, and the 'Crusaders' gave vent to it in a general slaughter of non-combatants at Rahova inside Bulgarian territory. After a month's march the force arrived at Nikopolis on the Danube, to find Bayezid the Thunderbolt waiting behind a hill on the river's right bank.

On the morning of 25 September a body of French knights spotted a Turkish cavalry squadron atop the hill and, probably without orders, spurred their horses to an attack. It was a classic example of Crusader *naiveté* of the kind that had brought their predecessors to grief so often in the past, and one is justified in wondering whether anyone in Sigismund's army realized it. The French knights quickly found themselves encircled by the Turks, who after dealing bloodily with them charged down the hill onto the main force. Rank after rank of Crusaders were mown down like wheat; some 10,000 of those who survived to be captured were led to Bayezid and beheaded in his presence. About 300 others were kept alive as slaves.

Naillac, the Grand Master-elect of the Hospitallers, was one of the lucky few to escape along with King Sigismund. Both somehow found a Venetian ship to carry them down to the mouth of the Danube and into the Mediterranean via Constantinople and the Dardanelles. It was as they were passing through this strait that they became aware of an eerie hooting sound: the Turks had lined up their Crusader captives on the shore and ordered them to jeer the fleeing king of Hungary. As for Naillac, the discomfiture at Nikopolis was a tumultuous start to a twenty-five year rule as Grand Master that saw the building of the most enduring military legacy of the Knights of Rhodes, their fortifications.

Six centuries after their construction, the Hospitaller fortifications of Rhodes still inspire awe in the many thousands of visitors who flock to the island each year. The Old Town of Rhodes is still in many ways a vast fort, and if one can mentally block out the clamour of the tourist shops and bars, it's possible to get the feel, albeit faint, of what it must have been like to live as a Hospitaller within those ramparts. They were built on pre-existing Byzantine structures that probably were not altered very much until the time of Grand Master Heredia, who is believed to have first brought in Italian and Greek master masons (*muratores*). The motive was most likely the introduction of firearms, which, as we have seen, became a firm fixture of warfare in the mid-fourteenth century and had shown what they could do in the intermittent campaigns against the Turks. At about this time work was also started on the Grand Master's Palace on the highest point of the port town on the site of the Byzantine citadel, as evidenced by Grand Master Hélion de Villeneuve's (1319–1346) sculpted coat of arms still visible on the western wall.

It was Philibert de Naillac, confirmed in his post of Grand Master after his lucky escape from Nikopolis, who began the work of fortifying Rhodes in earnest; the remains of the harbour tower bearing his name can be seen today. His successor, the Spaniard Antonio de Fluvia (1421–1437) erected most of the landward bastions that are so impressive today, especially the towers of Saint George, Saint Athanasios and Saint John and the double wall based on the design of the great Theodosian Wall of Constantinople but employing Spanish-Portuguese features. The chief defensive innovation was a partial separation of the towers from the rest of the wall so that the defenders in the towers could have a wider field of fire; also, if the tower were to be battered down, it wouldn't have to take a section of wall with it.[21] The Saint George Tower, completed in 1437, had apertures for cannon. The next Grand Master, Jean de Lastic (1437–1454) built up the north-west *enceinte* around the Grand Master's Palace, adding the Saint Anthony Gate and the Battery of Olives. Under Lastic and the next three Grand Masters, the ring of ramparts was progressively strengthened and expanded in time for the first great battle the Knights of Rhodes had to face, for by 1480 the Ottoman Turks had decided to rid themselves of this Christian military island in the middle of their rapidly expanding domain.

Chapter 10

Rhodes: The Sieges

Timur Kesh takes Smyrna – the Ottoman threat grows – Rhodes fortified – the siege of 1480 – Pierre d'Aubusson – a forty-year reprieve – debacle at Lesbos – Suleyman I – the siege of 1522 – the fall of Rhodes

The fifteenth century had so far gone well for the Turks. But it had not seemed that way in the beginning, when hardly had the Turks seen off the last Crusaders at Nikopolis than, like a whirlwind out of nowhere, the Mongol chieftain Timur of Kesh (Timurlane or Timur the Lame) descended with a huge force on the Ottomans' eastern flank. Timur, a descendant of Jenghiz Khan and already in his sixties, swept down on Sivas in Asia Minor, where Ottoman Sultan Bayezid I had his base. The Mongols, despite the intervening century in which they had been preoccupied with internal issues, had never ceased to regard the Turks as their vassals, and now, under Timur, they were dynamically renewing their claim. Fully as ruthless and unstoppable as his predecessors, Timur regarded the Turkish domains as just the first step in his plan for western conquest. In July 1402 Bayezid tried to stop him on the plain of Angora (now Ankara), but his men lacked spirit; instead of fighting Christians, they were being called upon to shed the blood of fellow-Muslims. Nonetheless, Bayezid himself and his 10,000 Janissaries fought bravely until overrun. The sultan who had personally supervised the beheading of thousands of Crusaders at Nikopolis ended his days shut up in a grille trundled along in Timur's entourage, while his wife was forced, we are told, to wait on tables naked.

The Turkish menace motivated the Knights Hospitaller to seek out a new stronghold on the Asia Minor coast not too far from Rhodes. They picked Bodrum, the former Greek city of Halikarnassos and birthplace of the pioneering ancient Greek historian Herodotus. Once permission was secured from Bayezid's successor Mehmet I, a German Knight, Heinrich Schlegelholt, put his architectural talents to work building a castle and complex that would rival that of Rhodes. Saint Peter's Castle, as it was called, featured the most advanced defensive fortifications of the time, including fourteen rainwater cisterns in the basement and a complex system of passages. It would withstand Ottoman attacks for more than a hundred years.[1]

In December 1402 Timur appeared before the Hospitaller castle at Smyrna. The garrison was confident of holding out, thanks to the deep ditch separating the castle from the mainland, while supplies and reinforcements could come by sea. The Mongol leader brought three corps to bear on the city and castle. While his engineers built a huge platform set on wooden piles in the sea to block the port, and the right and left corps joined up with the central, Timur began a massive and incessant bombardment. The Bible-reading defenders compared the rain of projectiles to the rain of the proverbial Flood.[2] Timur's sappers got busy undermining the foundations of the walls of Smyrna; within two days they had dug the mines and set fire to the wooden supports, collapsing the tunnels and the masonry above. As the Mongols surged into the city through the gap, slaughtering indiscriminately, the Hospitaller garrison fled to what ships had dared to risk the bombardment of Timur's mangonels. The Knights reassembled at Bodrum, about 100 miles to the south.

Timur's star fell as quickly as it had risen. Three years after Angora and Smyrna he died while on campaign against the Chinese, giving the Ottoman Turks a reprieve. At the time dynastic disputes weakened the sultan's family, and it wasn't until 1430 that Murad II renewed the Turkish power drive through the Balkans, sacking Salonika and re-peopling it with Muslims, and reaching Romania, where John Hunyadi of Hungary finally halted him. The news prompted Pope Eugenius IV to proclaim yet another Crusade, which scored a spectacular victory against Murad's forces at Jalowac in Bulgaria in December 1443. Though the victory was not followed up, the Albanians under George Kastriota Skanderbeg tied the Turks down, forcing Murad to sue for peace. The pope, however, persuaded Hunyadi to break the truce, and nearly a year later the Turks were trounced again at Varna. But that was the last Ottoman reverse. Murad II was succeeded by his ruthless son Mehmet II, whose chief trait was a monomaniacal desire to seize Constantinople, which he accomplished in a ferocious bloodbath on 29 May 1453. The last Greek emperor, Constantine XI, died heroically defending his city, and with him perished the 1,100-year-old Byzantine Empire, the light of Christian culture in south-east Europe. For the Knights Hospitaller in Rhodes, 'the only power in the [Aegean] archipelago which had not yet submitted to

The Blessed Gerard. (*Order of Malta*)

Krak des Chevaliers. (*Order of Malta*)

The siege of Tyre, 1187, a later artist's impression. (*Order of Malta*)

The siege of Acre, 1291, by Louis Papety.
(*Order of Malta*)

Grand Master's Palace, Rhodes, southern entrance. (*Ekdotike Athinon*)

Pierre d'Aubusson. (*Ekdotike Athinon*)

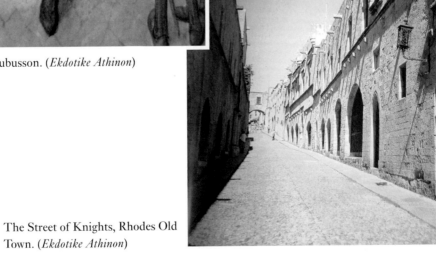

The Street of Knights, Rhodes Old Town. (*Ekdotike Athinon*)

Philippe Villiers de l'Isle Adam. (*Ekdotike Athinon*)

The siege of Rhodes, 1480: the Turkish attack on the St Nicholas Tower. (*Ekdotike Athinon*)

A galley of the Navy of the Religion. (*Henry Sire*)

The siege of Valletta, 1565, by Matteo Perez d'Aleccio. (*Ekdotike Athinon*)

A modern re-enactment of the siege of Malta at Fort St Elmo. (*Order of Malta*)

Napoleon's invasion of Malta, 1798. (*Order of Malta*)

Our Lady of Philermos. (*www.greekcatholicmalta.com*)

The Italian Corpo Militare, 1887. (*Gangemi Editore*)

An Order-run German hospital train of the First World War. (*Gangemi Editore*)

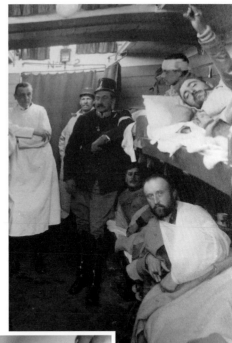

Inside Hospital Train No. 1, Second World War. (*Gangemi Editore*)

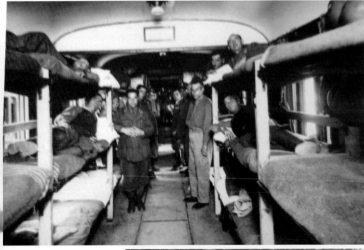

Converted Siai-Marchetti SM-82 bomber preserved in Order markings, at the Italian Air Force Museum, Vigna di Valle. (*Author's photo*)

The Order's headquarters at Via Condotti, Rome. (*Author's photo*)

The 79th and present Grand Master, Matthew Festing. (*Order of Malta*)

Ottoman rule,'³ the writing was on the wall; the fanatical young sultan, all of twenty-one, would surely not spare them now.

While Mehmet concentrated on absorbing and appropriating the administration of the defunct Byzantine Empire, the Knights had time to beef up their own defences against the expected onslaught. The Mamluks of Egypt maintained a navy strong enough to periodically threaten Hospitaller possessions in Cyprus and on at least one occasion, in 1444, had reached Rhodes itself. Attempts at an exploratory truce with the sultan fell through after he demanded 2,000 ducats a year in tribute; several Turkish raids on the neighbouring islands of Tilos, Nisyros, Leros and Kalymnos followed, plus an audacious attack on Archangelos near Lindos on the east coast of Rhodes. Grand Master Jacques de Milly responded by bringing much of the population of those islands to Rhodes.

As if troubles with the Turks were not enough, severe hostility was brewing between the Knights and their main rival for Mediterranean commerce, the Venetians. A dynastic dispute in Cyprus sparked the rivalry into open war; after the death of the Cypriot King John III Lusignan the Knights backed the cause of his daughter Charlotte against that of the king's illegitimate son James, championed by Venice (and incidentally by the Mamluks of Egypt). In 1460 Admiral Luigi Loredano of Venice staged a raid on Rhodes in retaliation for the Order's seizure of two Venetian galleys. The tension was soon defused by negotiations. A second Turkish demand for tribute was rebuffed in 1462, by which time the need for money became urgent. To pay for works on the fortifications and imports of weaponry Grand Master Raimundo Zacosta imposed a two per cent tax on all imports (known as the Chain Tax, as payment had to be made before incoming vessels passed the chain sealing off the port), while appealing desperately for aid from the European Priories.

The next Grand Master, Giovanni Battista Orsini, elected in 1467, gave each Tongue responsibility for beefing up its own section of walls and moat under the general direction of Pierre d'Aubusson, a capable military engineer. When d'Aubusson himself succeeded to the supreme office in 1476, the influx of volunteers from western Europe accelerated. In a parallel diplomatic offensive, treaties were signed with Muslim Egypt and Tunisia to minimize any danger from that quarter. At about that time an emissary from Mehmet II arrived with a proposal for an entente; nothing came of the move, as both sides knew that war would come, and soon. In the winter of 1479 an Ottoman flotilla under Mishak Pasha (sometimes referred to as Misac Pasha), a renegade Greek related to the Byzantine ex-imperial family, landed at a remote point on Rhodes and began to ravage the countryside. The force included a squadron of mounted sipahis, the Turkish equivalent of knights, which, however, were beaten off by the Hospitallers. Most likely the landing was a mere reconnaissance-in-force, but the Knights would have had some advance warning; as far as is known, they maintained an intelligence organization of some efficiency throughout the Aegean, including a network of island-spanning fire signallers.

The main attack on Rhodes materialized on 23 May 1480, when Mishak Pasha led 170 ships carrying perhaps 20,000 troops to a landing south of the port city.[4] As frightened peasants flocked to the castles at Lindos, Faraklos and Monolithos, Mishak Pasha tightened the noose around the port's sea approaches, the aim being to starve Rhodes into weakness after which an attempt would be made on the sea walls. The defenders, well supplied with provisions, were confident of holding out. An Augustinian monk, Father de Curti, noted with satisfaction the 'many crossbows and both heavy and light guns and earthenware fire-pots and receptacles for boiling oil and Greek Fire and pots full of pitch lashed together'.[5] It was clear that the Turks were going to get a hot reception, but the garrison would need all the technical help it could get. At the very best the Knights and their troops were outnumbered ten to one, as they could field only about 2,500 men, of whom a mere 600 or so were brother-knights and brother-sergeants, reinforced by crossbowmen and cavalry. After landing at Trianda Bay Mishak Pasha led his troops up to the Rhodes city walls. The defenders watched as sixteen enormous siege engines were trundled up as well as a large number of wheeled siege cannon and mortars. On the following day the Ottoman commander, scrupulously observing the preliminaries, called on the Knights to surrender; as he probably expected, the call was rejected out of hand. Whereupon he gave the order to his artillery to start the bombardment.

The Ottomans had made fast progress in their use of cannon since they first employed it to batter down the walls of Constantinople twenty-seven years before. The typical gun was a formidable instrument, with a thick bronze barrel more than 4m long, weighing 15t and able to hurl a ball weighing more than 280kg. Mishak Pasha aimed them not only at the walls but also beyond them into the Greek districts, as he hoped to get the Greek population to rebel against the Knights. The tactic failed, thanks largely to the foresight and ability of d'Aubusson who organized squads to douse the fires ignited by the Turks' incendiary projectiles and gather the non-combatants in shelters. This way, losses along the walls in the city could be minimized. D'Aubusson at the time was 57 years old. He had joined the

Order in his twenties after gaining military experience fighting the English, and in the following decades had displayed sound leadership qualities in the diplomatic field as well. And it was here, in the defence of Rhodes, that he would secure his fame.

But it was from the sea that Mishak Pasha hoped to decide the issue. He well knew that Rhodes lived mostly off imports, and one of his first moves, as we have seen, was to blockade the port. When he judged that the defence had been sufficiently weakened, he planned to order an assault on the sea walls. But it wasn't going to be easy. The chief obstacle was the round Saint Nicholas Tower on a mole dominating the two sections of Rhodes harbour, the commercial one and Mandraki to the north. Mishak had to have Mandraki to protect his left flank while attacking the northern section of wall – including the Grand Master's Palace – held by the French Tongue. To eliminate the Saint Nicholas Tower the Ottoman commander placed three large cannon on the shore opposite.

Day after day the cannon pounded the tower which stubbornly insisted on staying up. Each gun could not fire more than about a dozen shots a day, as cooling and reloading were time-consuming procedures. Their crews, moreover, were vulnerable to snipers on the wall and along the mole connecting the tower with the Saint Paul Tower and the Collachium, the Knights' quarter. It took more than a week's bombardment, in which at least 300 balls were expended, for the Saint Nicholas Tower to begin to split under the incessant impact. Its defenders under Fabrizio del Carretto performed wonders of improvisation refurbishing the ruined bits into a new rampart – aided by the unstinting contribution of many ordinary people who gladly risked, and sometimes gave, their lives to build a submerged defensive palisade in the shallow seabed around the beleaguered tower. Sometime around the beginning of June Mishak Pasha decided it was time to storm the position.

The task was given to the fleet, some of whose galleys had been converted into assault craft: masts, sails and most of the rigging had been removed, while the sides were strengthened and cannon platforms placed in the bow. Several of these, crammed like landing craft with assault troops, bore down on the tower accompanied by an indescribable din of drums, cymbals, pipes and hoarse battle cries. The attack was a bold one, pressed forward with great determination, but the defenders had the advantage from the first. Fire-pots and deadly spurts of Greek Fire – whose technique had now spread to the Hospitallers from the Byzantines and the Muslims – whizzed smoking over the water and slammed into Mishak Pasha's packed ships, dealing blazing death and destruction. Murderous crossbow and longbow fire from shore, plus cannon fire from the French section of the battlements, also ploughed into the attackers. One ship was lost, though the others managed to row close to the Saint Nicholas Tower; where the water was shallow enough, the first landing parties jumped off. Some of the Ottoman troops blundered into the underwater stakes and were drowned; the rest staggered ashore and into a desperate hand-to-hand struggle. The attackers, however, had to buckle under the sheer power of the defence led by Fabrizio del Carretto and the Knights in the front rank, and after sustaining severe casualties fled back to the boats. (The date of this initial action is uncertain. Most accounts place the heaviest attack on the Saint Nicholas Tower on the evening of 18 June, though according to some, the last attempt took place no later than 9 June. It remains a moot point.)[6]

Having come close, as he thought, to victory, the Ottoman commander launched two more assaults on the tower, both of which were repulsed with heavy losses. After that, he decided to switch tactics. Apparently figuring that the Knights had concentrated their main force at the French sector in the south, he moved round to the Italian sector of the wall in the north-east hoping to find a weak spot. On 7 June Mishak Pasha opened a heavy bombardment of the Italian wall and the Tower of the Windmills on the adjoining narrow promontory (where the ferry and freighter dock is today), and the Jewish quarter of the city within the wall. As balls and incendiaries rained down on the Italians, the wall began to crumble. Faced with a probable breach, d'Aubusson ordered the Jews out of their quarter and their houses razed to make way for a defensive ditch and new wall. As with the Saint Nicholas Tower earlier, all manner of people – 'knights, slaves, women, children and monks' – laboured on the ditch and wall around the clock.[7]

D'Aubusson spared no effort to make the Italian position as formidable as possible. Between the outer *enceinte* wall and the new rampart he had trap pits dug, camouflaged with twigs and soil. Barrels of tar, sulphur and the fearsome Greek Fire were stockpiled atop the wall, plus examples of a new weapon called a fire-wheel. This was a hoop – probably made of wood – coated with wax and soaked in pitch, set afire and rolled onto the enemy. The composition of this combustible material, like Greek Fire, was such that water was useless against it, therefore its effect on timber and human flesh was devastating. More curiously, a Basque seaman named Juan Aniboa built an old-fashioned trebuchet siege engine which, though impressive to look at, was now obsolete in the age of gunpowder. Very likely it was intended to hurl fire-pots against the Turkish positions, though there is no evidence that it was actually used for this, or even used at all.[8]

While the Knights were busy with the defences in the Italian sector Mishak Pasha took another crack at the Saint Nicholas Tower on 9 June. The attack was quite as costly as the first; some 600 Ottomans were reported killed, against very light casualties among the defenders and likely none among the Knights themselves. Mishak Pasha then tried a different tack, building a siege tower at Mandraki harbour from which archery and arquebus fire poured onto the defenders. Under cover of four days of this fire the Turks threw a pontoon bridge, wide enough for six men to march abreast, across the small bay. The pontoon was progressing rapidly when on the night of 17 June one Roger Jervis, described as an English seaman stationed at the Saint Nicholas Tower, heard the water being disturbed, dived in for a closer look and discovered that the pontoon was closer than anyone thought. To delay its progress he cut through its guide ropes.

However valorous the deed – Jervis was rewarded with a bag of gold from the grateful Grand Master – it was only a momentary check on the Ottoman offensive. After darkness fell the following evening, the pontoon was completed and some thirty of Mishak Pasha's galleys, including those fitted out for assault, moved up in almost total silence. Del Carretto and his knights were asleep in their armour when the alarm was sounded and by the time they woke up, the Janissaries in ranks six abreast were thundering across the pontoon and already at the Tower. At the same time, galleys landed irregular troops on the other side. The garrison of the French sector, however, was alert and began bombarding the attackers. One ball landed squarely onto the pontoon, breaching it and throwing many Janissaries into the water. D'Aubusson's defences now kicked in, with fireboats floating up to the Turkish galleys, destroying at least four. Still, the waves of Ottomans surged forward, illuminated by the fires and gunflashes and flaming arrows.

Pierre d'Aubusson, though past his prime, now showed of what stuff he was made. Not daring to weaken the Italian sector that was still under threat, he personally sped to the Saint Nicholas Tower and took up the fight in the front rank, firing the men with his courage. A cannonball fragment knocked his helmet off but on he fought through the night until he and the defenders had the satisfaction of seeing the Ottomans finally break off the action in midmorning, the sea red with their blood and choked with their bodies. For three days the Knights were able to rest from the battle, while Mishak Pasha is reported to have stayed in his tent refusing to talk to anyone.

After that sulk of several days, smouldering with Ottoman pride and refusing to admit defeat, the Turkish commander unleashed a fresh assault on the Italian sector. Cannon were brought up almost to the cusp of the ditch in front of the sector wall to hammer the masonry into rubble until only the Tower of Italy resembled anything standing upright. The defenders waited for a night with no moon and sent a squad of Italian Knights on a commando mission to spike the Turkish battery. The mission was successful, as evidenced by the heads of the Turkish artillerymen brought back triumphantly on the points of the Knights' lances. (We must never forget that military tactics we might consider unacceptably barbarous in our age were then normal procedure, even for warrior-monks.)

The beheadings further enraged Mishak Pasha who grimly ordered the black flag hoisted from his command post – the dread signal that Rhodes would be given no quarter. The Hospitallers well knew what this meant – the people would be massacred or sold into slavery, while they themselves would be impaled. Messages fired into the city on arrows provided all the gruesome detail for the benefit of any doubting optimists. At dawn on 27 June a single cannot shot sounded over the silent, apprehensive city: the signal for the all-out attack. It followed the pattern that had worked for Mehmet II when he stormed Constantinople: first the Bashi-Bazouk shock troops, screaming and yelling, were sent in to disorient and confuse the defenders; then the highly-disciplined Janissaries, who could be expected to keep their formation under even the heaviest fire, would follow up. This time the Janissaries lived up to their reputation, keeping steady under a hail of missiles from the Provençal sector.

D'Aubusson realized that the battered Italian sector of the wall was in no shape to hold back even a single determined infantryman, and ordered a withdrawal to the retrenchment. Here the Italians could count on the help of Knights from other Tongues such as the adjacent Provençals, Aragonese and English, whose sectors extended to the west. The unruly but all-but-unstoppable Bashi Bazouks swarmed over the ruined wall and planted their standard on the Tower of Italy. In their wake came some 300 Janissaries who had an open pathway to inside the city. A ferocious battle raged around the Tower of Italy which ended only as d'Aubusson, shrugging off an arrow in the hip, and a handful of Knights flung themselves with supreme courage against the Turks holding the tower. The Grand Master, turning himself into 'a living banner', suffered four more wounds but drove off the Bashi Bazouks and ripped their Ottoman standard from where it had been planted.[9] One of those wounds, however, was severe: a Turkish spear point had slammed through his breastplate, piercing a lung.

As he was carried away, the Grand Master had the satisfaction of seeing that his counterattack had an immediate effect. The Bashi-Bazouks had been renowned more for their enthusiasm than their discipline, and their retreat from the Italian wall quickly turned into a rout. Advancing Janissaries slashed at them to stop them running, killing some, but in vain. The few hundred Janissaries inside Rhodes found themselves cut off and were massacred. Seeing this, the defenders took new heart, and Knights from all the Tongues – French, Spanish, Italian, English, German – joined in a general northward counter-attack. When they reached the main Ottoman camp on the slopes of Mount Saint Stephen they gave no quarter – Mishak Pasha's black flag had redounded onto the heads of his own soldiers. When the killing was over (perhaps 3,000 Ottomans had fallen) the victors returned to the city with the usual gruesome trophies of victory stuck on their spear points – Turkish heads, of which there were plenty to go around. Also among the takings was Sultan Mehmet's gold and silver standard.

Pierre d'Aubusson was the undoubted hero of the day. He recovered from his wounds to be the Grand Master for twenty-three more honoured years. No face is more familiar from the illustrations of the time than his. Whether seated in his palace receiving envoys, or on horseback with a retinue of Knights behind him, he is portrayed having a solemn but not unpleasant expression, slightly hooded eyes lending an air of aristocratic calm, and a mouth set in sober thought over a long, but well-trimmed, greying beard. One portrait shows him seated on a gold-draped throne, dressed in a long red robe; over his shoulders is a black surplice bearing the white Hospitaller cross on the left shoulder. Holding a large rosary in his left hand, he is acknowledging the work of a chronicler on his knees before him. The setting may be one of typical majesty, but nowhere has the artist added the slightest sign of haughtiness or arrogance to d'Aubusson's features. Hospitaller historians say he enforced simple dress even among the wealthy and daily attendance at church services for all, and hoped until his last breath that another crusade might materialize to give his Knights a *raison d'être*.[10]

Mishak Pasha toyed with the idea of renewing the offensive, but in the middle of August he gave it up. It must not have been an easy decision, as the ruthless sultan had ruthless ways of dealing with commanders who failed. (Mehmet indeed condemned Mishak Pasha to death, but later commuted the sentence.) As the Ottoman ships vanished over the horizon, the dazed Knights and people of Rhodes began the task of reconstruction. Large parts of the city were in ruins, especially the ex-Jewish quarter in the south by the Italian sector wall. The Grand Master's Palace and what remained of the Saint Nicholas Tower also needed extensive repairs. Matters were not helped by a powerful earthquake in 1481 that destroyed much of what had been left standing. D'Aubusson displayed his leadership qualities by ordering a church, Our Lady of Victory, built on or near the site where his timely intervention with a handful of men had turned the tide of battle. (The Grand Master, undoubtedly a well-read man, may have followed the example of Constantinople in 626, when the Virgin Mary had been thanked for delivering the city from a siege by the pagan Avars.) In gratitude to the Greeks of Rhodes, who by all accounts had fought alongside the Hospitallers despite doctrinal differences, he exempted them from taxation for three years. The local Greeks had suffered the most of all from the Turkish raids, and many in the countryside were facing starvation. He could well afford the generosity, as the Order was swamped with donations and gifts from Priories all over Europe. But underlying the relief was the sobering knowledge that the Muslims had not given up their aim, and would certainly be back.

Mehmet II, the conqueror of Constantinople and scourge of Christians, died unexpectedly on campaign in 1481. His sons Bayezid and Cem (pronounced Jem) fought for the throne. Cem, the loser, fled to Rhodes, placing d'Aubusson in a delicate position. The exhausted Knights were in no position to get involved in an Ottoman dynastic tussle. But the Grand Master knew how to make the situation work for the Order. He knew that Sultan Bayezid II could not rest knowing that a rival brother was lurking in the region, and promising to keep Prince Cem out of mischief, d'Aubusson accepted 45,000 Venetian ducats a year from the sultan. Pope Innocent VIII then stepped in, offering a lot more money – plus a cardinal's hat for d'Aubusson – for the privilege of keeping Cem in reserve for a possible attack on the Ottomans. The Grand Master, however, preferred Rhodes to Rome, and sent Cem on to his cousin Guy de Blanchefort for safety in Auvergne, France. For seven years Prince Cem was kept a virtual prisoner there; eventually Innocent VIII got round to arranging his hoped-for crusade and took the Turkish runaway prince under his wing to help plan it. But the pope died before anything could be done and his successor, Alexander VI, handed the Turk over to King Charles VIII of France who was besieging Rome. Charles, unlike the popes, cultivated the favour of the Ottoman sultans, and it is quite likely that with Bayezid's involvement, the hapless Prince Cem was poisoned in Naples in 1495.[11]

D'Aubusson kept a watchful eye on developments in the Ottoman Empire on the pope's behalf. Along with Pope Innocent's money he had kept the red hat, and was given the authority to make papal decisions on his own. Yet the experience of 1480 burned into him a chronic urge for vengeance, which he put into action in 1501 with a raid on the Turkish positions at Mytilene, the chief port of the island of Lesbos. Dissension in the Hospitaller ranks, however, upset his plans and forced him to withdraw. The humiliation embittered him; he tried to explain his failure by imagining he was not fighting hard enough for Christendom, and in apparent expiation for this he expelled the Jews of Rhodes (whose quarter had been flattened anyway in 1480) and forcibly baptized those of their children who remained. He died in 1503, his dream of rolling back the Muslim tide unfulfilled.

For it was indeed a tide, and rolling on towards its high-water mark. In the year of d'Aubusson's death Bayezid II, who admittedly tried to avoid war whenever he could, bought several areas on the western Greek and Albanian coast from the Venetians. His armies, meanwhile, were mopping up more of the Balkans, with Bosnia the latest addition to the sultan's domains. To give credit to Bayezid, there is no evidence that he planned another campaign against Rhodes or any other Christian possession in the eastern Mediterranean; but the same cannot be said for his aggressive and ambitious younger son Selim, who rebelled in 1511 with the support of most of the army and attempted to seize power. Bayezid, though old and infirm, defeated Selim in battle, but the son reappeared before Constantinople the following spring and with the army's help deposed his father – having him poisoned for good measure.

Selim I Yavuz – the Grim, as he was accurately called – now set his sights on the great Muslim rival power, the Mamluks of Egypt. Throughout the Muslim world, it was customary for the most powerful regional ruler to have the privilege of caring for the Arabian holy places and the constant stream of pilgrims on the obligatory *haj* to Mecca. In Selim's view the Mamluks had enjoyed this exalted and lucrative status for too long. The Ottomans, who were now indisputably the main standard-bearers of the Prophet's faith, needed to take over. Selim was willing to allow the Mamluks to remain in power as long as they recognized him as their sovereign, with his image on their coins and his name in their Friday prayers. Mamluk Sultan Tumanbey refused, and Selim had the excuse he needed.

On 21 January 1517 Selim and his Ottoman army appeared before Cairo; by now the Turks had become proficient in the use of cannon, a weapon that the Mamluks had completely neglected to develop. On the following day the Ottoman guns put the Egyptians to flight, but only after fierce street fighting did Cairo fall. Tumanbey, after trying to escape, was caught and hanged. This left Selim free now to abolish the old Baghdad-based Abbasid caliphate, which had lived on in shadowy form for centuries, and assume the title of caliph for himself. The remaining Mamluk bigwigs, content to live in luxury on their large estates, gave him no more trouble. On his return to his capital at Adrianople (now Edirne) Selim the Grim began to plan the elimination of the Knights of Saint John on Rhodes. Their very presence was a blot on the Ottoman reputation. But before he could put the plans into effect he himself was eliminated by illness in September 1520. The throne passed to his hugely able son Suleyman I, soon to become known as the Magnificent.

In the opening years of the sixteenth century the Knights of Rhodes had not slackened in their vigilance. Under d'Aubusson's successor, Grand Master Emery d'Amboise, the Hospitaller Navy scored a coup in 1507 by capturing a large Egyptian carrack merchantman, the *Mogarbina* (claimed to be the biggest ship afloat), off Crete with its passengers and cargo. The vessel was converted into a warship, renamed the *Santa Maria*, and employed on other operations, such as a daring raid on the port of Alexandria under Philippe Villiers de l'Isle Adam and André d'Amaral three years later; no fewer than fourteen captured galleys were towed to Rhodes with their crews and cargoes. On Amboise's death in 1512, the late d'Aubusson's cousin Guy de Blanchefort – he who had been entrusted with the custody of the unfortunate Ottoman Prince Cem – was elected Grand Master but died while on his way from France. In his place was elected the indefatigable defender of the Saint Nicholas Tower in 1480, Fabrizio del Carretto.

Suleyman I's priority at his accession was to secure the northern frontiers of his expanding empire, of which a key objective was the seizure of Belgrade in 1521. Once this was accomplished he could turn his attention to the Knights of Saint John, whom he appeared to regard as little more than a nuisance preying on his shipping – 'pirates bearing crosses which vaunt themselves to be the bulwark of Christendom'.[12] Whether his description of the Hospitallers was accurate or not – and he was probably at least partly right – no Ottoman sultan of any pride could put up with their activity. Meanwhile, del Carretto had continued building up the defences of Rhodes, a task that on his death in 1521 devolved upon the equally capable Grand Master Villiers de l'Isle Adam who had helped lead the audacious raid on Alexandria nine years earlier. But there must have been a sense of time running out, as de l'Isle Adam, before his election to the top job, had travelled to western Europe with appeals for help. King Francis I of France was embroiled in a dispute with Holy Roman Emperor Charles V, a general balance-of-power contest that swept up most of the other lesser European states on one side or the other; yet he was concerned enough to send weapons and perhaps some knights; the Dutchman Pope Adrian VI also responded with some help. But given the unstable politics among the European states, many of the Hospitallers' European Priories (see below) proved unable to effectively aid their Rhodian headquarters in any way.

What of the Venetians, the wealthiest Christian power in the Mediterranean? Hopes for their help were soon dashed, as it was shockingly obvious that much of their wealth was earned precisely from trade with the Turks, and they were not about to jeopardize it for the sake of a bunch of military monks whose very crusading spirit seemed outdated anyway. Yet fellow-Christian feeling was not entirely absent among the Italians, as at about the time Suleyman the future Magnificent was taking Belgrade, Marco Minio, the Venetian envoy in Constantinople, sent word to de l'Isle Adam of feverish shipbuilding in the city's dockyards. From what de l'Isle Adam's intelligence could gather, there was little mention of Rhodes as the target for such a fleet, but that could just have been good security.

The Grand Master rightly assumed the worst and ordered steady but urgent work on the port defences, the walls and the surrounding moat. The sectors allocated to the Tongues were almost identical to what they had been in the siege of 1480, except that the French were given a slightly wider arc to include the Grand Master's Palace; also, the Spanish and English Tongues exchanged places, the latter moving north-east to take the place of the Aragonese, who seem to have been merged with the Spaniards. The Provençals and the Italians maintained their old positions along the north of the wall, from about the Saint John Tower to the Tower of the Windmills at the tip of the promontory of the commercial port. The harbour itself, its chain stretched between the Tower of the Windmills and the Naillac Tower, was defended jointly by the Castilians and Portuguese.[13] Ship hulls full of stones were sunk in Mandraki harbour, leaving only a narrow navigable channel. As the villagers of the northern part of the island flocked within the walls (the others sought refuge in the castles of Lindos, Faraklos and Monolithos), 500 or so brother-knights and brother-sergeants rallied some 7,000 turcopoles and mercenaries to brace for the expected Turkish assault.

It was not long in coming. On 26 June 1522 the first of what would eventually become at least 400 galleys bore down on Kallithea Bay, about ten miles south of the port of Rhodes. The stream increased steadily for the next six weeks, under the Sultan's second vizier and son-in-law, Mustafa Pasha, until some 200,000 Ottomans (if the figures given by the chroniclers are to be believed) had landed, including 10,000 Janissaries and about 60,000 experienced sappers and tunnellers recruited from Bosnia and Wallachia, specialists in undermining fortifications. (These figures are almost certainly exaggerated, but in the absence of any others, we need to take note of them at least.) Mustafa Pasha was not about to make the mistake of his predecessor Mishak Pasha and come to grief through attempted amphibious assaults on the harbour towers; this time the hammer blows would be delivered by land from the west coast, directly against the south and east sectors of the city wall, while the fleet would blockade the port from the sea. On 28 July, a month after the first landings, Sultan Suleyman himself arrived to personally take charge of the siege.

As the defenders watched from the walls, the Turks hauled about sixty cannon into place opposite the English and Spanish sectors flanking the Virgin Mary and Saint Athanasios towers. Eight of the cannon were disconcertingly huge, but any such effect that their size might have created was dissipated when the Turks began their bombardment without adequate protective works. The defenders' response was ferocious, quickly putting a couple of Turkish batteries out of action. But this was just the beginning; the cannonade continued throughout August, when an estimated 1,800 cannonballs fell into the city. The defenders' casualties were light – twenty-five men reported killed. (Some of the balls, still embedded in the masonry, can be seen today.)

The incessant Turkish bombardment was meant in part to mask the furious mining of the walls that was a key element in the sultan's strategy. But the Knights had good engineers, too, and one of them, the Italian Gabriele Tadini da Martinengo, had the idea of finding out where the tunnelling was by the use of ingenious mine detectors. These were drums hung on interior walls and adorned with little bells; any vibration from below, ordinarily undetectable, would cause the parchment drumheads to vibrate, ringing the bells. The louder the ring, the closer the mine. These gadgets seem to have been effective, as we know that the Knights were able to detect and destroy many tunnels by counter-sapping.

The small German sector between the d'Amboise Gate and the Saint George Bastion withstood ten days of heavy pounding after which the Ottoman battery in that sector was transferred to Mandraki harbour to attack the rebuilt Saint Nicholas Tower. The reason for the transfer is unclear; perhaps the tower was threatening the blockading Ottoman fleet.

At any rate, someone in the Turkish command recalled the debacle of 1480 and judged the effort to be not worth its potential benefits; the batteries were moved round to the north to boost those aimed at the English and Spanish sectors. These continued their destructive work until by mid–August severe breaches had appeared in the English, Spanish and Provençal wall sectors. When soon afterwards the Italian wall was breached, Tadini, the inventor of the mine–detector, displayed his battlefield as well as his engineering skills by leading 200 brother–knights and brother–sergeants in a charge on the nearest Ottoman battery, destroying several field pieces and killing some sappers, whose turbaned heads – on this as well as three subsequent occasions – were of course brought back on spear points.

The underground battle was just as relentless as that being fought on the surface. As September began, tunnels had been dug under most of the length of the city wall. Tadini countered by digging transverse tunnels parallel to the wall and beneath its foundations for about a mile and a half from the d'Amboise Gate almost to the coast in the Italian sector. One Turkish mine was thus discovered under the Provençal sector and put out of commission, but another, undetected, under the English sector was fired by the attackers on 4 September. The resulting massive blast shook the entire city and opened a 10m wide breach through which the Turks poured, only to come up against a wall of determined English who in the most desperate close–order combat thrust the enemy back, killing up to 2,000 of them. Five days later another undetected mine under the English position went up; again the attackers poured into the gap, to be repulsed again by the English. This time, however, the Turks held on to the outer side of the ditch, from where their snipers inflicted severe casualties on the defenders.

Tadini, meanwhile, added a sophisticated twist to his counter-mining efforts by having a series of vents dug outwards to channel some of the blast from any mines away from the walls. This tactic had a partial success on 22 September when a massive mine was blown beneath the Auvergne sector and some of the wall there, at least, stayed up. On the Turkish side there were equally crafty innovations. One was the introduction of 'dirty' gunpowder to billow into a smokescreen for an infantry attack when the cannon were fired, and it was with this surprise that Suleyman opened his violent assault at daybreak on 24 September.

All along the wall, from sea to sea, the Ottoman guns opened up, wreathing the walls in thick black smoke. With the defenders' visibility nearly nil, and as the sultan himself sat watching on an elevated platform in the rear (shades of the Persian Xerxes observing the Battle of Salamis a millennium before), the first Janissary troops surged out of the murk onto the Spanish sector and planted a few dozen banners on the ruined wall. This was the signal for a general charge on the Spanish, English, Provençal and Italian sectors in the north. The Ottomans pressed forward with great courage under the deadly hail of fire from the wall. Right in the thick of the combat de l'Isle Adam put in a personal appearance to direct the defence – at 57 years old, he was the exact age that d'Aubusson had been when he had defended the ramparts from the same spot in 1480. And the result, after six hours of the most desperate slashing, close-order combat, in which the Spanish sector changed hands twice and where Rhodians of all ages and both sexes did their part from actual fighting from tending to the wounded and bringing up ammunition, food and water, was the same – the Ottomans had to fall back, whipped to shreds. Some 15,000 of them lay dead, their blood dyeing the waters near the Italian sector. Casualties among the defenders were reported at some 200 killed and 150 wounded.

Suleyman, considerably shaken by this bloody debacle, was on the point of deciding to lift the siege when that singular weapon against which no-one is invulnerable – treachery – came to play its part. Not all the Hospitallers, it seems, were as devoted to the Christian cause as Grand Master de l'Isle Adam. Since 1461 the roster of high posts in the administration had included the Grand Chancellor, a kind of private secretary to the Grand Master. Occupying the post in 1522 was a Castilian, Andrea d'Amaral, who for reasons of his own decided he'd had enough. Those reasons can only be guessed at, though prominent among them must have been a good deal of personal privation. Sometime in October d'Amaral wrote messages to the sultan and fastened them to arrows fired in the Turks' direction by his Spanish manservant. In them he painted an accurate but treacherous picture of the sad state of the defenders' resistance. On 27 October the servant was caught in the act of sending one of those messages flying on its way to the Ottoman lines. Under interrogation he implicated his boss d'Amaral who had allegedly plotted for the Ottomans to enter Rhodes on 1 November. On 5 November master and servant paid for their treachery on the scaffold.

By December the sheer overwhelming fatigue among the Rhodians and their defenders had begun to tell. The entire northern section of the wall was in ruins. Ammunition was running dangerously low, with no chance of resupply as little could get through the harbour blockade. Tadini's counter-sappers needed timber to shore up their tunnels, but all the trees in the city had been cut down, and Tadini himself was on the verge of despair. He could only watch helplessly as the Ottomans beavered away at their own tunnels, popping up brazenly inside the city and threatening the Knights from the rear. The Knights' servants and slaves had also suffered grievous losses, and few were by now available to do the manual tasks. The siege had settled into a pattern of intermittent bombardment supplemented by the mining of the walls. In October and November the Turks made a few unsuccessful sallies against the northern sectors, but the pressure had begun to tell, especially on the decimated English contingent. A French Knight, Jean Bin de Malincorne, was deputed to command what was left of the English, bringing with him reinforcements from the other Tongues. On 9 November two ships ran the Ottoman blockade to bring in a dozen knights and about 100 auxiliaries from Bodrum Castle on the Asia Minor coast, plus food and war materials; a week later a similar reinforcement sailed up from Lindos. But these were mere stop-gap measures.

The Ottomans, too, were feeling the strain. Losses had been very heavy, and food supplies were running short; there were rumours that France and the papacy were sending help to the beleaguered Knights. To force the issue, Suleyman decided on a bit of psychological warfare. Well aware, from the efforts of d'Amaral as well as deserters, that the Rhodians were suffering intensely, he appealed to them, quite literally over the Knights' heads, by firing arrows into the city bearing promises of leniency in case of surrender – or fire and sword if they continued to resist and were defeated.

A good many of the ordinary Rhodians were quite prepared to consider the offer, even from a Muslim potentate. Starving, ill, cold and exhausted, they were reported close to rebelling against the Knights who had been their masters for more than 200 years, and extended peace feelers to the sultan. Moreover, the local Greek Orthodox had never been fully at ease with the Catholicism of the Knights; their leading prelate, Metropolitan Clement, led a delegation to the Grand Master urging him to consider capitulating. At first de l'Isle Adam would not hear of it, but seeing the misery stalking the city, he agreed to a three-day truce starting on 11 December. The previous day Suleyman had made the first offer by having a white flag raised; de l'Isle Adam responded by raising one of his own on the Provençal sector wall. The sultan reiterated his generous terms: all surviving Knights of Saint John would be allowed to leave Rhodes within twelve days with their assets and weapons, except for their bronze cannon; any Rhodian natives who chose could also go with them, and were given a generous three years to decide. Finally – and this more than anything else reconciled the native Greek Orthodox to the Turkish conquest – the Greeks left behind would be allowed to freely practice their religion while, for good measure, enjoying exemption from taxation for five years.

Of course, the reaction among many was one of distrust: it sounded too good to be true, and moreover, how could a Muslim of the likes of Suleyman be trusted? There was, of course, no answer to that question, and while the Knights dithered, the sultan ordered bombardments to resume. When on 17 December the Turks seized and held the Tower of Spain, the game was, to all intents and purposes, up. On 22 December a joint delegation of Knights and Greeks, representing the two communities of Rhodes, appeared before the sultan to accept his terms. Around Christmas Day 400 Janissaries formally marched into the city of Rhodes while fifty knights and prominent Rhodians were escorted to the sultan's camp as hostages to guarantee the Knights' good behaviour before leaving. All other Ottoman troops were pulled back one mile from their advanced positions to reduce the chance of a skirmish while Suleyman and de l'Isle Adam cemented a correct diplomatic relationship by conferring and exchanging gifts. Suleyman genuinely praised his adversary's courage and lamented that he was 'obliged to force this Christian in his old age to abandon his home and his belongings'.[14] On the first day of 1523 the Grand Master, his 180 remaining Hospitaller Knights, and some 5,000 Rhodians who elected to go with them (among them Metropolitan Clement who in the end preferred not to take his chances with the Turks), marched in formation out of the city, drums beating and banners flying at half-staff, to board their galleys. With their precious few religious relics – the icon of Our Lady of Philermos, the purported right hand of John the Baptist and a fragment of the True Cross that had been found by the mother of Roman-Byzantine Emperor Constantine I – they sailed away from a glorious chapter of their history that they would never know again.

The 1522 siege of Rhodes broke new ground in military science. It has been called 'an excellent example of siege warfare of the Renaissance period'.[15] It marked the watershed between the use of mangonels, catapults and other mechanical siege engines going back to antiquity and the new invention of firearms. Gunpowder was also essential in supplying the force for blowing up the mines. Yet the fact that the vastly outnumbered defenders were able to hold out for six months – during which Suleyman became seriously disheartened more than once – shows how stoutly the fortifications of Rhodes had been built and how advanced the defensive system was for its time.

Chapter 11

The Order in Europe

The Reconquista in Spain – Spanish knights and orders – decline in France – papal distractions in Europe – the English Hospitallers – the Great Revolt – the execution of Robert Hales – milites Christi in Germany

Before we take up the story of the Knights of Saint John after their expulsion from Rhodes, a brief look would be in order at what the Hospitallers had been doing in the rest of Europe throughout the thirteenth and fourteenth centuries. Though not as historically renowned as the Knights who fought the Muslims in the Middle East and eastern Mediterranean, the Hospitallers of the twenty-three European Priories, from Ireland to Poland and from Portugal to Greece, were no less active in upholding a sense of Christian duty, fighting for the faith where necessary, and in various intangible ways helping restrain the tendency to barbarism that was unfortunately common among powerful rulers.

In Spain the Hospitallers forged a devout and solemn organization that was the spearhead of the fabled *Reconquista*, the re-conquest of southern Spain from the Muslims, and the subsequent rise of the Spanish noble knightly ideal. As far back as 1113, the very year in which the Blessed Gerard was established as the first Grand Master in Jerusalem, the Queen of Castile had given the Order the village of Paradinas near Salamanca. Eleven more villages were added over the next three years near La Boveda de Toro – all on the well-trodden pilgrim route to the shrine of Santiago de Compostela in north-west Spain. As in the environs of faraway Jerusalem, pilgrims here too required succour and protection from robbers and disease.

The first Muslims had surged into Spain across the Strait of Gibraltar in 711 under Tariq ibn-Ziyad (who gave his name to the rock – Jabr al-Tariq, or Gibraltar). The advance of the Moors (as they became known) was stalled at Covadonga eight years later and at the famous Battle of Tours in 732, but not before they had founded a durable Muslim state, al-Andalus, in the south of the country. From then on the steady aim of the Christian kings of Spain was to rid the Iberian peninsula of the alien Arabs. Around the beginning of the ninth century a shepherd in the mountains of north-west Spain claimed to have been guided by a star to discover a coffin containing the remains of James, the brother of Jesus. Word of the site quickly spread, and before long a great cathedral had gone up at Santiago de Compostela, or Saint James of the Field of the Star. Saint James was made the patron saint of Spain, and when the Knights of Saint John came into being at the opposite end of the Mediterranean three centuries later, it was fitting that the popes would set up a branch in Spain. The Order, thanks to royal aid, built a pilgrims' hospice on the Jerusalem model at Atapuerca near Santiago.

By the start of the twelfth century, with the help of some French Templars, three military orders had been set up: the Knights of Calatrava, Santiago and Alcántara, with their own Commanderies, dedicated to helping the kings of Spain drive out the Muslims. There was, to be sure, a degree of rivalry between those orders and the Hospitallers, though their general purpose was identical. The Hospitallers and Templars carved out a sphere of influence in Aragon, though they were by no means absent from the other Spanish districts. For example, as a reward for success in Catalonia, in 1157 King Raymond Berenguer IV (revered as 'The Saint') handed the Hospitallers one-tenth of all territory seized from the Moors. As the thirteenth century progressed, and while the Hospitallers in the Holy Land and Egypt were kept busy, Christian forces decimated the Moors at Las Navas de Tolosa, and one by one the main Muslim cities fell – Cordova in 1236, Valencia in 1238, Seville in 1248 and Cadiz in 1250, leaving only the fabled Granada in Moorish hands. The Hospitallers were a small but potent contingent in these campaigns, supplying perhaps a few dozen brother-knights to fend off Moorish offensives around Valencia and Granada.

Around the middle of the thirteenth century the *Reconquista* appeared to run out of steam for a couple of centuries as the kings of Castile, Leon and Navarre considered one another greater enemies than the Muslims and turned their attention to who would be the greatest power in Christian Spain. The main Hospitaller Priories in the Iberian peninsula at this time were those of Portugal, Castile and Navarre in the north-east, with the Castellany of Amposta acting as a separate Priory in what is now Catalonia. Grand Master Juan Fernandez de Heredia, who made his mark in Rhodes, was a Castilian, as was Father Prior Alfonso Ortiz, who suffered a crushing naval defeat at Moroccan hands off Algeciras in 1340. A Portuguese Hospitaller, Father Iñigo d'Alvaro, led the hopeless defence of Smyrna against Timur Kesh; he survived to defend the Aragonese Castle at Alcañiz nine years later.

Not much distinguished the Portuguese from the Spanish Hospitallers; in Portugal there was an Order of Christ which performed much the same function and which helped to capture Ceuta, on the African side of the Strait of Gibraltar, in 1415.

While the political and religious aims of the Knights of Saint John in the Middle East and the Iberian peninsula were generally identical, on closer examination there were differences. Whereas French nobles accounted for the great majority of Hospitaller Knights in Palestine and Rhodes, for example, those in Spain and Portugal tended to have humbler origins. The great advantage of this was that they were free of much of the blind anti-Muslim prejudice that typified the newly-arrived Knight in the East.[1] On the other hand, the overriding duty of the *Reconquista* reinforced the idea and practice of *hidalguia*, best described as a kind of elitist nobility and all-pervasive sense of honour that has marked the Spanish character ever since. Luttrell avers that there grew up a 'domineering anti-economic' mentality among the Spanish knighthood that mutated 'far from the original monk-warrior ideal'.[2] The *hidalguia* may have been a psychological defence against the rising power of the Spanish kings and the centralization of the state, especially after the expulsion of the Moors in 1492. The Order, moreover, gradually ceased to fit into any clear political or civil structure; the members were subject to sometimes conflicting allegiances to their Order, the king and of course the popes. As a result it coalesced into a closed nepotist organization, extremely jealous of its privileges – though the Prories never failed to remit their *responsiones*, or required share of revenues, to the headquarters at Rhodes.

In France, the spiritual birthplace of the Hospitallers, the Order was withering away. In part this was because royal centralized power was on the increase and also because the best recruits tended to ship overseas to where the real action was. The kings of France requisitioned several Hospitaller castles. Moreover, the Order found itself embroiled in such conflicts as the already-mentioned Papal Schism and the 'crusade' against the Albigensians. This latter was a particularly nasty episode in French history in which thousands of 'heretics' – meaning those who wished to live in evangelical simplicity – were hounded and burned at the stake. As a force nominally loyal to the papacy, the relatively few active Hospitallers in France would have been expected to help crush the movement, but they also had good relations with the counts of Toulouse, who were sympathetic to the Albigensians. It is unclear how many of the Order joined in the 'crusade', which proved quite as murderous as those against the Muslims – some 20,000 Christian men, women and children of the city of Béziers were slaughtered indiscriminately. It took thirty years for the sect to be finally subdued.

The popes, in fact, had never viewed the Hospitallers as a force with which they could do as they liked. They had too much respect for them and their abilities to keep the Middle Eastern Muslims at bay, which is why the Order played little part in those perennial power struggles between the papacy and European secular powers, especially the Holy Roman Empire. A few individual Knights were employed in the Pope's personal military entourage in Rome and some leading figures in the Order were sent as envoys to mediate major disputes; as we have seen, Juan Fernandez de Heredia attempted one such mission on the eve of the Battle of Poitiers in the Hundred Years' War, narrowly escaping execution for his pains. But these were exceptions to the general rule that the Hospitallers should be left unmolested in the eastern Mediterranean where every man was valuable. The occasional Italian knight might break the virtual French monopoly on the highest office, such as Giovanni Battista Orsini of the noble Roman family, elected Grand Master in 1467. Italy-based Hospitallers in general helped sponsor artists and writers in that flowering of culture that we know as the Renaissance.

The first Hospitaller known to have stepped on English soil is named as Gerald Jebarre, who was sent there in 1135 to retrieve Raymond de Poitiers as a consort for the heiress of Antioch. King Henry I (1100–1135) approved the creation of the English Priory; his successor Henry II on his death in 1187 left a large amount of money to recruit Hospitallers and Templars for Holy Land expeditions. Until about 1140 the English Priory had been run from Messina in Sicily and Saint-Gilles in France; thirty years later the Priory came under the control of the Grand Commander Outremer. Partly as a result of the first two Crusades, English society in the twelfth century experienced 'a great surge in devotion'.[3] While the Crusades were freshly in fashion, the relationship between the English crown and the Knights Hospitaller was a mutually beneficial one, especially under Prior Roger de Vere. But it began to sour towards the close of the thirteenth century, when King Edward I suspected that the Order might have conflicting loyalties to pope and English king. When in 1275 Grand Master Hugh Revel, 'one of the greatest administrators ever to have governed the order',[4] ordered the Prior of Ireland to travel to Palestine to reinforce Outremer against the Egyptian Mamluk threat, King Edward countermanded the decree, threatening to seize all Hospitaller estates if the prior made a move, which he didn't.[5]

In actuality the Knights of the English Tongue in Rhodes never seem to have had much of an affinity with the Priory of England. It was an example of how Rhodes had become a state of its own, claiming its own allegiance over and above ethnic homeland loyalties. Probably in the king's view, any knight who journeyed to Rhodes represented one less knight available to defend England and its king in the perennial tensions and conflicts with France. When the Earl of Derby (the future Henry IV) visited Rhodes he helped re-ignite interest somewhat, but by 1455 the English Tongue on Rhodes numbered only about seventeen brother-knights and brother-sergeants with scant probability that the number would increase.

In England proper, however, the Order was comfortably off thanks to generous donations by the nobility. English Hospitaller houses tended to be on the small side, with at most perhaps a dozen Knights holding feudal rights over the surrounding areas. The largest were at Chippenham and Clerkenwell. Several preceptories, such as those of Dingley in Northamptonshire and Temple Balsall in Warwickshire (this latter inherited from the dissolved Templars, as its name implies), survive into our own time. The brother-knights themselves, as a sort of holy officer class, made up between a quarter and a third of all the brothers in a Priory. The Priory of England maintained control of the Priory of Ireland, based at Kilmainham, and the Commandery of Scotland at Torpichen near Edinburgh, at least until the middle of the fourteenth century.

Any actual military activity engaged in by the Hospitallers of the British Isles was extremely limited, and confined mainly to Ireland. In 1318 Prior Roger Utlagh of Ireland helped fight a Scottish invasion under Robert Bruce, apparently incurring some losses; but that was an exception to the general rule by which the Irish Knights served mainly as the king's justiciars whose job was to help enforce order in the lawless parts of Ireland.[6] The Hospitallers, as far as we know, posed no threat to the rebellious Welsh, Highland Scots or Irish Celts. In England proper, the Order was happy to keep a low political profile as its nominal suzerain, the papacy, was becoming highly unpopular as the champion of arch-foe France. (The Papal Schism undoubtedly contributed to this bad publicity: the rival popes were widely accused of 'rending the garment of Christ'.) But this benign stance was called into serious question when in 1381 the Knights Hospitaller were dragged into their greatest English crisis in the form of the Great Revolt.

Given their preoccupation with doing God's work, and their solid membership in what was now England's squire class, few Hospitallers would have known or cared much about economic and labour issues. But England in 1381 was a very different place from what it had been a half-century before. Great ravages had been wrought by the Black Death in 1349, which wiped out perhaps one-third of the population and upended the relationship between capital and labour, triggering a massive burst of social unrest that began in Essex and Kent and engulfed London and its environs before it was suppressed. Many were the manors and castles burned to the ground in the turbulent summer of 1381, and the extensive properties of the Knights Hospitaller, associated as they were in the rebels' minds with rent-collectors and a privileged and sheltered way of life, did not escape the destruction.

Among the first targets of the insurrectionists was the Knights' preceptory at Cressing Temple, a former Templar possession, near Bocking in Essex. It was a wealthy holding of more than 1,500 acres of prime farmland and five mills that earned handsome profits for its Hospitaller Warden, John Luterell. The preceptory's courts also brought in income from fines, and this may well have stained its reputation in the eyes of poorer folk. An armed mob broke into the premises and stripped it of anything valuable they could get their hands on, including armour and precious metals, and burned the manor records. The one man the insurrectionists really wanted to get their hands on, however, was the English Prior Robert Hales.

We have met Father Hales before, as a leader in the bloody sack of Alexandria of 1365, for which he was presumably rewarded with the English Priory. His subsequent military and naval record in England, however, was not so notable, and can be said to have contributed to excessive royal war expenditures that he had the idea of recouping by heavy taxation. On 1 February 1381 the king had appointed him Treasurer, which placed him in a position to make himself highly unpopular with the mass of the people. Hales accompanied 14-year-old King Richard II when the latter consented to meet a delegation of the rebels on a barge in the River Thames at Rotherhithe; the sheer number of aggressive rebels on the south bank, however, struck such fear into the king's entourage that they sped him back to the safety of the Tower. The rebels under Wat Tyler of Kent surged into London and on 13 June, after sacking Savoy Palace, the home of the absent John of Gaunt, headed for the Hospitaller Priory at Clerkenwell.

Described as 'more like a village than a religious house', the Priory covered ten acres of north London real estate.[7] With a mere handful of Knights in residence, the Priory was easily taken, thoroughly looted and put to the torch. The records cite one John Hallingbury of Wandsworth, charged later with stealing a good deal of Priory property and burning more, and Robert Gardiner of Holborn, who was accused of murdering seven Flemish artisans or merchants on the premises and stealing a valuable chalice, as the perpetrators of 'enormities against the king's peace'. Perhaps not surprisingly, Hales' servant John Gamelyn and falconer John Webbe, and probably his prosperous steward, Richard Mory, were later tried on charges of instigating and abetting in the destruction. The Priory burned for a full week, leaving only the stone church intact. Not since the sack of Acre had the Knights Hospitaller experienced such grievous devastation – and at the hands of Englishmen at that.

Hales may or may not have been guilty of the charges of mismanagement laid at his door, but in the atmosphere of the time, he was a marked man. The Kentish and London rebels demanded the head of Hales, whom they vilified as 'Hob the Robber', along with those of Gaunt and fourteen other royal councillors deemed responsible for the hated poll tax. Hales' own whereabouts at this time are uncertain; probably he was holed up in the Tower of London. When in the middle of June the king rode out to Mile End for an epochal confrontation with the rebels, most of whom were still prepared to support young Richard against the oppressive nobles, Hales stayed in the Tower for safety. At Mile End King Richard signed an agreement to meet most of the rebels' demands and the insurrection appeared to be over.

But this did not prevent a rebel band from forcing its way into the Tower. Hales knew what was coming; after confession in the small chapel of Saint John on the second floor, he was dragged out to Tower Hill and beheaded with a handful of others including Bishop Simon Sudbury. Their bodies were left at the scene, as no one dared bury them, and the heads stuck on poles and displayed on London Bridge. The bloody spectacle, if anything, triggered fresh insurrectionist hysteria. The main victims this time were prosperous Flemish merchants and artisans in London. Though the king made a point of personally seeing to the Hospitallers' protection after Hales' murder, it took some time, as the revolt subsided, for the various preceptories in England to get back on their economic feet. They survived until 1540, when King Henry VIII suppressed the Order along with the monasteries in 1540, plundering their wealth in the process.

In Germany the Knights Hospitaller had maintained a presence at least since 1122, but later were all but eclipsed by the Order of Teutonic Knights, who had taken over the fight for the faith in north-east Europe and the Baltic regions. Various independent nobles ensured the Order of political and financial support. Yet the German Hospitallers' real strength lay in the nation's 'deeply-rooted concept of military service to God' which nurtured what became known as *milites Christi*, or Knights of Christ.[8] The Order was popular in Bavaria and Bohemia, though in neighbouring Hungary, as in Croatia, it was the French and Italians who took the lead in setting up the Priory. In military terms, the prime function of these various European Priories was to form a reserve of manpower for the headquarters at Rhodes which, after all, was where the action was.

Chapter 12

Malta and Lepanto

The search for another home – Charles V – settling in Malta – the Barbary Pirates – reverses in the Mediterranean – the siege of Malta – La Valette – a floating palace – defeat off Sicily – the Battle of Lepanto

Rien n'est plus connu comme le siege de Malte. Nothing is better known than the siege of Malta. – Voltaire

What now? That must have been the question on the lips of Philippe Villiers de l'Isle Adam and the other Knights sailing into the unknown as the familiar mountainous outline of Rhodes, their home for more than two centuries, receded into the distance. They still believed they had an important part to play in the defence of Christendom in the Mediterranean; there were enough Muslim and Ottoman traders and corsairs scudding about to provide fair game. But many members of the Order must also have reflected that such activity would be a significant come-down from the high-minded action of the Crusades. The most they could do in the morale department was to try to recreate the noble warrior-monk society that they had developed with such success in Rhodes.

But where? The eastern Mediterranean was now almost totally in Ottoman hands. The Muslim capture of Rhodes had followed Selim the Grim's elimination of the Egyptian Mamluks in 1517, giving the Turks control over the entire eastern Mediterranean seaboard from Greece in the north and west to the border of Libya in the south. The island of Crete, however, still held out against the Turkish tide, and that's where de l'Isle Adam and his men originally headed. The choice was, however, short-lived, as the Venetians in Crete and the Aegean were fighting a losing war against the advancing Ottomans, and so the Knights decided they might be safer in mainland Italy. The Hospitallers set up their headquarters at Viterbo, a central Italian town north of Rome, where the austerely devout Pope Adrian VI named de l'Isle Adam Defender of the Faith.

It proved to be a stopgap measure at best. Italy at the time was a highly unstable battleground among the French, Spaniards and Germans, with the Papal States caught in the middle. Viterbo, inside the Papal States' boundary, presumably could be protected by the popes; but as the papacy itself was none too secure at this time, the advantage of the location was minimal. Between 1523 and 1527 the Hospitallers maintained a precarious existence at Viterbo as de l'Isle Adam struggled to keep the Order intact amid problematic finances, internal power intrigues, doctrinal arguments and the inevitable slump in recruitment. Adrian VI's successor as pope, Clement VII, used this crisis to argue for turning the Order into an exclusive papal guard. This idea was successfully resisted. But in 1527 twin blows struck: an outbreak of plague which forced the Hospitallers to temporarily move to Nice, and the sack of Rome by Holy Roman Empire troops.

Clement VII, a member of the Medici family and the very antithesis of his frugal Dutch predecessor, had high diplomatic ambitions for Europe which he hoped to wean away from the teachings of Martin Luther. But he appears to have underestimated the power of Holy Roman Emperor Charles V who administered more of Europe than any ruler before or since, and who viewed the papacy's alliance with France with some alarm. The emperor therefore had no compunction in sending an army of 30,000 men, many of them Lutherans, against Rome. Hordes of German Landsknechte troops (called Lanzichenecchi by the terrified Romans) burst into the city in an orgy of murder, rape, looting and desecration of holy sites. The pope, after holing himself up in the Castel Sant'Angelo for six months, managed to escape disguised as a travelling salesman. The Imperial troops left in February 1528, after losing half their number to plague. The lesson for the Hospitallers was that Rome and its environs, devastated as they were, could no longer be relied upon.

Whereupon Charles V (who also reigned as Charles I of Spain) took matters in hand. Much has been written about this singular Habsburg monarch, 'of commonplace abilities and melancholy temperament, the son of a mentally defective mother', who found himself by chance the ruler of most of the continent of Europe apart from France, Portugal and parts of Italy.[1] Charles' position made him the natural foil for the Ottoman Suleyman the Magnificent, who lorded it over a similar-sized Muslim empire in the East and in 1526 had advanced as far as Budapest. For this Charles had to avoid the trap of Lutheranism and stick to the official Roman Catholic Church, mending fences as far as he could with France. As the Knights of Saint John also occupied a place in his thinking, he hit upon the idea of offering Malta as their new home as a kind of substitute Rhodes, an island domain from which they could harass Muslim shipping as their contribution to the never-ending fight against the infidel. After the failure of Crete and Viterbo to offer any durable sanctuary, de l'Isle Adam had to agree, and in 1530, eight years after the expulsion from Rhodes, the Order finally settled down to a fresh start. All that Charles V required in return for this favour was a single Maltese gerfalcon as tribute each year, to be delivered each November, on All Souls' Day, to the emperor's Viceroy of Sicily.

After Rhodes Malta was, to put it mildly, a disappointment. There was hardly any vegetation to break the monotony of the ochre-coloured rocky terrain. It was just a hunk of sandstone in the middle of nowhere. The only redeeming value of Malta was that it had a few good natural harbours, the best of which appeared to be that of Birgu, a fishing village dominated by the ruins of the Sant'Angelo Tower. The Knights got busily to work repairing the tower and building a hospital.[2] By this time the Order was as much a naval as a military power, and along naval lines they sought to reconstruct the privileged life of holy arms-bearing they had known in Rhodes. Only there wasn't much scope for it. Crusading was by now distinctly unfashionable. In the interests of trade western Europe preferred to maintain a stable balance of power with the Ottomans in the East; moreover, new vistas for conquest were opening up in the New World, to where European adventurers turned their attention. Within western Europe itself, kings and parliaments were preoccupied with jockeying for dominance among themselves and few had the inclination to measure swords anew with the Muslim.

The change of attitude was most striking in the ethnic and cultural cradle of the Hospitaller Order, France. In 1515 Francis I had become king. Courtly, charming and courageous, displaying the outward virtues of a knight but politically and emotionally rather shallow, Francis assumed the French throne while the country was enjoying a period of economic growth. Despite his love of luxury and the finer points of life, the young king displayed his martial qualities by pulling his troops from the cusp of defeat to a shattering victory over Milan's Swiss mercenaries at Marignano, gaining the grateful alliance of Pope Leo X. But Francis had wider issues in mind – nothing less than the European balance of power. He was especially worried by the power and reach of Holy Roman Emperor Charles V, who was also Charles I of Spain, and hence had the power to keep Germany, Spain and northern Italy pressing on France like a three-sided vice.

While the Hospitallers were fighting their last desperate battles in Rhodes, Francis I was battling Imperial forces in Italy, with himself fearlessly in the front line. An attempt to seize Milan resulted in his capture. 'There is nothing in the world left to me but my honour and my life,' the imprisoned French king wrote to his regent mother.[3] He was taken to Madrid and there confined, falling seriously ill. But his cunning was unimpaired. He recovered to name his 8-year-old eldest son Francis as his successor, and pretended to submit to Charles V's demands that he abdicate. Freed and back on French soil, Francis leaped on a horse crying, 'I'm king again!' and proceeded to be just that. Now he could indulge in grand strategy against the Habsburg emperor who had shut him up for a year, and for that he had to look farther east.

While still a prisoner of Charles V, Francis had written to Suleyman I, the Magnificent, asking him to attack Hungary to draw off Imperial forces in that direction. 'Our horse is saddled, our sword is girt on,' the sultan is reported to have written back; in fact, Suleyman, three years after Rhodes, had been planning just such a campaign. At Mohacs in 1526 he shattered the Hungarians, took Budapest and surged on to the outskirts of Vienna, but on 15 October 1529 a lack of supplies forced him to pull back. Nonetheless, panic seized Europe, but not Francis, who in July 1541 sent emissaries to the Ottoman sultan, who responded by sending a fleet to besiege Imperial-held Nice. Francis' alliance with the Turks arguably checked the spread of Charles V's power and thus fulfilled its purpose. Suleyman I died in 1566 while making another attempt on Hungary, but his successors maintained friendly ties with France for many more years.

Deprived of support from France, the Knights Hospitaller tried to make the best of their new situation in Malta, a less-than-ideal environment. Other locations had been looked at, such as Minorca and Ibiza as well as Ischia off the Italian coast, but the authorities on those islands raised a wall of objection. Malta seemed a poor choice for a base; timber was scarce, with the result that cow-dung and thistles were often used as fuel in the early days. The Knights encountered a sullen hostility from the Maltese nobility of Norman, Italian and Catalan origin who ruled over some 12,000 Arabic-speaking peasants and artisans. But there were compensations in the form of a large cotton industry that could procure ship sails. The harbour of Birgu itself, rivalling the best in the central Mediterranean, was slowly built up.

The French distrusted the Order as a potential ally of the King of Spain, even though a number of brother-knights opted to go on joint French-Turkish naval operations. The other practical military option open to the Hospitallers was to attack Muslim shipping in the Mediterranean. The severest threat was posed by the Muslim pirates based in Tunis, which was wrested from the Spaniards by the redoubtable Ottoman admiral, Hayreddin Barbarossa, in 1534. These Barbary pirates, 'as ruffianly a lot of cutthroats as history can offer', practised a relentless jihadi-type naval warfare based on the Koranic prescription:

[T]hat all nations who should not have acknowledged their authority were sinners … that it was [the pirates'] right and duty to make war upon them wherever they could be found, and to make slaves of all they could take as prisoners; and that every [Muslim] who was slain in battle was sure to go to Paradise.[4]

'God save you from the galleys of Tripoli!' the Italians would routinely warn anyone embarking at a port.[5]

The Knights' Navy joined an Imperial fleet of Spanish, papal and Genoese galleys, seventy-four ships strong plus some 300 other vessels, which bore down on troublesome Tunis in May 1535 and ejected Barbarossa's forces. Six years later Charles V, having secured a truce with France, sent fifty galleys, 150 transports and 24,000 men against the 6,000-strong Muslim garrison of Algiers. A severe storm all but destroyed this armada before it could reach its objective, allowing the Muslim regimes to stay on in North Africa and in fact strengthen their presence; the corsair chieftain, Dragut Reis, snatched Tripoli from the Hospitallers in 1551, but by then the Holy Roman Empire was preoccupied with crises closer to home.

The most aggressively successful Hospitaller naval commander at this time was Mathurin d'Aux de Lescout Romegas, who performed prodigies of valour against the Muslim corsairs. He was on his galley in port one night when a ferocious storm sank every vessel moored there, including his. When shocked rescuers came on the scene the following morning they heard a knocking sound from inside one of the overturned hulls: it was Romegas who had survived in an air pocket along with his pet monkey. The incident, though, had badly shaken him to the extent that for the rest of his life he could not drink anything without his trembling hand spilling the contents.[6] His exploits coincided with the election in 1557 of one of the most famous Grand Masters, Jean Parisot de la Valette. A stern disciplinarian whose naval experience had included a year as a slave on a Turkish galley, la Valette tightened up the Knights' morals; gambling, duelling and visiting prostitutes were banned, while finances were cleaned up. He brought in military engineers from several lands to design and build new fortifications, including San Michele Castle and Fort Saint Elmo at the tip of the peninsula guarding the main harbour.

In 1564 Romegas captured the galley of Suleyman the Magnificent's chief eunuch. The sultan decided he'd had enough of the 'pirates bearing crosses', a description that is not wide of the mark but rather ignored the purpose behind the Hospitallers' piracy, which was precisely to help keep the Mediterranean open for Christian shipping. There was always an underlying hope that somehow they could retake Rhodes, or failing that, establish a securer base in Sicily. Grand Master de l'Isle Adam had died in 1534, after a long and distinguished career; his steady leadership no doubt kept the Order together in the uneasy years between Rhodes and Malta. Grand Master Juan de Homedes y Coscon had the humiliation of having to let go of Tripoli, yet the loss enabled him to concentrate on fortifying Malta proper for the Ottoman attack on the 'Maltese pirates' that everyone was sure would come.

The French alliance with the Ottomans against the interests of the Holy Roman Empire, Spain, and independent Italian powers such as Florence and Venice was a recipe for constant tension in the Mediterranean, and the Hospitallers, of course, found themselves in the middle of it. We have already seen how some Knights – probably just to do anything to ease their ennui – had enlisted under French standards. But these were almost certainly a minority, as the Order of Malta preferred to retain its allegiance to the more traditionally Catholic Spaniards and Italians. The Turks, on the other hand, could not be budged from their control of most of eastern Europe and the eastern Mediterranean, a fact that fuelled much diplomatic dickering among the powers. King Philip II of Spain, however, had no intention of allowing Suleyman to keep any North African bases that could serve as potential jumping-off points for another Muslim invasion of Spain, and in 1559 he struck.

The result was repeated disaster. The first expedition against Tripoli was trounced with heavy loss of ships and men at Djerba. A year later Dragut Reis captured a dozen Italian galleys, after which another storm shattered the fleet of Juan de Mendoza, again with heavy loss. In the space of a couple of years Philip II, the Hospitallers' feudal overlord, had lost thousands of experienced soldiers and sailors. The lack of manpower soon made itself felt in the summer of 1565 when Suleyman, bored with peace, mobilized 40,000 men under Dragut Reis to sail to Malta and stamp out the hornets' nest of Christian corsairs – and hopefully gain a base from which to invade Italy.[7] Grand Master Jean Parisot de la Valette braced for the Turkish onslaught with about 540 brother-knights and brother-sergeants, plus 400 Spanish troops and perhaps 4,000 Maltese auxiliaries for what promised to be a showdown to rival the defence of Rhodes.[8]

A year previously, the Knights had helped Don Garcia de Toledo, the Spanish king's new and capable navy commander, claw back the small island of Velez de la Gomera off the Moroccan coast from the Muslims. Toledo was a careful planner who never made hasty moves, and his success earned him a promotion to Viceroy of Sicily, from which position he could return the favour to Malta. Acutely aware of the danger the island was in, Toledo had sailed to Malta in April 1565 to meet la Valette to discuss the disquieting news that a large Ottoman fleet had sailed from Constantinople. Philip II had promised troops, of which there was yet no sign, so Toledo promised 1,000 men – one-third of his Sicily garrison – and returned to his base. He left behind his son Fadrique de Toledo, who took the oath of a Knight of Saint John.

Favourable winds sped the Ottoman fleet past Greece and on 19 May the first squadrons landed on Malta. This, however, was not to be a reprise of Rhodes. The Turks this time were a long way from their bases, and supply by sea would prove problematic over the long run. Therefore the operation had to be a quick one before winter and rough seas set in. The Birgu, the chief town of Malta, was ill-positioned to withstand a determined siege employing the best military engineering the age could boast. The defenders, even by the most favourable estimate, were outnumbered by at least four to one. Toledo in Sicily agonized over the imbalance; he had asked for 25,000 men from the king of Spain, but Philip could scrape together just 16,000, composed of Spain's Italian garrisons and a few thousand new recruits gathered during the Spanish fleet's voyage from Seville to Sicily. This fleet of sixty galleys was just one-third of the size of the Ottoman.

The eyes of all Europe were now on Malta. Whoever controlled this barren speck of rock controlled the sea lanes of the Mediterranean. In Ottoman hands it could strangle east-west trade and provide a base for a Muslim invasion of Italy. Toledo was no doubt acutely aware of what was riding on the defence of Malta and redoubled his natural caution. His first concern was to elude the Turks and land his force on Malta, to lend initial encouragement to the Hospitallers who were determined to mount a stern defence. But Toledo also could not afford to completely denude Sicily of men, with the result that some Knights became disgruntled at the paucity of the reinforcements they were getting. They claimed that Toledo had actually forbidden some of the Knights in Messina from sailing to join the rest of the Order in Malta.[9] La Valette, for his part, braced for an expected Turkish attack on Fort Saint Elmo that commanded the entrance to Marsamxett harbour and whose loss to the Hospitallers would be a severe blow.

Fort Saint Elmo at the tip of the Sciberras promontory dominating Marsamxett had been built specifically to withstand an attack from the sea. Its ramparts were in the shape of a four-pointed star reinforced by a V-shaped ravelin, or outer work with ditch, on the seaward side. To protect the more vulnerable landward side la Valette had built a free-standing tower outside the western wall. Soon after their arrival the Turks began their bombardment of the fort from its south-western side; though the casualties were severe, replacement troops could be brought in by night. At the end of May Dragut Reis arrived to personally assume command of the Ottoman force, judged the offensive so far to be too feeble and extended his bombardments to the whole perimeter of the fort. On 4 August, when he judged the fort's defences to have been sufficiently weakened, Dragut ordered an audacious night attack by picked Janissaries on the ravelin. By dawn the assault had succeeded, as covering fire from other Turkish units suppressed the resistance. With one of the fort's strongpoints seized, the tower on the landward side was the next objective. Artillery fire soon reduced the tower to rubble, scattering its defenders. The ravelin ditch was filled in and the encircled defenders had no hope of holding on.

La Valette received the despairing messages from Fort Saint Elmo but could not afford to be swayed by them into frittering away his own forces; in two weeks, he knew (or hoped) about 600 crack soldiers and artillerymen promised by Toledo would arrive, and if the fort fell by then, they would have nowhere to land. He ordered the fort's defenders to keep fighting, whatever the cost – which they did for an incredible three weeks, while Turkish shot rained down on them from the sea and enemy infantry stood ready to pour in from the land side. Toledo's units failed to arrive on the promised date, 20 June, and three days later Dragut unleashed a major assault. A full day of desperate combat cost the defenders 200 out of 260 men, but the fort held. The exhausted survivors presented a tragic spectacle that evening as they took Communion in the chapel:

Not one of them remained unwounded: bodies were blasted into strange contortions by their injuries and eyes stared out wildly from faces blackened by gunpowder. Two of the knights who were too crippled to walk had themselves carried onto the walls in chairs to face the enemy.[10]

The Turks, who at first had blithely expected to capture Saint Elmo in three days, by the morning of 24 June had lost some 5,000 men. One of them was Dragut himself, killed by a Hospitaller cannonball while directing operations on Sciberras promontory. But Fort Saint Elmo, for all the fierce valour of its defenders, was finished. One hour's fighting in the morning decided the issue. Mustafa Pasha, the new Turkish commander, gazed at the ruined fort and is said to have exclaimed, 'What will the parent [Malta] cost when the child [the fort] has been purchased at so heavy a price!'[11] He ordered the bodies of fallen Knights nailed to crosses and thrown into the harbour for their comrades to view. La Valette retaliated by beheading his Turkish prisoners and using their heads as cannonballs to be fired into the enemy lines.

The Grand Master's outburst of ruthless fury can be understood; besides the effect of the sacrilegious atrocity committed by Mustafa Pasha, the crack troops promised by Toledo had failed to arrive in time to save the fort. But perhaps he had no way of knowing that the promised force, under Melchor de Robles, had tried unsuccessfully to reach Malta three times, driven back by Ottoman squadrons. Eventually Robles made it, but was just too late by a matter of hours. But arrive he did, disembarking his men on the north side of Malta, entering the Birgu under cover of fog on the night of 29 June. To the defenders, who had lost at least 1,500 men, this Piccolo Soccorso, or 'Small Relief', as it is known to history, was most welcome. Mustafa Pasha, his force greatly decimated by the weeks of action against Fort Saint Elmo, failed to extend his siege lines to the Birgu in time, a lapse that most likely cost him the campaign.

But in the middle of July it seemed that the Ottomans were on the verge of success. Mustafa launched a massed amphibious attack on the Birgu and Senglea in the Grand Harbour. It came to grief on the tips of underwater stakes off Senglea, while Hospitaller artillery hidden in the Castel Sant'Angelo smashed a Turkish squadron that was trying to sneak into the anchorage of the defenders' galleys. Week after week the Turks poured fire into the defenders' positions, and on 7 August Mustafa Pasha thought he had a chance to decide the issue when he hurled an overwhelming mass of troops against San Michele Castle at Senglea defended by Pietro del Monte. He might well have attained his objective had not a squadron of fresh Hospitaller cavalry caused a diversion by raiding the Ottoman camp, forcing Mustafa to pull back from the very cusp of victory.

As the Ottoman siege dragged on into September, Mustafa Pasha began to worry. With winter approaching he would have to start thinking about winter quarters, which would require breaking off the action. On the other hand, he must have known of the desperate situation the defenders were in; the Hospitallers and their auxiliaries had lost some 5,000 men, including 219 Knights and Fadrique de Toledo, the gallant son of Don Garcia. Six hundred able-bodied men at most were still able to man the ramparts. It seemed to Mustafa as if one more determined push would earn him the island, but at dawn on 7 September, exactly one month after the attack on Senglea Castle, the long-awaited 16,000 men under Garcia de Toledo sailed into Mellieha Bay. They had made an audacious night crossing from Sicily, sailing in what was the sixteenth century equivalent of radio silence – not a single crew member was allowed to make the slightest noise – to elude the watchful Turks. It took two hours to disembark the first 8,000 men, and by the time the Turks were alerted to what was happening the rest had also been ferried ashore.

Panic seized the fatigued Ottomans. The following day the first ranks broke and ran for their ships. Mustafa, knowing that he still outnumbered the Christians, tried to stop the flight but his orders were ignored. In a matter of hours the Ottoman fleet was on its way back to Constantinople and quite suddenly, after a four-month ordeal that appeared to be the end of the Knights Hospitaller, Malta was free. Christian Europe could breathe again. A grateful Philip II kept Don Garcia de Toledo in place as Viceroy of Sicily until 1568, when he was made Duke of Fernandina and Prince of Montalban.[12] For the Knights, it was by far their finest hour, surpassing in valour and endurance the sieges of Acre and Rhodes. The victory was all the more impressive for being unexpected. Malta was the equivalent of Constantinople (717) and Tours (732) in slamming the door to a Muslim incursion into Europe. If Malta had fallen to the Ottomans, what would have become of the Hospitallers? Writes Henry Sire, a modern-day Knight of the Order:

> [T]heir reputation as the shield of Christian Europe could hardly have survived. The Order would doubtless have disintegrated into national fragments, an obsolete relic of the past … The fame of 1565 was to make the Knights of Malta the acknowledged paragons of Christian chivalry for as long as that ideal held sway in Europe.[13]

The salvation of Malta was literally the 'news of the century' for an astounded Europe. Even 200 years later the French philosopher Voltaire could write that 'nothing is better known than the siege of Malta'. The

Knights whose lives revolved around the age-old vow of poverty, chastity and obedience were now flooded with money from grateful governments. Most of this largesse went into designing and building a new city. Hardly had the battered Order recovered from its ordeal than Pope Pius IV sent an engineer, Francesco Laparelli, a student of Michelangelo, to give form to what Sir Walter Scott would much later call 'a city built by gentlemen for gentlemen'.[14] Laparelli turned the Sciberras promontory into a veritable fortress with Fort Saint Elmo at the tip. Within the walls the new town was laid out in an efficient grid; in what was state-of-the-art city planning of the time, each house had its own water tank and sewer, while every Knight was given a financial incentive to build a fine house. The promontory itself was clad in formidable walls through which a single gate led into the city from the landward side, flanked by two towers and a deep, wide ditch.

La Valette at first hesitated to splash out so abundantly. Though Spain guaranteed Malta against any more Muslim attacks, only after Philip II urged him to go ahead did the Grand Master give the green light; on 28 March 1566 la Valette laid the foundation stone of the city that henceforth was to bear his name – Valletta. Two years later he died, to be succeeded by Pietro del Monte, who had distinguished himself in the defence of Senglea Castle. Laparelli had returned to Italy, to be replaced by a native Maltese, Girolamo Cassar, who can be considered the true architect of Valletta, which replaced the Birgu as the Hospitallers' capital. By March 1571 del Monte was well-established in newly-built quarters in the centre of Valletta, but the Knights' complacency was short-lived, as that year the Ottomans again made a bid to dominate the Mediterranean.

The *Santa Anna* was the most remarkable warship of its time – perhaps of all time. Built to order by the Hospitallers in Nice just after their expulsion from Rhodes, when it was launched in 1524 it dwarfed anything else afloat: longer than any other ship of war, with four towering masts, bearing fifty heavy cannon on twin gun-decks and able to carry 600 soldiers, and – a full three centuries before the ironclads of the nineteenth century – a metal-sheathed bottom. It was nothing short of a floating palace, of which Grand Master de l'Isle Adam made good use to escape the plague at Nice. It had its own bakery and on-board grove of trees for shade and fresh fruit and numerous hearths that could be kept alight around the clock.

The ship of which the *Santa Anna* was the pinnacle was called a great carrack, a larger and stronger version of the galley, though more useful for transport and logistics than for the lightness and manoeuvrability of battle. The Order had already gained valuable experience with the great carrack

Santa Maria, which, it will be recalled, was the captured former Egyptian vessel *Mogarbina*. For sixteen years the *Santa Anna* had been the pride of the Hospitaller Navy, taking part in all the main encounters with the Ottoman fleet, including the capture of Tunis in 1635. Yet by that date her age was already beginning to show. Warship design in Europe was advancing rapidly, with the carrack and galley outclassed by the newer galleon, and in 1540 the *Santa Anna* went to the breakers' yard. From then on the Order acquired galleons, ordering a new one every dozen years or so, whenever finances would permit, to build a fleet that was henceforth known as the Navy of the Religion.

The galley, however, continued to be the mainstay of the Navy, which became known for the size of its galleys, better able than most to withstand winter weather in the Mediterranean. They became a byword among Spanish seafarers, for example, who would tell of storms 'that only the galleys of Malta could weather'.[15] A typical Maltese galley would be propelled by between 150 and 180 oars and two large lateen (triangular) sails; its shallow draught enabled it to chase pirates into coves and inlets. The grand sight of 'six galleys of Malta coming in all their pomp' impressed at least one English visitor as he sailed out of Valletta. Such a sight, says Henry Sire, 'must have thrilled Christian hearts and swollen the pride of the Order all over the Mediterranean world'. This new might would soon be put to good use.

After the salvation of Malta naval operations continued unabated. One of Grand Master del Monte's first acts after his accession in 1568 was to send four galleys to aid the Venetians against the Turks. However, once this detachment under François de Saint Clément got as far as Sicily, its commander appeared more concerned with loading up with supplies of wine and heading home than staying on guard against an Ottoman fleet under Uluç Ali that was hovering nearby. Saint Clément paid the price for his folly in the morning of 15 July, when he stumbled on the Ottoman ships off Gozo and had to turn around and hasten back to Sicily. After making sure that the four Maltese galleys were not the vanguard of a larger Venetian fleet, Uluç Ali gave chase. At first the wind aided Saint Clément, but when it dropped the Turks caught up with his small squadron. Two of the Order's ships, the *Santa Maria della Vittoria* and the *Sant'Anna* (presumably not to be confused with the hulking *Santa Anna* that had been scrapped eighteen years before) made a break for the open sea. Saint Clément and his two remaining galleys sped for the Sicilian coast.

The splitting manoeuvre didn't work. The Ottoman galliots quickly overhauled the *Sant'Anna* whose sails became tangled during a futile attempt at a counter-attack and which was seized after a long and fierce fight with heavy casualties. The *Santa Maria della Vittoria* escaped and found refuge in the Sicilian port of Agrigento. But Saint Clément and his remaining two ships were doomed. The Knights employed hundreds of Muslim war captives as slaves to man the galley oars, and these slaves now deliberately lingered over their oars, letting the main Turkish fleet catch up. When Uluç Ali captured the *San Giovanni* Saint Clément in desperation ran the flagship aground. This was the signal for the Muslim oarsmen to attack the Christian crew with axes. Taking refuge in a tower, the Christians watched helplessly as Uluç Ali hauled the Knights' flagship back into the water, to use it as his own. Saint Clément himself, preoccupied with retrieving his gold and silver, forgot about the standard of Saint John, which was saved by a quick-witted crewmember named Michele Calli, helped by the brother-knight Bongianni Gianfiliazzi.[16] The loss of three fighting ships crippled the Navy of the Religion right on the eve of when it was needed the most.

Meanwhile, Suleyman the Magnificent had died, to be succeeded by his far less capable son Selim II, whose bibulous proclivities earned him the lasting sobriquet of Selim the Drunkard, but who was no less dangerous than his father, as he was easily led by his hawkish advisers. In February 1568 his government signed a peace treaty with Austria defining the limits of Ottoman expansion into central Europe. But two years later the sultan's influential Jewish adviser Joseph Nasi talked him into trying to grab Cyprus from its Venetian masters. The temptation was great, as Cyprus was the last major Venetian bastion in the eastern Mediterranean. The Turks succeeded in landing a force on the island, but the move triggered a pact among Venice, the papacy and Spain, which put together a Christian fleet that gathered at Messina in August 1571 under the 26-year-old Don John of Austria, Philip II's half-brother. On 16 September Don John's fleet of 231 vessels set off for Corfu on the first leg of their voyage. On board were some 50,000 seamen – many of them slaves chained to their rowing benches – and about 30,000 fighting soldiers at a liberal estimate. The fleet included six large galleasses, each of them bristling with thirty guns, that were given the task of forming a screen half a mile ahead of the main force.

The Ottoman fleet under Müezzinzâde Ali Pasha assembled at the western entrance to the Gulf of Patras in western Greece; with 250 vessels it outnumbered the Christians, but the Ottoman ships were not as well armed. The Turkish soldiers also lacked firearms, whereas the Christians were armed with the arquebus. On the morning of 7 October Don John's fleet came within sight of the Ottomans in line abreast blocking the entrance to the gulf about twenty-five miles west of the Greek town of Navpaktos – corrupted into Lepanto by the Italians. Don John arranged the ships in a battle-order line three miles long. He himself commanded the centre with sixty-three galleys; on the left he placed Agostino Barbarigo with sixty-three more, while the Hospitallers' three galleys – all they could muster after the humiliation off Sicily – were assigned a place of honour on the right, among the sixty-four ships under the command of Giovanni Andrea Doria. In charge of the three Hospitaller ships was General Pietro Giustiniani.

The young Don John was a popular commander. He had earned his spurs fighting the Muslims at Granada and against Algerian pirates. His diplomatic talents soothed countless spats among the quarrelsome Italians and Spaniards. He was a stickler for instruction, explaining tactics on a blackboard, and would often sail around his squadrons in a fast brigantine to show himself and keep up morale – a gesture that was hugely appreciated.[17] Now, with battle imminent, he spiritedly exhorted his sailors and soldiers to acquit themselves well, and to set a personal example of morale, called for his pipers and danced in full armour on the deck of his flagship, the *Real*. On the other side Müezzinzâde Ali Pasha employed his vocal talents – as his name implies, he was a former muezzin whose prayer time chants had so charmed one of the sultan's wives that she made him a high-ranking admiral – to stiffen the resolve of the warriors for the Prophet.

Serving as commander of the papal galleys was Hospitaller Knight Lescaut de Romegas, who had miraculously survived the terrible storm in the Birgu sixteen years before. Romegas had been spying out the Turkish force as it sailed out of Lepanto and warned Don John that the enemy appeared stronger than was initially thought. Don John didn't quite believe the Hospitaller, but the first light on 7 October showed that Romegas was right; the whole Ottoman fleet was bearing down on the Christians. Don John called for the green alert flag to be raised on his ship, and a warning gun to be fired. But he appears to have been unwilling to join battle so early and asked Romegas what he thought he should do. The grizzled Hospitaller replied that he must fight, and now. 'If the emperor your father had seen such an armada like ours,' he told his commander, 'he would not have stopped until he had become emperor of Constantinople.' The debate continued for a while longer until Don John cut it short. 'Now's not the time to discuss, but to fight.'[18]

The advance galleasses on the Christian left opened the action with a bombardment of the Turkish right wing under Mehmet Scirocco, one of whose fifty-five ships was sunk. Scirocco then moved to try and outflank the hulking galleasses, but they backed water and turned to pour a withering fire into the Turks. Though severely mauled, the rest of Scirocco's formation clashed with Barbarigo's ships. In the ensuing hour-long struggle, Barbarigo was killed but his crews fought on, eventually pushing Scirocco back. At that point some of the Christian slave-rowers in the Ottoman fleet managed to pry off their chains and overcome their masters. This turned the Turkish retreat into a rout; some galleys were driven to the beetling cliffs of the north shore of the Gulf of Patras, others were sunk and the rest captured. But at other parts of the line the encounter was not so favourable to the Christians.

As soon as the signal to advance had been given, the Christian and Ottoman flagships made directly for one another, accompanied by their flanking vessels. The clash was fierce, soon extending to perhaps thirty ships of both fleets in one grand, confused and noisy melee. More than once it seemed as if Ali Pasha was on the point of seizing Don John's galley – some Ottoman troops actually jumped onto the forecastle – but the Christian commander had wisely kept a reserve of thirty-five galleys under the Marquis of Santa Cruz in the rear. Santa Cruz at this critical point sent 200 men to reinforce the Christian centre, and this may have saved it, because even then it took ninety minutes for the Ottoman centre to give way. Romegas, on the papal flagship, saw his chance for a make-or-break gesture. While sister vessels turned to help the embattled *Real*, Romegas seized the tiller of his vessel and steered it towards Ali's own flagship, the *Sultana*. The move enabled the Christian soldiers to board Ali Pasha's flagship, which was finally put out of action by being rammed. Ali Pasha fought fanatically to the last, shooting arrows at his attackers as he fell. Some accounts say he took an arquebus ball in the head; others say a Spanish soldier sliced off his head or he slashed his own throat in despair. Don John, shrugging off an ankle wound, captured the ex-muezzin's standard. By noon, the battle in the centre, too, was over.

On Don John's right the situation was more perilous. Opposite this sector was the Hospitallers' recent bugbear, Uluç Ali, who had humiliated Saint Clément off Sicily the previous year. His line outflanked that of Doria, with the result that the Genoese commander sidled to the right to even out the lines. The Ottoman commander kept his distance from the two powerful galleasses screening Doria's wing. Doria appears to have wanted to stop Uluç Ali from joining the battle in the centre, but to some of his skippers he seemed to be not moving fast enough. The Ottomans sped to the attack, overwhelming eleven of the fifteen galleys, including the Hospitaller *Capitana*, with little trouble.

The sight of the Hospitaller standard, writes one modern historian, to Uluç Ali 'had the effect of a red rag to a bull'.[19] Four Ottoman galleys descended on Giustiniani's flagship, whose crew fought back so fiercely that just two Knights survived badly wounded, plus Giustiniani with five arrows in him. It would later be said that Giustiniani's Muslim slave rescued him by pulling him below decks and barricading the door with blankets. In return, the slave was reportedly given his freedom, but preferred instead to stay and serve his master; the story, however attractive, cannot be authenticated.[20] Don Martin de Herrera of Aragon, the flagship standard-bearer, lost his whole left arm, a piece of his shoulder and part of his face to a horrific sword-blow; nonetheless he would survive into an honoured old age. It is almost certain that the Hospitaller standard was captured, though there continues to be some dispute about this. The *Capitana* itself was saved from seizure by the timely intervention of a squadron under Don Juan de Cardona. One of Doria's crewmen was a literary-minded Spaniard named Miguel de Cervantes, whose left hand was shattered by an arquebus shot, but who lived to use his right hand to pen the epochal *Don Quixote*.

The turning point came when one Christian captain, Benedetto Soranzo, carried out the equivalent of a suicide bombing, torching his ship's powder magazine and immolating several of the enemy along with himself and his crew. Momentarily checked by this, Uluç Ali veered towards the main fight in the centre, but by this time that battle had turned decisively in the Christians' favour. Moreover, Doria had brought his ships around from the right to assail the Ottomans from the rear while Santa Cruz's reserves hammered them from in front. By mid-afternoon Uluç Ali realized the battle was lost and did the sensible thing, pulling his squadrons out fast; besides, a thunderstorm was seen to be approaching and the urgent task now was to seek safe anchorages. The Christians captured 117 Turkish galleys more or less intact and 274 guns. Floating Ottoman bodies by the hundred were looted, though one Italian commander commendably refused to take part, saying he had 'not come to steal, but instead to fight and serve Our Lord'. (From what we know, he was not a Hospitaller.)

The significance of the Battle of Lepanto for European history has been endlessly debated, with recent writers tending to minimize its actual consequences. Montgomery calls it 'a negative victory' that may have kept Muslim powers temporarily at bay in the Mediterranean yet was not followed up by a naval offensive that could have eliminated or reduced the threat of the still-powerful Ottoman fleet.[21] Three years later Uluç Ali annexed Tunis, almost as if Lepanto had never happened. But for the Knights of Saint John, Lepanto proved their worth as much as the siege of Malta had six years before. Both battles showed that their commitment to upholding Christendom in the Mediterranean area was undimmed, and that their reserves of courage in carrying out that unchanging mission were a long way from being exhausted. The Navy of the Religion had helped firm up the Muslim-Christian boundaries in the Mediterranean, allowing Spain to turn its naval attention to its English and Dutch rivals.

Chapter 13

The Navy of the Religion

The Navy and the corso – suppressing the pirates – a strictly noble class – career of a Knight – the Italian ascendancy – the War of Candia – Turks in Europe – the Knights at their apex

Though the splendid performance of the few Hospitaller crews against overwhelming odds at Lepanto added to the Order's military lustre, the Knights of Malta had little time to rest on their laurels. By now the Maltese Navy had acquired a reputation for excellence in the courts and chancelleries of Europe; indeed, so important was its contribution to keeping the ever-present Muslim corsairs at bay that it became known as the Navy of the Religion. Though the Knights never formally considered themselves sailors, with a base like Malta the sea was the only field of combat open to them. The main foe continued to be the Ottoman outlying provinces along the North African coast and the pirate nests that they nurtured.

In point of fact, the Navy of the Religion was in effect an arm of the Spanish Navy, deputed to maintain order in the Mediterranean while Philip II could concentrate on building his Armada to hopefully subjugate England and safeguard the seaborne wealth flowing in from the New World. But maintaining order was easier said than done, as the Barbary pirates were growing in power and reach. Uluç Ali's capture of Tunis in 1574 began that town's career as a corsair centre that was to last more than two centuries; even bigger was Algiers, which served as a homeport for more than a hundred Muslim pirate ships. The Tunisian pirates copied the Hospitallers' large, strong galleys, and used them to savage a Maltese fleet near Sicily in 1625. Under the redoubtable Yusuf Dey, Tunis served as a base even for Dutch and English pirates who despised the Catholics quite as much as the Muslims did. By 1640 the Barbary pirates operated about 150 corsair ships, most of them small and manoeuvrable, known as bertons and actually introduced by the English and Dutch. These vessels were the scourge of the southern

Spanish and southern Italian coasts, where they would often land in search of plunder and slaves.

As the seventeenth century got into its stride a relentless and deadly game of cat and mouse played out in the Mediterranean Sea between the Muslim corsairs, abetted by the Ottoman Sultan on the one hand, and the Maltese Navy of the Religion on the other. The naval campaigns on both sides were known as the *corso*, roughly translated as the 'running'. By now the Knights of Saint John needed to be fully conversant with the techniques of naval combat. Every Knight without exception was expected to serve three six-month stints on a galley of the Order in order to amass enough experience to qualify for a Commandery (previously known as a Preceptory). Each stint was called a 'caravan', hence the term *caravanisti* for a galley complement of up to twenty Knights. Being young, they were generally aggressive enough, while rivalry among the Tongues sharpened their combat skills; a competent Knight who distinguished himself in the *corso* could expect to be made a general even in his twenties.

Once a galley of the Order captured a Muslim corsair vessel the booty and captives went direct to the Malta headquarters; the crew received nothing except their regular pay. But an ambitious captain who could afford it would pay the operating expenses of his ship in the hope of obtaining a Commandery and the rank of general, on which the benefice money would come pouring in. Financially, though, it was a risky venture. As one Hospitaller historian notes: 'It [is not] likely that the wealth the knights drew from their eventual dignities really repaid the outlay in qualifying for them.'[1] Far more important to the average Knight was not what he could pocket from his activities but how he could serve Christendom with his sword and courage.

This is not to say, however, that the *caravanisti* always resisted the temptation to imitate their pirate foes. Privateering, though not officially a part of the Order's strategy, was frequent. The Mediterranean swarmed with pirates of several nationalities. At times it would have been hard to tell apart a Maltese from a Muslim vessel, though the Christian crews concentrated more on fighting than on raiding and looting. Sometimes the Navy of the Religion veered out of line, as on one occasion when it attacked Spanish ships during the French-Spanish War and Grand Master Juan de Lascaris-Castellar stepped in to halt the practice. Some ships attacked English and Dutch merchantmen trading with Turkey, though in most cases compensation was eventually paid.

Though the Knights of Saint John appeared to have gained a new lease on life with their value as Mediterranean piracy-suppressors, Europe was changing politically. In France the monarchy reclaimed its old prestige in the person of King Henry IV of Navarre, who sensibly ended an intermittent war with Spain and started France on the road to royal absolutism. In England, however, the opposite was happening: the death in 1603 of the last Tudor, Elizabeth I, was the signal for the dilution of royal power under her much lesser successors, James I and his son Charles I, who in 1649 paid with his head and an eleven-year Cromwellian interlude. But in both countries the effect on the military establishment was identical; both France and England built up national armies whose allegiance was not to any warlord or duke or freebooting Italian *condottiere*, but to the nation's sovereign and flag. It was the start of the process by which nationalism would replace religion as the prime motive for warfare, and in such an environment the Knights Hospitaller, with their noble yet archaic principle of fighting for the Christian religion – which in their eyes was now exclusively the Roman Catholic Church – were becoming fast outmoded.

Along with motivation, the quality of recruits to the Order of Malta declined steadily in the seventeenth century. Admits the Hospitaller historian Sire:

> The cross of profession, which had retained in Rhodes and the [Birgu] its religious severity, beckoned to every mettlesome young nobleman, and a tone of debauchery and riot blemished the last decades of the century.[2]

A more recent parallel can be found in the French Foreign Legion of the twentieth century, which attracted plenty of restless young soldiers of fortune from many nationalities. As early as the 1570s Grand Master Jean de la Cassiere failed to re-establish the old discipline and indeed was toppled from his post. His successor Hugues Loubenx de Verdala had no better luck, having to spend a great deal of time out of harm's way in Rome; had it not been for the firm backing of the papacy he, too, would have suffered la Cassiere's fate. How, then, can we reconcile this reported decline in the quality of the Knights with their success in manning and operating the Navy of the Religion? Part of the answer could lie in the sterner stuff of which the Grand Masters were made in the seventeenth century. In the lull between the Battle of Lepanto and the successes against the Muslim corsairs, senior Knights had the chance to re-polish their command and combat skills and bring the experience to the highest office of the Order.

The Order's heightened prestige after Lepanto was reflected in a new building programme for Valletta and the Grand Master's palace. La Cassiere and Verdala in particular might have been despised, but they can take credit for some of the lavish architecture and decoration we can see in the Knights' former premises today. Verdala built himself a miniature castle on the Boschetto, the highest point of Malta, to use as a lodge for hunting whatever wild life could be found on the island. The Tongues built corresponding auberges on the Rhodes model, though they have been architecturally criticized as boxy and unattractive in comparison with the more gracious Rhodian buildings. More controversially, the Knights elevated themselves to a superior aristocracy lording it over the native Maltese population of some 65,000, whose own nobles, known as the Barons, refused all contact with the Order and secluded themselves behind the walls of their town, the Notabile. The Knights' wealth did, however, trickle down to the local people, as the new buildings and ships gave steady jobs to many. The Maltese *corso*, in fact, is believed to have given direct and indirect employment to up to one-quarter of Malta's population.[3]

So far the Hospitaller Order had been run along the lines laid down in the early fourteenth century, though in the meantime two new offices, those of Grand Bailiff and Chancellor, had been added to the original seven (Grand Master, Grand Commander, Marshal, Grand Hospitaller, Admiral, Treasurer and Grand Turcopolier). The last-named office, traditionally a prerogative of the English Tongue, became ambiguous after the Rhodes years, as the western Mediterranean had no Levantine turcopoles to enlist. However, the head of the English Tongue in Malta continued to formally hold that title, which was applied to the guardianship of the watchtowers – until it was taken over by Grand Master de Verdala in 1582. Ethnic criteria continued to apply as of old, with a Provençal almost invariably occupying the office of Grand Commander, an Auvergnais as Marshal, a Frenchman as Grand Hospitaller, a Spaniard as Conservator (the renamed office of Drapier), an Italian as Admiral, a Castilian as Chancellor (responsible for diplomacy and foreign relations) and a German as Grand Bailiff (responsible for fortifications). In addition to these senior officials the Grand Master employed what was called the Venerable Council, including the Bishop of Malta and the Prior of Saint John, as a body that he could turn to when he needed fast advice.

The Chapter General, consisting of all these officials, continued to meet every five years. During the Malta years it was kept quite busy examining and authorizing naval expenditures, with sixteen days being the limit for any debate, no doubt to prevent filibustering. Much mental energy and cunning was expended on forestalling any intrigues by the popes, especially in the election of a new Grand Master, which explains why it was limited to a three-day process. The knighthood itself, along with its aggressive independence from the papacy, was becoming increasingly exclusive. A political crisis of this sort erupted in 1581 when Romegas, flushed with renown after his exploits at Lepanto, joined – or may have masterminded – a mutiny that toppled Grand Master Jean de la Cassiere, who was confined in Sant'Angelo Castle. The papacy refused to put up with such disobedience and toppled the plotters in turn. Romegas, who probably saw his chance of becoming Grand Master gone for good, died a broken man soon afterwards.

Whereas in the original rules of 1206 a Knight was required to be the legitimate son of a knightly family, the requirement was tightened around 1350 to include proof of nobility in the mother's line as well, and in 1428 an applicant knight had to prove at least four generations of nobility in his lineage on both sides – a practice that seems little different from 'the breeding of a good hunting-hound or war horse'. No one else, however wealthy or influential, could make it into the hallowed ranks of the Order. 'With no more than a horse and a sword to his name,' one of confirmed noble pedigree 'received preference over the son of some duke of ample acres who happened to have been guilty of a *mésalliance* [extramarital affair]'.[4] The Spanish and Portuguese, for their part, excluded anyone with even a suspected drop of Jewish or Moorish blood; the Italians and Germans went even further and demanded up to 200 years' proven and unbroken nobility. This stifling racism, cemented into an ironclad rule by the Chapter General of 1598, was the law through most of the seventeenth century. To be sure, there were many instances, especially among the Italians, where a knighthood in the Order was surreptitiously purchased by some wealthy but formally unqualified family, which could then flaunt the appointment as proof of long membership in the *noblesse d'épée*, literally 'nobility of the sword', that carried a somewhat higher social cachet than the *noblesse de robe*, or 'nobility of learning'.

A young aspirant to the Order, assuming his pedigree was adequate, would be accepted as a novitiate in his late teens; for an even earlier head start, a boy as young as 12 could become a Page of the Grand Master. The job of page became so sought-after that at least 100 boys were received in 1631; however, when they reached 16 they had to go through the novitiate stage like everyone else. The novitiate would undergo training and instruction in arms for twelve months, after which he would take a preliminary vow as a Knight and be sent on his first caravan, one of three on which he was required to serve that year (upped to four in the seventeenth century) before taking a more solemn vow at age 21. At this stage a Knight would stay five years in the Convent in Malta, busy with administration or whatever duty he was assigned. His record here would be decisive in determining whether he was fit to command a galley, and if he was so deemed, then in his Hospitaller career he can be said to have 'arrived'. As we have seen, a competent galley commander who scored victories could aspire to a Commandery, and at this point he would be expected to acquire his own home and theoretically join the potential pool of candidates for an eventual grand mastership. Before that, however, a Knight lived in the auberge of his particular Tongue, helped by a servant or batman but otherwise observing military austerity. Henry Sire describes the atmosphere of a typical auberge dining hall, where some luxury was permitted:

> [The] knights ... sat among tapestries, brocade and trophies, and ate from solid silver dishes. Grand Crosses [generals] ... had the privilege of a velvet-covered bench, and the Pilier [head of a Tongue] presided alone on a raised dais, with a carpet and cushion at his feet, seated in a blue velvet armchair ... On his munificence depended the richness of the fare that reposed on his brethren's silverware.[5]

The Order's jealously-guarded independence and prestige were probable factors in the elevation of several prominent Grand Masters in the seventeenth century. Alof de Wignacourt, elected in 1601, was a hands-on leader if ever there was one. By sheer talent and force of personality this stern-browed Grand Master reorganized a crippled and weakened administration while pressing the continuous war effort against the Ottomans and the Muslim corsairs. His initial strategy of bearding the pirates in their North African lairs, however, was a failure; better success attended similar efforts to mop up the islands off Italy and Spain, where the corsairs would often winter. In 1614 he and a Spanish force thwarted another Ottoman attempt on Malta. Three years later Wignacourt had the Order's biggest vessel so far, the galleon *Gran Galeone*, built in Amsterdam. A flurry of excitement had occurred in 1606 when a colourful figure appeared in Valletta. This was the 31-year-old Italian artist Michelangelo Merisi da Caravaggio, whose talent for brawling and getting into trouble was overmatched only by his brilliance on canvas. After stabbing a man to death in Rome he fled to Malta where Wignacourt approved his appointment – on his fame alone rather than his lineage, one imagines – as an honorary Knight of Grace. The triumph was not to last long. Two years later Caravaggio seriously wounded a fellow-Knight in a quarrel and was jailed and booted out of the Order as a 'putrid and fetid limb' – but not before leaving behind some of the greatest paintings of his brief and turbulent life.[6]

Grand Master Antoine de Paule, elected in 1623, presided over a period in which, though recruitment for the Order steadily declined in the face of growing nationalism in Europe, he built the third magisterial palace of Malta, that of Sant'Antonio. De Paule was also responsible for the elaborate Floriana fortifications designed by the accomplished Italian military architect Pietro Floriani. The assignment reflects a mounting Italian influence in the Order at the expense of the once-dominant French, perhaps a natural geographical development, as Italy was the nearest country. A roster of personnel drawn up in 1631 shows the Italians as the plurality, with 584 Knights out of a total 1,755. The Provençals and Auvergnais were still considered distinct from the French proper, with 272 and 143 Knights respectively; the French had 361, the Aragonese 110, the Castilians 239 and the Germans 46. The striking absences from this list are the English, who must have been too few to count separately. It would not be surprising, as by now England had plenty of scope for its own knightly pursuits.[7]

Though the Italian Knights predominated, the office of Grand Master was more often than not the preserve of the Spanish. Of the eleven Grand Masters who ruled in the seventeenth century, six were Spaniards, four French and one Italian. The French thereafter would lose influence as the French state, as in England, absorbed the ambitions of young nobles with a flair for fighting. Spain itself was beginning to decline in power, and the preference for Spanish Grand Masters may have been a compensation for waning prestige at home. They certainly acted the part. The Navarrese Martin de Redín drew the comment from one observer that, of the holders of the Hospitallers' highest office, 'you would have called them Princes, they were so well set up, they marched so arrogantly, with so fine a grace'.[8] Their force of personality may have been one reason why the Grand Chapter meetings were discontinued after 1631, not to resume for 145 years. The brothers Rafael and Nicolás Cotoner, who served as Grand Masters from 1660 to 1680, heaped decoration on Valletta and its churches.

In the middle of the seventeenth century the national English and Dutch navies, followed by the French, began flexing more muscle against the corsairs in the Mediterranean. This development encouraged the Order to cast its glance eastwards, towards the old Outremer of venerable memory. As the Tunisian and Algerian pirate fleets were de-fanged, the Order began to eye Ottoman targets in the eastern Mediterranean. The first victory in that sector was the capture of a large Turkish official galley off Rhodes by Gabriel de Meaux de Boisboudran in 1644. One of the distinguished captives was the infant son of one of Sultan Ibrahim's mistresses; the child was taken to Malta and brought up as a Dominican monk dubbed the Padre Ottomano, or Ottoman Father. The stunt may have been a feather in the Hospitallers' cap, yet it aroused the ire not so much of the Turks as of the Venetians, who saw themselves as controllers of what Christian seas remained in the region and didn't want their power usurped by a handful of warrior-monks. In fact, Ibrahim himself considered the Venetians largely to blame for the affront, and therefore he decided that the long Venetian presence in Crete had to end.

On 1 June 1645 Ibrahim commenced hostilities against Venice. Any Venetians living within the Ottoman Empire were arrested and their property seized. A Turkish army landed at the Cretan city of Canea (modern Chania) and moved inland, though at such a slow pace that Ibrahim was blamed for incompetence and strangled to death, to be replaced by his young son Mehmet IV. Thereafter, the Ottoman campaign in Crete languished. As fellow-Christians, the Hospitallers felt duty-bound to aid their rivals the Venetians, and the twenty-four year War of Candia was on.[9] For some years the fortunes of this conflict surged back and forth, with neither side able to gain a real advantage – unless it was the value of caravan training and experience for young Knights. A Venetian fleet trounced the Ottomans off the Greek island of Paros in 1651, triggering a coup in Constantinople where Mehmet Köprülü, a low-born Albanian who had risen to the post of Grand Vizier and was already around 80 years old, seized the reins for some savage yet effective reforms. The reforms, however, were not enough to avert another major disaster for the Turkish Navy at the hands of Hospitaller General Gregorio Carafa at the mouth of the Dardanelles in 1656, where the sultan lost seventy-four galleys and forty-six other vessels.

But the Turks remained strong around the waters of Crete, and by 1669 Candia (modern Heraklion) was in desperate straits. That year in the early summer a Maltese relief expedition sailed up to assume the defence of Candia's Sant'Andrea bastion, which was in a parlous state. A French volunteer group also manning the defences lost heart and pulled out after their first sight of the Ottoman ships offshore, compelling the Knights to follow. There followed a bitter observation by the city's Venetian governor that he 'lost more by the departure of these few but most brave warriors than by that of all the other forces'. To complete the debacle, the Turks seized all of Crete, not to give it up until the early twentieth century.

The Turks were also on a roll in mainland Europe, as the energetic Köprülü (and his son Ahmet after him) had injected fresh vigour into the Ottoman state, partly by reviving the old jihadist drive to fight the Christians to the death. Transylvania came under Ottoman control, triggering a reaction in Europe reminiscent of that which had ignited the Crusades. Hostilities in Europe erupted in April 1663 when Sultan Mehmet IV launched his Muslim armies on Hungary and Austria. Christian forces under the irresolute Holy Roman Emperor Leopold I, backed by the French, beat back the invaders in a famous clash at Saint Gotthard; but that was only a temporary reprieve, as within thirteen years the Ottomans would overrun Crete and push their conquests as far north as Ukraine, directly threatening Poland. Ahmet Köprülü was now poised for the biggest push of all, an overwhelming blow against Vienna with 150,000 fanatic troops from all parts of the empire who converged on the walls of the city in June 1683 under Umar Mustafa. (France's Louis XIV had enabled this to happen by looking the other way, loth to risk his profitable ties with the Sultan – a short-sighted policy if ever there was one.) For two months Mustafa besieged Vienna, after which King John Sobieski of Poland and a large German army decisively hammered the Ottomans at Kahlenberg and western Europe – again – was saved.

The failure of the siege of Vienna was the beginning of the end for the Ottoman Empire, which would linger on in decline for another 250 or so years. With Pope Innocent XI doing the cheerleading, imperial German forces freed the Hungarian city of Buda from a century and a half of Turkish rule. Venice, with the help of the Hospitallers, joined in from the sea. Belgrade was the next eastern European capital to be wrested from the Turks, but only for a couple of years as the third scion of the Köprülü family, Mustafa, rallied his forces for another crack at the Christian powers. But eventually in 1699 Sultan Mustafa II, under pressure from the Holy Roman Empire, Savoy and Russia, relinquished most of his eastern European gains by the Treaty of Karlowitz.

The Navy of the Religion was a willing and vigorous participant in the anti-Turkish campaigns. Between 1684 and 1694, in alliance with the Papal States and Venice, its galley fleet – including eight of the biggest and strongest afloat – chalked up a string of victories off the western Greek coast: Santa Maura, Preveza, Korone, Navarino, Castelnovo, Malvasia and Valona. Some of these were almost certainly the result of the Knights' experience and spirit. It was a war that was sometimes cold, but mostly hot, stretching intermittently over more than two centuries, a relentless struggle between Christian and Muslim over control of what was still the world's most important strategic and commercial body of water – and barely remarked on in most conventional European histories.

On Malta itself the Knights enjoyed a cachet that they would never again know. The island was in a perfect geographical position to benefit from the freeing up of large parts of the Mediterranean to western trade, and the Grand Masters made sure the world knew it. As the seventeenth century gave way to the eighteenth, Malta became the mandatory quarantine halt for all commercial vessels sailing between Africa and Europe. The Grand Master most associated with Malta's heightened prestige is the Portuguese Antonio Manoel de Vilhena (1722–1736), who ordered major architectural improvements to accompany his status as a sovereign prince. De Vilhena was the first to fully develop the concept of total sovereignty of the Knights of Saint John as no one now remembered the old vassalage to Sicily and the King of Spain; he was, in fact, the first Grand Master to authorize the portrayal of his head on the Maltese coinage. The Knights and associate classes enjoyed a lively cultural and social life, acting in plays and operas staged in Valletta's new and ornate theatre. True, the simmering conflicts with the Ottoman Empire and what was left of the Barbary pirates was far from over. Yet before long, tumultuous developments closer to home would soon turn the life of the Knights Hospitaller upside down yet again.

Chapter 14

The Price of Louis' Head

The Order in European power struggles – Barbary resurgence – upgrading the fleet – the French Revolution – paying to save Louis XVI – financial blows – the predicament of von Hompesch – Bonaparte steamrollers Malta – the final capitulation

If it appeared to some that the Knights Hospitaller were living in a Maltese microcosm of their own, where one's rank in the Order, and in society as a whole, was rigidly defined, where nobility was its own reward and where military and spiritual virtues were fused into a solid reality that admitted of no other, they would by and large have been right. The senior Knights were doubtless aware of the political currents and wars roiling the continent of Europe, but still they viewed the Muslims – in the form of the ever-present Ottoman Empire and the Barbary pirates – as the main menace, no doubt correctly from their point of view. As long as this was true, political and social discipline could not be relaxed. The kings and queens and princes and dukes of Europe may have been playing their political and religious power games, but except for the great Ottoman threat to Vienna in 1683, it may well have seemed to the Knights of Saint John that they were the only true defenders of the faith regularly staving off the Muslims on the front line, as it were. In fact, the eighteenth century was one of almost constant naval tussles with the Muslims in the Mediterranean.

An attempt by the Ottomans in 1714 to recover their European losses after the Treaty of Karlowitz led to another showdown with Venice, and for some months it looked as if the Turks would succeed. But Prince Eugene Habsburg defeated the Turks in Hungary and Serbia; the result was a truce in which the Turks gave up Belgrade, though the Venetians had to hand back their possessions in southern Greece to the sultan. Hospitaller ships were among those that joined the papal fleet in savaging the Ottoman Navy in that conflict, to all intents and purposes putting the seal on Turkish naval decline. The Ottoman Empire's concurrent problems with its Asian vassals was probably a factor in an unofficial truce between the Order and the Ottomans in 1723. Yet such a truce also suited the Hospitallers, as it freed them from the obligation to patrol the eastern Mediterranean so they could concentrate their energies closer to home against the Barbary pirates, whose power was again on the rise.

All the North African Muslim states were nominally vassals of the Ottoman sultan as inheritor of the old Arab caliphate, but by the early decades of the eighteenth century they had carved out considerable autonomy for themselves. The main Barbary centres were Algiers and Tripoli, where the Karamanli dynasty concentrated on building up a strong pirate naval power. Working in favour of the Barbary states was the waning of Spanish influence in southern Europe, and a corresponding decline in Spanish naval protection. This left the Knights of Malta as the main naval bulwark against the Barbary depredations.[1]

Even before the brief Venetian–Ottoman war of 1714–16, the need became apparent to modernize the Order's fleet. Until now the Venetians had provided most of the Christian galleys for Mediterranean campaigns, but with the mounting threat from Tripoli, some diversification would be necessary. Some of the older galleys were scrapped or sold off, leaving four, while four newer ships of the line were built, each armed with up to sixty guns; a fifth was added by capture. The new fleet was ready for an attempt by Castel de Saint-Pierre in 1705 to clear the Mediterranean of the pirates once and for all. Unfortunately, his hope of getting the help of European navies backfired – the nations of Europe were too busy with their own rivalries – and the grand strategy failed to launch.

Most European navies, it is fair to say, had made their unspoken accommodations with the Karamanlis of Tripoli, chiefly through their governments' paying protection money. It was probably cheaper than fighting, and besides, countries such as England, France and Spain, not to mention the splinter states in Italy, had sea trade networks to protect, and covert money in the right places more often than not did the job. The Knights of Saint John, on the other hand, had no such national structure and economic diplomacy to fall back on; all they had was their tiny inhospitable island and the eight-pointed cross and an unswerving dedication to maintaining the Christian faith in a sea bounded to the south and east by infidels. And there was no lack of Knights able and willing to carry out this often thankless and unsung task. In 1710 Joseph de Langon died while capturing a large galley from the pirates, renamed the *Soleil d'Or* (Golden Sun). But it wasn't until 1723, when Malta and the Ottoman Empire agreed to bury the hatchet, that the Navy of the Religion cast off its subordinate status to Venice and began to operate independently, the first time it was fully able to do so since the glory years of Rhodes.

Malta found itself with arguably the strongest navy in the western Mediterranean, outgunning those of its nearest neighbours Sardinia, Naples and the Papal States. The Knights' naval expertise was recognized far beyond the shores of Malta; if the abovementioned Italian states and others had not sent promising officers to Malta for training, they 'would have had no officer corps worth looking at without the Knights of Saint John'.[2] Only the Knights, it seemed, knew the secrets of tackling the Barbary pirates in their own waters. It is now acknowledged that the skill and persistence of the Navy of the Religion was the key to preventing the Tripolitanian pirates from parlaying their pirate fleet into what otherwise would have become a force fully the size of the fleets of England and France. One of the first telling blows was struck by Jacques François de Chambray, the captain of the fifty-two-gun *Saint-Vincent*. On his first command in 1723 he came upon a strong Tripolitanian force off Pantelleria; undaunted, his 300-man crew boarded the flagship of the Muslim vice admiral after a hard fight. It was merely the start of a fighting career for de Chambray lasting a quarter of a century; in the 1740s, as commander of the Maltese Navy, he built it to a peak of strength and power, with four 60-gun galleons and four galleys. He retired in 1749, but may not have lived to see the accommodation between the Knights and Ali Karamanli of Tripoli that ended the long-running naval feud with the Barbary pirates.

This truce may have restored peace in the central Mediterranean, but it gave the Knights rather less to do. The Navy of the Religion was gradually pared down; the boom and flame of set sea battles was replaced by the cannonading of North African ports, most often in conjunction with a major European navy. This was the scenario in 1770 when the Order helped the French bombard Tunis. The Hospitallers also fired their cannon at Algiers – the sole remaining corsair base after the pact with Tripoli – in 1772, 1775, 1783 and 1784 as part of a continuing Spanish offensive. In the last-named year a Maltese squadron remained on patrol off Algiers to prepare to join another planned Spanish attack. Instead, Madrid opted to make a deal with the Algerians – a bad move as the Algerian pirates were free to make themselves a nuisance for another half-century. Moreover, Tunis and Tripoli were reviving their old bellicosity. Therefore the Knights resumed their *corsi*, capturing eight corsair vessels between 1793 and 1798. In 1797 alone Valletta licensed nine privateers. But the following year, just as it seemed that the Order of Saint John was needed more than ever, a blow fell from a most unexpected quarter.

In 1789, during the rule of Grand Master Emmanuel de Rohan-Polduc, while telling blows were being administered to the North African corsair fleets, the Hospitallers' original ethnic homeland of France erupted in social revolt. The French Revolution should not have come as surprise to many in Europe, especially the Knights of Saint John, whose French component was surely aware of what was going on in France. Some may well have sympathized with the purported idealistic aims of the insurrectionists that appeared to be in line with Christian principles. For example, Pierre-André de Suffren de Saint-Tropez, a Knight of the Order, served with the French Navy in aid of the rebels in the American War of Independence. Louis XVI himself had indicated a willingness to consider the demands for more liberty and democracy, especially after the storming of the Bastille in Paris. However, any initial Hospitaller sympathy for the French revolutionists must have evaporated when in November 1789 the rebel-dominated National Assembly in Paris confiscated all church property in France to pay off a huge national debt. French Catholic clergy were compelled to swear allegiance to the new civil constitution or be de-frocked; monks and nuns were told to find other jobs.

It seemed wise to Grand Master de Rohan-Polduc at this stage to try and divorce the Order from any connection with the French nobility, and thus it was at this time that the term 'Sovereign Order of Malta' came into use to stress the independence of the Maltese establishment. If the move was designed to mislead or mollify the French revolutionists, it didn't work. A rather large part of the Order's revenues at that stage derived from tithes and feudal dues paid by the French upper classes. But in August 1789 all those payments had been abolished, triggering a most serious financial problem. In France a new constitution clipping the prerogatives of Louis XVI was promulgated in 1791. The Order had maintained a precarious diplomatic representation in Paris under Chevalier d'Estourmel. This man lent Louis 12,000 francs of the Hospitallers' money (about £500 at the time) to help the king escape to Varennes, from where he hoped to lead royalist forces back to Paris and quash the revolution. D'Estourmel almost certainly acted with the Grand Master's approval. Louis' escape backfired; he and his family were apprehended at Varennes and imprisoned. De Rohan-Polduc suffered a stroke on hearing the news; his right side was paralysed and he remained an invalid for the remaining six years of his life, incapacitated just when the Order was coming under the most serious threat since the siege of Malta.

Worse was to come. The initial moderate French revolutionists were soon elbowed aside by the radical fire-eaters who hauled Louis XVI to the guillotine in January 1793. Before his execution the king had been held in Hospitaller-owned property, his Swiss Guard having been massacred. D'Estourmel protested at what he called a violation of the Order's sovereign status; the republican regime's response was to seize all £5m worth of the Order's properties in France, eliminating in one stroke three-fifths of all Hospitaller revenues from the continent of Europe.[3] The already incapacitated de Rohan-Polduc found himself in the position of literally having to sell the family silver, but shied away from more aggressive cost-cutting measures. He sold off all his personal jewellery, asking only that he be allowed 'one scudo a day for the expenses of my table' and the rest of his money to go 'to my distressed brethren'.[4] To his credit he did not touch the grain subsidy which ensured the Maltese poor a daily supply of bread; the downside, however, was that the Order's sovereign debt began to skyrocket. D'Estourmel, impoverished by the revolutionists' confiscations, had to leave Paris by the end of 1792, but not before he had used some of what little money he had left by helping some dispossessed Hospitaller nuns. It was a steep (but some might say healthy) come-down from the Knights' recent life of relative luxury.

The beheading of Louis XVI confirmed the Order's utter hostility to what the French Revolution had wrought. De Rohan-Polduc maintained a French royal envoy in Valletta, refusing to recognize the Paris regime. He believed he had a chance to strike back in August 1793 when French royalists with British support seized the town of Toulon on the Mediterranean coast. De Rohan-Polduc offered to help with 600 Knights and the Navy, but the British turned him down, probably because they discounted the Knights of Saint John as a credible force. The Grand Master himself was too ill to press the issue; all he could do in the French royalist cause was close Valletta to French ships when Naples declared war on the French republic. Historians of the Order fault Loras, the Marshal, for not initiating more vigorous measures.

At any rate, the French regime prevailed against European efforts to unseat it. De Rohan-Polduc withheld support from the French counter-revolutionaries as leading nowhere. However, one Knight, Chevalier de Thuisy, proposed a pact with Britain that would open Valletta to the Royal Navy in return for a Maltese force to help garrison Corsica, a new British possession. The plan for some reason did not appeal to de Rohan-Polduc, who caved in to the other side and accepted a French republican envoy. At the end of 1796 there was a single ray of hope from a totally unexpected source: Orthodox Russia. The new tsar, Paul I, had never hidden his admiration of the Catholic Knights of Saint John, and at his accession he had showered money on the Priory of Poland, whose responsions in turn definitely helped the finances of the headquarters in Malta. But that was the only bright spot in a worsening political landscape: Spanish pressure forced the British out of Corsica and a rising young French artillery officer by the name of Napoleon Bonaparte, now in charge of the French republic's army, conquered Venice and its strong fleet with which he seized the Ionian islands of Greece and thrust French power decisively into the Mediterranean. At this unhappy juncture, Grand Master de Rohan-Polduc passed away.

The Knights this time were hard put to find a worthy successor. A Neapolitan Knight named Frisari was considered and rejected out of fear that Naples might dominate the Order. The French, as members of a nation at war, had effectively put themselves out of the running. Eyes then turned to a nation that so far had not had a single Grand Master to its credit – Germany. For centuries this nation had been on the fringe of the Order, so to speak, with the Teutonic Knights absorbing the energies of its young nobles with a taste for adventure. The Holy Roman Empire was a mere shadow of its grand former self, prompting the poet Johann Wolfgang von Goethe to wonder in verse: 'The dear old Holy Roman Realm, how does it hold together …?'[5] Though still theoretically on the books, the Empire had fragmented into more than 300 more or less independent polities. The strongest of these was the Electorate of Brandenburg, out of whose Hohenzollern family came the strong-willed Frederick William I (1713–1740) who helped forge the kingdom of Prussia. It seemed at the time that 'destiny had selected the Hohenzollern dynasty to retrieve Germany from disintegration'.[6] The feeling was borne out by Frederick William's son and successor, Frederick II, known as the Great. This monarch did more than anyone else to build Prussia into a formidable European power, and at his death in 1786 had lent much-needed prestige to the neglected German Tongue among the Knights of Saint John.

In 1797 Napoleon Bonaparte had imposed France's will on Austria and the Italian states by the Treaty of Campo Formio. The revolutionary regime in Paris had softened its previous excesses, and there were hopes even that the monarchy might be restored. The late de Rohan-Polduc's decision to recognize the French Republic, it seemed, had turned out to be the only feasible one. But the Knights' position never ceased to be precarious, and it was felt that a German might revive the Order's flagging morale by symbolizing a new direction. The only available candidate for Grand Master was a rather vacuous and none-too-honest diplomat who had joined the Order the easy way – through money and influence rather than the more rigorous process of fighting and public service. Ferdinand von Hompesch zu Bolheim has been described by a leading Hospitaller historian as 'empty-headed, with a shrewd sense of whom it was valuable to cultivate, much attached to pomps and ceremonies, ingratiating and spineless'.[7] In short, a typical political lackey. Von Hompesch had previously served as Holy Roman Emperor Joseph II's envoy to Valletta, earning several German Commanderies. From this position he spent a great deal of other people's money, running up enormous debts, which by 1796 had earned him a Grand Cross. And since von Hompesch was the only German Grand Cross living in Valletta, he was duly elected the seventy-first Grand Master of the Order of Hospitallers.

His unimpressive eleven-month record is far from flattering. First, despite his exalted status and double-barrelled Teutonic name, he had no military experience to speak of, certainly nothing connected with service in the Order. He was not a soldier but a diplomat, and an inadequate one at that. Von Hompesch, though canny enough to cultivate a certain popularity among the Maltese, had little idea of how to defend Malta. French ambitions in the Mediterranean had become clear by Bonaparte's seizure of the Ionian Islands; the whole sea, in fact, was about to become a battleground between France and its foes, led by Britain. Malta's strategic position, it was clear, would engulf it in any regional conflict. France, Britain and even Naples could swallow the island in one gulp. Von Hompesch made efforts to strengthen the defences of Valletta, but they were late and half-hearted. Moreover, Napoleon Bonaparte was not about to let Malta go to his enemies. In the spring of 1797 he had argued strongly for its seizure, but was heeded only six months later. The possession of Malta, he claimed, would help the French 'become masters of the whole Mediterranean'.

Bonaparte planned the move craftily. At the time he was preparing for his Egyptian campaign, and sent an agent masquerading as a scientific adviser to Malta to secretly contact several, mainly French, Knights believed to be sympathetic to the French Republic and dissatisfied with von Hompesch's rule. The agent reported that he found fifteen Knights with French republican sympathies, of whom just three could be expected to actively work with the French conquest – though these three were high officials in the Order's administration. In all fairness, however, it must be said that the great majority of the approximately 300 Knights of Malta were loyal to the

Grand Master and as determined to fight an invader as they had been when Suleyman the Magnificent's fleet had loomed over the horizon more than two centuries before. However, the republican sympathizers in the Order included Louis-Ovide Doublet, who had served as de Rohan-Polduc's secretary for French affairs and is believed to have advised the French on how to proceed. In March 1798 a seventeen-ship fleet under Admiral Brueys made a show of strength off the Maltese coast. The following month the French Directory, the ruling body in Paris, ordered Bonaparte to seize Malta on his way to Egypt. The final act in the 700-year active military history of the Hospitallers was about to be played.

Bonaparte's invasion almost, but not quite, caught the Maltese by surprise. An alert German diplomat, who had served as a Knight in Malta, got wind of the impending invasion and sent a hasty message to von Hompesch.

> You will certainly be attacked [the letter read]. Take all measures to defend yourself suitably. [We] know that the fortress of Malta is impregnable, or at least in condition to resist for three months … If you yield without having defended yourself, you will be dishonoured in the eyes of all Europe.[8]

Von Hompesch read the letter on 4 June but shied away from realizing its import. All he could seem to do was urge his Knights to 'pray to God that we shall not be attacked'. Two days later, advance vessels of Bonaparte's French fleet were sighted off Malta.

Von Hompesch was no soldier, and was honest enough to admit it. But others, who were soldiers, seemed to be afflicted by a sudden lack of fighting spirit. Perhaps it was because the Maltese Navy could field just three ships against Bonaparte, perhaps a creeping defeatism was seeping through the Order, but Grand Marshal Loras could only bring himself to organize a weak demonstration against the French fleet. By now, too, many French Knights had openly gone over to the side of the French Republic and the man who seemed a winner – Napoleon Bonaparte. The Order's Financial Secretary (the former office of Treasurer), Jean-Baptiste Bosredon-Ransijeat, the man who held the purse-strings, was one of the three highly-placed conspirators whom the French agent had located and presumably cultivated. What was perhaps worse, the Spanish Knights had been ordered to stay out of the fray, as France and Spain had recently inked an alliance. Many of the 7,000 or so auxiliary Maltese troops were sunk in low morale. Some of them tried to murder one Chevalier Anthony O'Hara in the street; he was rescued, in fact, by the otherwise inactive Spaniards, 'rendering the only service given by their nation in the siege'.[9]

As Bonaparte's fleet of at least 500 ships carrying 29,000 men on their way to Egypt loomed before Malta, the defenders had some hope that their well-repaired fortifications bristling with 1,400 cannon might do some damage. The French proceeded cautiously. While Bonaparte was fancying himself a latter-day Alexander the Great 'on the road to Asia, perched on an elephant, a turban on my head',[10] on 7 June General Desaix sent a request for eighty ships to be allowed to take on water in Valletta; the Order's reply two days later was that the French could do so, though with just four ships at a time – a rule that had been in force for many years and applying to all navies. Bonaparte found an excuse now to abandon all pretences and declare Valletta an enemy city, which he obviously had intended all along. In the city Bosredon-Ransijeat realized he had to put his pro-French money where his mouth was; claiming that his vows obliged him to make war only on the Turks (and by implication on no one else), he resigned and was locked in a cell in Fort Sant'Angelo.

The French enjoyed a strong advantage from the start. In the morning of 10 June they focused a three-pronged attack on the bays of Saint Paul and Saint Julian, and the island of Gozo. The strategy of the defenders was unsound. They frittered away their forces instead of concentrating them at a few highly-defensible points such as Floriana and Cotonera. Gozo and Fort Rohan were ably defended, but sheer French numbers overcame them. At Saint Julian Bay the fight was at first more balanced: three Hospitaller ships sank a French landing craft, but General Vaubois, the French commander in the sector, forced back the defenders into Valletta. A surprise Maltese attack on the French on Floriana turned into a French ambush in which the Maltese lost their standard. There was plenty of Hospitaller courage to be found on that day. The octogenarian Bailli de Tigné had himself carried to the ramparts where he could feel he was part of the action; Giovanni Tommasi, an Italian Knight, led the fanatic defence of the Naxxar line with 400 green militiamen against a whole French division. But these were mere flashes in the pan. After barely a day of fighting the issue had been decided. Notabile surrendered, French guns were trained on Fort Tigné and Valletta was surrounded. Some Knights argued that there was still time for a robust resistance centring on Fort Tigné, but von Hompesch was confused. Around midnight several Knights went to the Grand Master to suggest a surrender. One of them, the Portuguese Carvalho Pinto, told von Hompesch to his face that he deserved to be hanged for his indecision.

The common soldiers of Malta now stepped in to do what their Grand Master could not. Throughout the previous weeks no one quite knew where the French Knights stood. French agents on Malta spread rumours intensifying the uncertainty. Early on 11 June the troops defending Cotonera mutinied, murdering two of their Knights. At Senglea seventeen Knights, faced with the wholesale desertion of their men, personally carried powder to their guns. But morale at the top had gone. Grand Marshal Loras pleaded with von Hompesch, even going down on his knees, to hold out; Admiral Nelson's British fleet, he said, was sailing south of France and in ten or so days would be nearing Malta. It was true that Nelson was proceeding with all speed to help the Maltese, though it is unclear just how much Loras knew. Ironically, what no one in Valletta did know was that Bonaparte planned to break off the siege of Malta if it threatened to derail the bigger objective of Egypt. Yet there was a general justified feeling in Valletta that Nelson would soon be along to help. So why did von Hompesch not consider this?

Various answers have been proposed. One Knight, the Bailli de la Tour du Pin Montauban, who had valiantly defended Senglea, hinted darkly that masonic lodges in Germany, jealous of the Hospitallers' fame, plotted to destroy them through their man von Hompesch. But that can never be proven, and indeed strains credulity. Most likely is that von Hompesch, an unwarlike man, came to the common-sense conclusion that the French would sooner or later take Malta and that military defence would be futile. Nonetheless, he seems to have had no intention of giving up his high office and apparently believed that he could come to some arrangement with Bonaparte to keep the Order where it was. He was, as one Hospitaller scholar admits, 'a man who had spent his life toadying to the powerful to the detriment of his Order'.[11] Thus on 11 June at 6.00 pm the head of the Spanish Tongue, Don Felipe de Amat, the Neapolitan Frisari who had once been in the running for Grand Master, and Bosredon-Ransijeat (the darling of the French) negotiated a ceasefire on board Bonaparte's flagship, *L'Orient*. Rough seas delayed their boarding the vessel, and when they did, de Amat did most of the talking. The others were too seasick to effectively take part in the deliberations which – and here the Spaniards must take most of the responsibility – surrendered Malta to the French.

Even von Hompesch was appalled at the French terms when he read them, but by now of course it was much too late to do anything. The terms included pensions for the French Knights only and a German principality for von Hompesch. Still, he vacillated, apparently unable to decide. La Tour du Pin chided him for his indecision, at which the Grand Master smiled wanly, replying, 'What would you do? All is lost.' The Knight bitterly agreed that all was lost, and 'honour above all'. That same day Bonaparte stepped off the *L'Orient* to make his triumphal walk into Valletta. His army's chief engineer, accompanying him, remarked on the robustness of the city's massive fortifications to the effect that 'it was well that someone was within to open the gates for us'. When Bonaparte returned to his ship, it was with all the Hospitaller treasures seized from the Grand Palace and the churches, and the silverware and medical instruments of the Hospital. He also took with him about fifty French Knights – including the sympathizers who had opened the door to Bonaparte – who had signed on for his Egyptian campaign and sailed on 19 June. These earned the contempt of the rest, expressed by Chevalier de Boisgelin: 'No situation, however desperate, can ever justify the commission of a dishonourable act.'[12] Left behind was a 3,000-man garrison under General Vaubois and a puppet government under Bosredon-Ransijeat. Von Hompesch was banished from Malta, and on that discouraging note the 700-year military history of the Knights Hospitaller was to all intents and purposes over.

Chapter 15

Swords into Ploughshares

Our Lady of Philermos – Russian interlude – the Sicilian years – Napoleon seizes Malta – new politics in Europe – a brief Greek dream – the era of the Lieutenants – settling in Rome – new life for the European Priories

O ne of the few precious objects that von Hompesch was allowed to take with him into exile was the icon of Our Lady of Philermos, and at this point it would be useful to devote some space to what at first glance might not fit into a military history but which played a profound, if unseen, role in the whole history of the Knights Hospitaller. The icon had been in the Order's possession for nearly 500 years, since it was discovered in a Greek Orthodox monastery in Rhodes at about the time the Knights moved there from Cyprus. Many devout Greeks believed it was painted by the Evangelist Luke himself, and that it was spirited away to Rhodes from Constantinople in the eighth century to escape the ban on icons imposed by Byzantine Emperor Leo I. The legend found plenty of believers among the Catholic Knights as well, and during the siege of Rhodes of 1480 we find the icon – an oblique face of the Virgin Mary painted in tempera on wood – playing a decisive part in the defence, as Grand Master Pierre d'Aubusson was firmly convinced that the icon's own supernatural powers helped repel the Turks; there were Knights who swore that Our Lady had been at the forefront of the defences along with John the Baptist.[1]

D'Aubusson in gratitude housed the icon in two purpose-built chapels at the Church of Saint Mark in Rhodes. During the second and final siege in 1522 the church was razed but somehow Our Lady of Philermos survived intact in the rubble. She went with the defeated Knights as they sailed away from Rhodes for the last time, finding a temporary home in the church of Saints Faustino and Giovina at Viterbo. In Malta the icon graced the church of Saint Lawrence in the Birgu, and when Valletta was built it was moved to the co-cathedral of Saint John. By then Our Lady of Philermos had been adorned with gold leaf and precious stones, leaving just her face uncovered.

Bonaparte made sure he included the coruscation in his booty, leaving von Hompesch with the bare portrait as it had been originally. Possibly because of the icon's Orthodox origin and associations, in 1798 it ended up in the only safe place the ejected Knights could think of – the court of Tsar Paul I of Russia, who now opened a rather curious chapter in Hospitaller history.

Russia seemed a natural destination for many out-of-work French Knights: it was a Christian power which, even though of the Eastern Orthodox persuasion, was closer to the idea of Catholic nobility than most western Protestant churches were. About fifty Knights chose to place themselves under the protection of the Tsar and the Russian Priory; the rest, it seems, dispersed themselves around Europe and the Mediterranean, some reduced to beggary. On 26 August 1798, two months after the ejection from Malta, the Russian Priory, closely followed by the German, claimed to have deposed von Hompesch from the post of Grand Master. The move lacked validity, as it had not been enacted by a Grand Chapter according to the rules. Nonetheless, after a three-month interregnum the Russian Priory elected Tsar Paul I – who, it must be admitted, had always had a high respect for the Hospitaller Order – as *de facto* Grand Master of the Order, as von Hompesch was still alive and hence *de jure* the holder of the office.

The elevation of a Russian tsar to lead the Order was technically absurd. Besides being a monarch of the Orthodox faith, he could never take any of the classic vows of poverty, chastity and obedience. Paul I soon displayed an authoritarian streak that affronted many Knights, especially German ones. He threatened to invade Bavaria with 50,000 men, intimidating the German opposition. At this, the papacy finally sat up; Pope Pius VI was most unhappy at the Russian usurpation of the Order of Saint John, and said so, but the tsar brushed the complaint aside, booting the papal nuncio out of Saint Petersburg for good measure. Napoleon Bonaparte, meanwhile, had messed up his Egyptian adventure, his fleet shattered by Lord Horatio Nelson in the Battle of the Nile. 'I allowed my imagination to interfere with my practice,' he declared emptily, abandoning his soldiers, and pledged not 'to let it run away with my judgement again'.[2] That said, he fled back to France to become the country's master in a *coup d'état*. Most remaining French Knights thus preferred to throw in their lot with the tsar, however less than ideal a leader he might be. Naples and Portugal soon followed suit, with only four Spanish Priories holding out against Russian control. In June 1799 von Hompesch, three years before his death, yielded to pressure by his German compatriots and abdicated.

Tsar Paul I, it is safe to say, was one of the worst occupants of the office of Grand Master. He appeared to have little notion of its essential meaning or *gravitas*. He was even in the habit of wearing his Grand Master's robe to call on his mistresses. In Malta, meanwhile, seven weeks of French repression and persecution of religion had triggered a popular revolt that holed up the French in Valletta, while the Maltese people received occasional help from Britain and Naples. The tsar could quite easily – and legitimately – have seized Malta for Russia at this stage, and a Russian fleet did make a demonstration in the Mediterranean. Britain would not have minded Russia taking over Malta – anyone but the French – but Nelson, London's enforcer in the Mediterranean, had other ideas. With the help of the Neapolitans he kept the Russian fleet away from the island. In 1800 Bonaparte made diplomatic overtures to Paul, which decided Nelson to forcibly seize Valletta and drive out the French. Paul complained that the island was legally his while plotting to seize it with French aid. By now, however, the tsar had become an unbalanced, even frightening figure, hugely unpopular at home and terrified for his life. The terror proved justified on 23 March 1801 when four Knights of Saint John in his entourage joined a band of conspirators to strangle him.

Tsar Alexander I, Paul's son and successor, realizing the bizarreness of Russia's control of the Order, appointed the Bailli Soltykov as interim Lieutenant pending a new election for a Grand Master. Alexander was realistic enough to perceive that the Knights deserved to get Malta back, as long as no British or French were among them. This was a condition of the Treaty of Amiens, which temporarily halted hostilities between Britain and France. It may have been that the idealistic and dreamy tsar wished to somehow 'purify' the Order of its chief warring elements. To ease the election of a new Grand Master, the Russian Priory waived its right to convene a Chapter General and surprisingly asked Pope Pius VII to do the honours. There followed a confused jostling for influence among Spain (four of whose Priories formally broke away), France, Russia and Bavaria; Bonaparte pushed his own candidate, the Italian Knight Bartolomeo Ruspoli who, however, declined the nomination. Months of delay and hesitation followed, with Pius VII unsure of what to do, until February 1803, when another Italian Knight who had fought bravely in the defence of Malta, Giovanni Tommasi, was elected Grand Master. Tommasi, living in Messina in Sicily, at once demanded that the Knights retrieve Malta as promised by the Treaty of Amiens.

The grim truth was, however, that at the dawn of the nineteenth century the Knights of Saint John had shrunk to international irrelevance. The erratic stewardship of Tsar Paul I had severely dented their reputation. Malta itself was just one of several bones of contention between Britain and France, prized by both for its strategic position. The British were determined to keep the island out of Napoleon Bonaparte's hands, but that did not mean the British were any more favourable to the Knights than the French were. When Tommasi staked his claim to return to Valletta the British coolly pointed out to him that the four palaces of the Order in Valletta were badly run down and hence not immediately habitable and that he was better off in Messina. Any remote hopes of returning to Valletta were definitely shelved in 1803, when Anglo-French hostilities resumed. No one, it was clear, any longer took the Hospitaller Order seriously as a political force.

Confined to Sicily, Grand Master Tommasi had his appointment ratified by a Chapter General and had the integrity to turn down a generous pension from Napoleon who had hoped to neutralize him with money. Tommasi, fearing that Napoleon might send a French fleet to Messina, slipped down the coast to Catania to live in luxury till his death in 1805. While Guevara Suardo was confirmed as Lieutenant the Chapter General elected Giuseppe Caracciolo dei Marchesi di Sant'Erano as Grand Master. But here they came up against the opposition of Pius VII. The reason was pure balance-of-power politics. Caracciolo, as a Neapolitan, would have been expected to promote the interests of the Kingdom of Naples, hence of its ally Britain, and this the pope did not want. Moreover, Pius was in the process of a strong diplomatic rapprochement with France that would give Napoleon a large chunk of central Italy. Oddly enough, the only great power leader to recognize Caracciolo was Tsar Alexander I, who approved a pension for him from the Russian Priory.

But Pius' veto was decisive, and thus Guevara Suardo, the Lieutenant, continued as effective head of the Order. There followed a sad period of disorganization and humiliation without a Grand Master to provide some sort of leadership, if only symbolic. On 2 December 1804 Bonaparte had crowned himself 'Emperor of the French', snatching the crown from a startled pope who was expecting to do the honours himself. Within five years the whole northern half of Italy was his, with Rome and the papacy itself reduced to French vassalage. Small wonder, then, that Suardo's attempt to move the Hospitaller headquarters to Rome was firmly stymied; the contents of the Treasury, transferred to Palermo, were confiscated by the Roman puppet administration and never returned. Britain finally took over Malta as a permanent possession in 1806, in one of several complex deals with France, as a southern buffer against Napoleon's relentless expansionism.

But this was not necessarily good news for the Order, the idea of which, it now seems, had fallen out of fashion everywhere. The European Priories, if not already dissolved or merged with other bodies, were shrivelling. In an age of ebullient nationalism, the very idea of knightly orders, of fighting monks, of crosses on surcoats and standards, seemed hopelessly mediaeval. The modern age was fast sweeping away all remnants of feudalism, however benign and honourable. Lord William Bentinck, a British general who was envoy to the Sicilian court at Palermo, saw himself as a missionary of sorts who would bring the blessings of British democracy to benighted southern Italy. Unsurprisingly he considered the Knights of Saint John useless and wanted to abolish them. Bentinck actually did manage to give the Sicilians a constitution in 1812, which lasted just four years until Sicily was reabsorbed into the Kingdom of Naples. But before he could turn his attention to the Knights, he was recalled to London. Nonetheless, Hospitaller money was regularly filched for the benefits of governments in London and for nine years Suardo, as Lieutenant, could do little except sadly witness the decline until his death in Catania. Then Caracciolo made another bid for Grand Master, but a perceived arrogance of his attitude alienated the majority of Knights who approved Andrea di Giovanni, a 72-year-old Sicilian, as new Lieutenant.

Napoleon Bonaparte's tumultuous career came to an inglorious end on the battlefield of Waterloo in June 1815. His elimination was the cue for the great powers of Europe to radically reorganize the continent to make sure that no one could disrupt the peace on such a scale again. But Europe had changed radically.

> For twenty-five years [writes an American authority on European history] Europe had been convulsed by war and social ferment, many landmarks of the old regime had been swept away, thrones had toppled, church lands had been secularized, nobles had lost their estates while hitherto unprivileged commoners climbed to power and office.[3]

Among the losers in this new state of affairs were the Knights Hospitaller. And at first they adjusted to it quite badly, even though conservative forces across Europe quickly rallied to provide a stable golden age that many applauded after the turmoil of the Napoleonic Wars. British, Austrian, Russian and Prussian diplomats dominated the 1815 Vienna Congress, as a result of which 'kings crept out again to feel the sun' as well as many nobles and churchmen. But the Knights of Saint John, though nominally participants in the Congress, could not make much of an impression there. Prince Camille de Rohan, the Prior of Aquitaine, had formed the French Tongues into a unified commission with the cautious support of France's new King Louis XVIII; the Spanish branches of the Order did likewise. But di Giovanni, the Lieutenant, failed to ally himself with these initiatives; as an Italian, he was too distrustful of the French and hated to see them regaining prominence within the Order. This division at a crucial moment deprived the Knights of any chance they may have had of restoring some of their sovereignty, even though Malta now was firmly in British hands and hence secure from war and unrest.

The fact that there was still no Grand Master in office (though Caracciolo never ceased to claim it) did much to undermine the Order's image and power. This was the fault primarily of Pope Pius VII, who is suspected by Hospitaller historians of planning to weaken the Order so much as to turn it into a direct instrument of the Papacy.[4] The lack of a Grand Master also encouraged centrifugal tendencies among the various Tongues, which gravitated towards their own national centres. While the headquarters remained at Catania the Italians naturally took over all the senior posts from the Lieutenancy on down – naturally with the pope's blessings. Pius VII wanted to control, not abolish, the Order and thus made sure that the Lieutenancy kept up the legal fiction of being a sovereign entity. The Austrian architect of the new European conservative order, Prince von Metternich, offered the Hospitallers Elba – the place of Napoleon's first exile – but on condition, that they submit themselves to the Habsburgs. The offer was politely rejected; the Knights would be independent or not at all.

It was in France, ironically, that the Order gained what seemed like a new lease on life. The restored monarchy of Louis XVIII approved pensions for surviving French Knights thanks to the efforts of Lasteyrie de Saillant, the Commission head. The French state was in possession of large tracts of woodland that had once belonged to the Order and promised to give the land back if the Hospitallers could find a new home (but not in France!). Elba was rejected for reasons we have just mentioned. There was some hope that Metternich's series of international congresses might solve the problem, but it soon became clear that the Austrian diplomatic mastermind, too, simply wanted the Knights of Saint John to be his puppets. In 1821 Metternich eased out the ineffectual di Giovanni and replaced him as Lieutenant (still no mention of a Grand Master!) with the 'calamitous' Austrian-Italian Antonio

Busca.[5] This man's attempt to push the French Knights out of the picture brought the Hospitallers briefly up against their old foe, the Ottoman Turks.

In the early nineteenth century, encouraged by first the American and then the French revolutions, the eastern and southern European peoples ruled by the Ottomans began to be restive. The first to openly revolt against the Turks were the Greeks, who were determined to revive their ancient glories after four centuries of deadening Turkish rule. They were also Orthodox Christians, adding to the crusade-like fervour of the uprising that started in March 1821. This was most unpalatable to Metternich and the conservative European powers that wanted to prop up the aging Ottoman Empire in the interests of political stability. Only the French were officially sympathetic to the Greeks, and a Greek rebel delegation called on Busca in 1822 to see if the Knights Hospitaller could add some military clout to this renewal of the old struggle against Christ's foes. Busca was embarrassed, though probably more by the poverty of his headquarters in Catania rather than for any other reason, and referred the Greeks to the French Commission. The Commission head, Marquis de Sainte-Croix-Molay, seized the opportunity, as dangling before him was the heady vision that the Order might one day get back its old home of romantic memory – Rhodes! Or if not that, any other of the Greek islands studded like jewels in the blue Aegean Sea.

In great secrecy, as Metternich and most of the rest of official Europe backed the Turks, in June 1823 the Order's French Commission and the Greek insurrectionists signed a pact for mutual military aid. In return for aiding the Greek cause and subsidizing a Greek rebel fleet, the Knights would receive Rhodes and several adjacent islands. But the Order had not reckoned on another power that in the early nineteenth century had risen to rival the importance of states and governments – the power of the press. It wasn't long before details of the scheme were leaked to newspapers across Europe; an embarrassed French government had to deny involvement in the pact and the money for a Greek naval force never materialized. Busca in Catania saw his chance to get rid of the meddlesome French Commission, whose members – despite statements of contrition by Sainte-Croix-Molay – were expelled from the Order of Saint John. The French brother-knights were finished. The Greeks won their independence in 1829 after an eight-year struggle – aided finally by Britain, France and Russia – and another member was added to the European family of free nations. But since the Order had technically failed to bring its forces to the military aid of the Greeks as per the agreement of 1823, and was discredited into the bargain, the Knights never did get back Rhodes.

The next ten years were sad ones for the Knights of Malta. Busca proved unable to stem the gradual disintegration of the Priories. The Spanish ones, for example, reverted to the control of the Spanish throne until confiscated in 1841, closely followed by that of Portugal. Most of the Italian Priories suffered similar fates except that of Rome, which had been revived in 1816 (and was to prove more important that anyone then could imagine). In France what remained of the Order pinned some hopes on King Charles X when he sent an army against Algiers and the Knights imagined they could settle there to continue the fight against the Barbary pirates, who were still active (but would soon be suppressed for good). But in 1830 a popular revolt toppled Charles and with him the Hospitallers' influence in his court. And that, to all intents and purposes, was the end of the Order in France.

Busca, who meanwhile had transferred the Order's headquarters from Sicily to Ferrara and thus alienated the Sicilians and southern Italians, died in 1834. As a Lieutenant he had been an abject failure, devoted solely to 'preserving the monopoly of power which chance and papal favour had placed in [his] hands'. His twenty years of rule had nothing whatever to recommend it – 'no Chapter General was held to reunite the Order, no novitiate was found to perpetuate its religious life, no hospital was promoted to carry on its original duty.'[6] And of course, despite the dreams of regaining Rhodes or setting up a base in Algiers, no military activity of any kind was at all possible. Well might Henry Sire, a leading Hospitaller historian, lambaste the Busca regime as 'a wretched clique'.

The Barbary pirates were still active. Under Yusuf Karamanli Tripoli remained a troublesome pirates' nest. Most European navies kept their vessels safe by paying bribes. Even the new United States Navy in 1805 could make little headway, and President Thomas Jefferson had to pay a handsome ransom to the Karamanlis to free some captive American sailors. It was not until the 1830s that the Barbary menace was at last fully suppressed. As for the Order, just as its future appeared darker than ever, a helping hand came from Pope Gregory XVI. The new Grand Priory of Rome, set up in 1816, had occupied the old Maltese envoys' headquarters in central Rome, a large and handsome palazzo fronting Via Condotti within shouting distance of the Piazza di Spagna. It was to this refuge that the pope invited the new Lieutenant he had appointed (no elections now!), Carlo Candida, to relocate from Ferrara in 1834. Candida, an experienced Knight who had been a commander in the Navy of the Religion before the fall of Malta, was a singularly good papal choice. Gregory himself did more than almost any pontiff before him in breathing new life into the Order of Saint John in

Italy; the first task was to follow in the footsteps of the very first Jerusalem Hospitallers by setting up the Cento Preti (Hundred Priests) hospice at the Ponte Sisto on the banks of the Tiber.

There followed a mushrooming of Commanderies – thirty new ones in Italy alone in the thirty years after 1834 – and a corresponding enthusiasm in other countries. Pope Gregory XVI sought to restore the office of Grand Master, but as long as the Austrian Metternich dominated the continent's politics it would be a vain hope. Then in 1848 large parts of Europe were convulsed by a social and political revolt that in the end accomplished little except putting an end to the career of Metternich and placing Napoleon III, the nephew of Napoleon I, on the French throne. The new Napoleon cultivated the favour of the Catholic Church, but by now the Knights of Malta were no longer recognized in France. To make matters worse, the helpful Gregory XVI had recently died, to be replaced by Pope Pius IX who, though strong-minded and capable, spent most of his long pontificate huddling under the protection of France while Italian nationalists under Giuseppe Garibaldi unified Italy and marched into Rome in September 1870. For eight years the sullen pope preferred to remain a virtual prisoner in the Vatican rather than recognize the new Italian national state.

Pius IX proved to have precious little interest in the fate of the Order. But the composition of the Order itself underwent profound changes. Gone were the days of the warrior monks who after solemn vows dedicated themselves to fighting for the Cross, who formed a separate and exclusive noble club to express the highest ideals of spiritual service and military duty. The great majority of Order members now took such names as Knights of Justice or Knights of Honour and Devotion. There is reason to assume that these did not practise the rigour and exclusivity of the old brother-knights, hence the ease with which these distinctions sprang up. Yet it is indisputable that they did much to revive the ideal of service for Saint John. One Austrian Knight of Justice, Gottfried von Schröter, harked back to the days of the Blessed Gerard by journeying to Jerusalem – still under Ottoman control – to set up a hospice. But Jerusalem then, as before and after, was a sensitive spot. The Crimean War had just been fought over who would protect the Latin Church in the Holy Land, and Napoleon III vetoed Schröter's plan unless Paris could be in charge. The hospital was not founded until 1869, and then at Tantur between Jerusalem and Bethlehem, thanks to a joint German-Austrian initiative by the Order.

Following in Schröter's footsteps was a German Catholic noble named August von Haxthausen, also a Knight of Justice. But this was the mid-nineteenth century, when Prussia rose to prominence in German affairs, and Prussia was very solidly Protestant. Von Haxthausen caved before strong Prussian pressure to transform the German Priory into an arm of the Prussian state, so it was his deputy, the blind but quite strong-willed Count von Hönsbröch, who successfully resisted the pressure. Besides, as the Protestant Teutonic Knights had long been the dominant order in that part of Europe, the German Priory felt it had to confirm its Catholicism along more religious than military lines. In 1864 Schröter took the helm once more. The Priory's new charter reflected its idealism, binding the members to 'do everything possible to make their homes a mirror of simplicity and Christian living', to conduct themselves 'as obedient and faithful subjects of the holy Church', and most especially, to 'strive in every way to further the Church's spiritual and secular interests'.[7]

There was nothing here about taking up the sword to fight for the Cross. On the contrary, the pacifist nature of the Order's German branch is expressly defined. Yet the eagerness with which the ideal was taken up by some East Prussian knights under Prince Hohenlohe-Waldenburg-Schillingsfürst, in the heart of militarist Juncker country, points to something else: there are ways in which once can fight for one's country not with swords and guns but, for example, with bandages and medicines for the wounded and dying. The Red Cross had just been formed and was in its infancy; much of the task of relieving battlefield suffering devolved on the Knights of Malta in the two main European conflicts of that time: the 1866 Austro-Prussian War and the Franco-German War of 1870–71. In the latter war, thanks to the efforts of people like Schröter, the Order's medical corpsmen, nurses, field hospitals and chaplains cared for one-third of all German wounded. The example spread; in 1859 the Italian Knights set up a hospital for incurables in Naples, while ten years later the Order of Saint John was recognized as a sovereign entity at the second International Conference of the Red Cross.

There were also stirrings in Britain, where the Order had been abolished in 1540 after two English Knights, Thomas Dingley and Adrian Fortescue, had been beheaded for refusing to swear to Henry VIII's claim to church supremacy. Another Knight, David Gunston, had been hanged, drawn and quartered the following year. But the idea remained alive through later centuries, and when in the 1820s the French Knights cast about for a new homeland after the loss of Malta, they found willing helpers across the Channel. Denis O'Sullivan, an Irish Knight among the French, was instrumental in reviving an English Priory under Sir Robert Peat (probably an assumed name) in the reign of King George IV. Yet the main Order under

Busca could not quite bring itself to take the new English Priory seriously, probably because the Priory had become Protestant-oriented and apparently not intensely charitable enough. The English Catholics stayed apart; in 1858 the Catholic baronet Sir George Bowyer became a Knight of Malta, putting the Maltese Cross on the tunics of the Sisters of Mercy whose labours resulted in the Hospital of Saint John and Saint Elizabeth in Saint John's Wood, London. The British Association of the Knights of Malta took shape in 1876. On the Protestant side, Queen Victoria granted a royal charter to the Venerable Order of Saint John, while the heir to the throne (the future Edward VII) assumed the office of Grand Prior – in fact the prince sported an Order-type costume at a fancy-dress ball at Devonshire House in 1897. Today this order runs Britain's Saint John's Ambulance Service along Hospitaller lines but is not a part of the official Hospitaller Order based in Rome.

Chapter 16

Back to the Wars

The Corpo Militare – First World War – Grand Master Chigi – Second World War – the saga of Hospital Train No. 1 – the Order saves an air force – soldiers of charity: the Hospitallers today

In 1877 an Italian association of the Order, the Corpo Militare, was formed for the specific purpose of directing the Order's military medical services. Similar Spanish and French (now that the hostile Napoleon III was out of the way) associations along the same lines soon appeared. And it was most likely the new prestige earned by the Knights of Saint John in the mid-nineteenth century European wars – now not as soldiers but as carers – that influenced Pope Leo XIII to at long last restore the Grand Master's office in 1879 after a gap of seventy-four years during which it often seemed that the Order was about to be extinguished. (It may also have influenced the choice by the US Army of the Maltese Cross as the emblem of the Fifth Corps in the American Civil War.) The Lieutenant at the time, Giovanni Battista Ceschi a Santa Croce, was elevated to be the seventy-third Grand Master of the Order.

The Order's medical and hospital services did sterling work in the First World War, under the administration of Grand Master Galeazzo von Thun und Hohenstein. The Grand Priory of Bohemia and Austria, to mention the most important organization, mobilized eight hospital trains at the outbreak of war in August 1914 for the German and Austro-Hungarian armies. By the war's end the trains, and the fifty-nine surgeons, sixteen chaplains and 103 volunteer nurses manning them, had completed more than 1,000 journeys totalling some 800,000km to care for nearly 250,000 wounded.[1] In France the Order set up a sixty-bed field hospital at Verdun which, after suffering a severe bombardment, was relocated to Châlons-sur-Marne. The Italian Corpo Militare placed four hospital trains and a 350-bed hospital in Rome at the disposal of the Italian Army; the trains made more than 600 trips to the Austrian front, bringing back almost 150,000 casualties. At least one senior officer of that war was a professed Knight of the Order, such as Count Alfred von Schlieffen who thought up the Schlieffen Plan that was intended to outflank the French from the north and bring the Imperial German Army down onto Paris like a scythe. In Italy the Corpo Militare remains an integral part of that country's military today. Its few hundred uniformed members serve the Order of Malta in disaster relief and recovery operations.

When Adolf Hitler took power in Germany in 1933 his Nazi Party banned its members from belonging to the Order. Yet Lieutenant Colonel Klaus Stauffenberg, who attempted to kill Hitler in July 1944 and paid with his life for it, was a Knight of Malta, as were other officers. In Russia the Bolsheviks, of course, eradicated any trace of the Order, and that was largely the situation in eastern Europe until 1989.

The experience of the First World War had brought out the need to coordinate the work of the various European Priories. The outbreak of the Second World War found the Order in the hands of Grand Master Ludovico Chigi Albani della Rovere, elected in 1931 at the height of the Great Depression when the need for succouring the poor and disadvantaged was greater than ever. Chigi, a kindly, white-goateed figure with a Roman family pedigree stretching back to the Renaissance, specifically referred to the Blessed Gerard in a 1935 speech in which he said that 'a soldier of Christ ... has a duty to provide health services in peace and war'.[2] The first drama occurred in September 1939, when Hitler invaded Poland and the commandant of the Order's hospital in Warsaw, Mielewski Lipkowski, barely had time to cable the Rome headquarters before all communications were cut that his hospital was 'doing its duty to the wounded soldiers'.[3] The following year, when Italy invaded Greece and began sustaining heavy casualties on the Albanian front, the Order's Hospital Train No. 1 made a total of fourteen trips down to the heel of Italy to take on more than 4,000 sick and wounded shipped back from Albania.

After the Germans knocked Greece out of the war in 1941, Train No. 1 was sent to the Russian front, arriving there on 5 November to take on 224 Italian wounded and carry them to Florence. The trip out and back was fraught with problems. Besides the ever-present danger from the surrounding hostilities, stations, lines and platforms along the route were found to have been destroyed and had to be repaired before the train could continue; water required for drinking and locomotive steam often froze. The train also carried ten female Red Cross volunteers who stayed with the field hospitals in the fearful Russian winter. An Order chaplain serving on that train, Don Pirro Scavizzi, described his experiences:

It was moving to see the volunteers helping the wounded, carrying stretchers, doing the most delicate and humble tasks, always alert and smiling, ready to grant every request even if they had spent more than one night sleepless in their duties or had to jump up from their mealtimes.'[4]

Train No. 1 chugged up to Russia again in January 1942, through temperatures dipping as low as -50°C, to bring home 290 wounded soldiers, many suffering the agonies and gangrenous hazards of frostbite. The third trip started in April, though this time instead of snow and ice there was intractable mud. At each stop on the return journey, throngs of hungry locals would mob the train for some scrap of food. Russian aircraft strafed the train more than once, fortunately without causing casualties.

At noon on 3 May 1942 Train No.1 with its full complement of sick and wounded was trundling through the Brenner Pass into Italian territory at the end of its third Russian trip. Though it was a Sunday and Padre Scavizzi had already performed one Mass, he decided on a second one to celebrate the homecoming. As one soldier played the organ, from the altar in the middle of the train Scavizzi intoned a prayer of thanks for deliverance. Then, flanked by a few soldiers and nurses bearing lighted candles, he walked slowly between the rows of the wounded, who joined him in a prayer for the souls of those who wouldn't be coming back.[5]

Eight months later, on the night of 12 January 1943, the same train was labouring through Poland on its way to the front when a violent explosion brought the train to a lurching halt. The personnel, shaken out of their bunks, peered out of the windows, but a thick layer of ice over the windows impeded their view. Several got out in the glacial night to find that a partisan mine had blown the train off the track. A snow-covered wilderness stretched in all directions. There seemed little to do but wait until the morning for someone to notice the mishap and bring help. At about 3.00 am the chaplain called the crew together for a Mass which, shortly afterwards, appeared to have had an effect as help unexpectedly turned up before dawn. By 9.00 am the train had been levered back onto the track and was able to resume its journey by late afternoon. More than 500 wounded Italian soldiers, waiting shivering at Donetsk in Ukraine, were able to crowd onto Train No. 1 that had just half that number of beds. Casualties were crammed into every single spare space. On the homeward route polar blizzards buffeted the train mercilessly, driving spirals of snow through even the most tightly closed windows; the heating stoves, working at full blast, could only preserve a temperature slightly above freezing. The next trip brought back hundreds of wounded of the Alpine Corps, limping on frostbitten stumps of feet. Two more hospital trains, Nos. 2 and 4, handled casualties from the Balkan fronts and Ukraine to back up Train No. 1. One can imagine the relief of those Italian soldiers, used to their homeland's warm sunshine and suffering excessively from the Russian winters, at the sight of the saviour trains with the Order's emblem painted boldly on the sides.

Many of the wounded were placed in Rome's Principe di Piemonte hospital, a former English ecclesiastical college converted in the space of one month. But with the fall of Benito Mussolini and the Allied landings in Italy of 1944, Italy was in danger of falling into social and economic chaos. Large parts of the country had fallen under communist partisan control. A large shantytown grew next to Rome's Trastevere Station to house hundreds of homeless and destitute Romans; here the Order was active, supplying food, medical care and spiritual guidance to whoever needed it.

At the war's end Italy, despite its late adherence to the Allied cause, was ordered to disarm its air force, the Regia Aeronautica, on the grounds that it had been an important offensive Axis force early in the war, and hand the aircraft over to the Allies for destruction. There wasn't much to hand over, but to the new Italian government of 1947 it was a gratuitous humiliation, and ways were sought around it. Then the Defence Ministry had the idea of handing the planes over to the Order of Malta. About 100 of them were hastily repainted with the Order's Maltese Cross emblem; technically as no longer Italian, the aircraft were no longer under Allied command jurisdiction. Thus the Italian flying college, the Centro Addestramento al Volo, presented the incongruous spectacle of its hardware sporting livery going back nearly 900 years! Under the Hospitaller Cross, then, the first pilots were trained for the new Italian air force, the Aeronautica Militare.[6] One of the larger planes, a converted Siai-Marchetti SM82 bomber – one of thirty that regularly flew on mercy missions for several years – now rests in the Italian Air Force Museum at Vigna di Valle north of Rome, still proudly wearing its Order insignia.

With the collapse of European communism, the activity of the Order in eastern Europe revived – and in a sudden and remarkable way, as Zoltan Bécsi, a Hungarian volunteer for the Order, could personally attest. Bécsi was vacationing in Budapest in August 1989 when the Hungarian communist government took the momentous step of dismantling its Cold War barrier with neighbouring Austria on the grounds that its upkeep was proving costly. Once the concrete and barbed wire came down, thousands of East

Germans flocked into Hungary to take advantage of that unexpected gap in the Iron Curtain. Totally embarrassed, the still-communist government of Hungary dared not call on the Red Cross for support. West Germany, as it was then, stepped in through its Hospitaller associations, along with the Austrian Priory and Hungary's own Order of Malta Charity Service – a foreign-based organization as communist governments had long banned the Order at home. Thanks largely to the Austrian Malteser Hilfsdienst (Malteser Aid Service), a major humanitarian crisis was averted. One of the helpers was Bécsi, who was put in charge of handling the flock of journalists who were descending on Budapest and told not to reveal that West Germany was issuing passports to the East Germans who were fleeing to the West. The Cold War was still technically on, and some things were still best kept under wraps.

On 19 August the Hungarian government cautiously allowed Hungarians and Austrians to mingle at the border for a picnic. The event was the idea of Walburga Douglas, the granddaughter of the last King of Hungary, who was present with a senior Hungarian government minister. Bécsi was also there. As part of the festivity the border was opened for three hours. It was the signal for hundreds of East Germans to charge madly through the opening, brushing aside the shocked border guards who could only watch helplessly. In a face-saving statement Hungary later would claim that it had opened the border to 'test' public reaction. But in a wider political sense, the horse had bolted. East Germany's communist leader, Erich Honecker, feeling control slipping away, resigned, and since then the world has been familiar with the spectacular fall of the Berlin Wall and European communism with it. In Bécsi's pithy judgement:

> There was something both hugely absurd and highly promising in this situation: a Catholic order was helping East German refugees in a communist country to flee to the west, while the granddaughter of the last King of Hungary was overseeing the opening of the Iron Curtain.[7]

Though the Order of Saint John is now wholly devoted to charitable works that do not involve fighting, the underlying military imagery is never lost sight of. In 1950, a year before his death, Grand Master Chigi gave a radio address in which he reminded his listeners: 'In place of the old military glory, we must aspire to another glory, in that the smile of someone who is saved shines brighter than the blade of a sword.'[8] The seventy-ninth and present Grand Master, Matthew Festing, has a military background.

Born in Northumberland in 1949, he is the son of Field Marshal Francis Festing, a past Chief of the Imperial General Staff. After studying history at Cambridge University, Matthew Festing served in the British Army's Grenadier Guards, reaching the rank of colonel. In later civilian life he was an art auctioneer while holding the office of Deputy Lieutenant of Northumberland. He can claim maternal descent from Adrian Fortescue, the Knight who was executed under Henry VIII and beatified in 1895, becoming the patron saint of the English Priory.

Festing was admitted to the Order in 1977, becoming a Knight of Justice eleven years later. In 1991 he took the perpetual vows of a Professed Knight of Malta: poverty, chastity and obedience. Two years later he was named Grand Prior of England – the first since Henry VIII's day – and took part in many humanitarian missions to the war-torn Balkans of the 1990s. He was elected Grand Master in 2008, the second Englishman to hold the supreme office. From his headquarters in the Rome headquarters on Via Condotti, Matthew Festing heads a roster of sixty-two Professed Knights (at this writing), each of whom has taken the abovementioned triple oath for life. The Knights are also bound to serve the spiritual interests of the Roman Catholic Church, though they insist that the association is voluntary only, and that the pope has no formal authority over the Order – an independence that the Order has upheld, though with difficulty, since the later Crusades.[9] In 2008 the Maltese government granted the Order a ninety-nine-year lease on Fort Sant' Angelo, in belated recognition of the Hospitallers' contribution to that island's history.

Epilogue

To the thousands of tourists strolling past the posh shops of Via Condotti in the heart of Rome, the large and apparently undistinguished palazzo within sight of Piazza di Spagna and those lounging and taking selfies on its storied steps seems to be just another office building. But step through the grilled gate in the central portico and you're in another country – literally. The Vatican City isn't the only separate city-state within the confines of Rome. The Order of Malta is far smaller, and far less well-known. And the people who live and work inside prefer it that way, out of the voracious eyes of the media.

From this building, however, the Order runs twelve Priories, forty-seven national associations, 133 diplomatic missions, one global relief agency and thirty-three national relief corps. The thousands of volunteers who are often sent to the world's crisis spots are known collectively as the Maltesers.[1] Much of the original administrative Hospitaller structure remains in place. Under the Grand Master are the Grand Commander, Grand Chancellor, Grand Hospitaller and Receiver of the Common Treasure; these correspond roughly to prime minister (head of government and religious superior), domestic and foreign minister, international charity head and finance minister. A six-member Sovereign Council oversees a Government Council, a Board of Auditors, a Board of Communications, a Juridical Council, a Magistral Court of First Instance, a Magistral Court of Appeal and a Commission for the Protection of Names and Emblems. The Order has permanent observer status at the United Nations and maintains diplomatic relations with over 100 countries, though surprisingly, few of the important ones. The United States, Britain, France, Russia and Germany, for example, do not recognize the Order diplomatically, following what seems to be a general practice of Protestant (e.g. Britain and Germany), Orthodox (e.g. Russia and Greece) and secular (e.g. France) countries. On one side of the headquarters, along Via Bocca di Leone, one can buy stamps of the Order and use them to post a letter. Since 1834 the Grand Master has enjoyed the use of an ornate Magistral Villa on the Aventine Hill high on the left bank of the Tiber overlooking the Trastevere district across the river and with a view of Saint Peter's.

The ideal of the warrior-monk as a knight-errant devoted to fighting evil in the world has persisted in literature and popular culture. To take one of the more recent examples, a British television series of the 1960s, *The Saint*, propelled actor Roger Moore to fame as the embodiment of such a figure – an upper-class adventurer of independent wealth who became the nemesis of baddies the world over, thanks to an ironclad moral code reminiscent of the Knights. The character's name, Simon Templar, was a direct reference to the Military Orders (though one must admit that Simon Hospitaller would not be as catchy). The series, and the preceding books written by Chinese-American ex-Hollywood screenwriter Leslie Charteris, have since come under liberal criticism for promoting 'class-based' and 'imperialist' values. Yet for all that, *The Saint* was highly popular, and sold in great quantities abroad, precisely for the knightly standard set by its main character.

The fame of the Order of Saint John has naturally spawned many imitators, especially in the United States. The Order makes clear that none of these have any connections with the real thing; indeed, several are, in the words of one modern Knight, 'fakes and scams'. As in this Internet age there is little to stop anyone from claiming anything, the only sure guide to the Order's history and activities is through its official website www.orderofmalta.int.

The icon of Our Lady of Philermos, which did so much to sustain the Hospitallers' morale in ages past, still exists but is no longer in the Order's possession. After the expulsion from Malta the icon found its way to Tsar Paul I who, as we have seen, had it richly decorated with gold and precious stones in the Orthodox tradition. After Paul's assassination it was stored in the Winter Palace at Saint Petersburg. There it remained for more than a century until the menace of the Bolshevik Revolution moved the Dowager Empress Maria Feodorovna to spirit it to safety in Denmark. From there Our Lady of Philermos found her way into the possession of the Yugoslav royal family. The icon was believed to have been destroyed by a German bombing raid, but it turned out that Serbian Orthodox monks had preserved it. When Marshal Josip Broz Tito established a communist dictatorship in Yugoslavia he reportedly tried to sell it in secret, but failed. For many years the icon's whereabouts were unknown until Richard Divall, Vice-Regent of the Subpriory of the Immaculate Conception of the Order of Malta in Australia, confirmed that he saw it in Montenegro in 1997. He found Our Lady of Philermos in good condition, though some of the decorative gems were missing. The icon has now been fully restored and can be seen in the Cetinje Museum near Podgorica in Montenegro.[2] Our Lady of Philermos remains, however, a patron of the Order along with Saint John the Baptist.

In August 2013 Israeli archaeologists announced that they had unearthed the foundations of a vast hospital covering some 150,000 square feet in Jerusalem's Old City and declared it to be the original Hospitaller medical facility plus the additions of some 200 years.[3] The date was exactly 900 years after Pope Paschal II established the Knights Hospitaller as a Military Order. The discovery symbolizes the full circle the Knights have come, from those turbulent eleventh century days of Jerusalem when the overriding purpose was wrapped up in the Latin phrase *tuitio fidei et obsequium pauperum* – to bear witness to the faith and give service to 'our Lords the Sick and Poor'. That again is the Order's mission. But it is worth bearing in mind that the official title – the Sovereign *Military* Hospitaller Order of Saint John of Jerusalem, of Rhodes and of Malta – remains. The twenty-first century is proving to be as turbulent as any that went before. Perhaps, after all, the Knights Hospitaller may have to prove themselves again.

Appendix

Grand Masters of the Knights Hospitaller (dating from the Order's official establishment in 1113)

It is usual in Hospitaller publications to prefix the names of Grand Masters, and most Knights, with Fra' (short for *frater*, or brother), as in Fra' Raymond du Puy or the present Grand Master, Fra' Matthew Festing. I have avoided this as being possibly confusing for the reader and perhaps pedantic as well.

Blessed Gerard (1113–1120)
Raymond du Puy (1120–*c.*1160)
Auger de Balben (*c.*1160–1162)
Arnaud de Comps (1162–1163)
Gilbert d'Assailly (1163–*c.*1170)
Gastone de Murols (*c.*1170–*c.*1172)
Gilbert [surname unknown] (*c.*1172–1177)
Roger de Moulins (1177–*c.*1187)
Armengaud d'Asp (1188–1190)
Garnier de Nablus (1190–1192)
Geoffrey de Donjon (1193–1202)
Alfonso de Portugal (1203–1206)
Geoffrey le Rat (1206–1207)
Garin de Montaigu (1207–*c.*1228)
Bertrand de Thessy (*c.*1228–1231)
Guerin [other names unknown] (1231–1236)
Bertrand de Comps (1236–*c.*1240)
Pierre de Vielle–Bride (*c.*1240–1242)
Guillaume de Châteauneuf (1242–1258)
Hugues de Revel (1258–1277)
Nicolas Lorgne (1277–1284)

Jean de Villiers (1284–*c.*1294)
Odon de Pins (1294–1296)
Guillaume de Villaret (1296–1305)
Fulk de Villaret (1305–1319)
Helion de Villeneuve (1319–1346)
Dieudonné de Gozon (1346–1353)
Pierre de Cornellian (1353–1355)
Roger de Pins (1355–1365)
Raymond Berenger (1365–1374)
Robert de Juliac (1374–1376)
Juan Fernandez de Heredia (1376–1396)
[with Riccardo Caracciolo (1383–1395)]
Philibert de Naillac (1396–1421)
Antonio Fluvian de Riviere (1421–1437)
Jean de Lastic (1437–1454)
Jacques de Milly (1454–1461)
Piero Raimondo Zacosta (1461–1467)
Giovanni Battista Orsini (1467–1476)
Pierre d'Aubusson (1476–1503)
Emery d'Amboise (1503–1512)
Guy de Blanchefort (1512–1513)
Fabrizio del Carretto (1513–1521)
Philippe de Villiers de l'Isle Adam (1521–1534)
Piero de Ponte (1534–1535)
Didier de Saint–Jaille (1535–1536)
Jean de Homedes (1536–1553)
Claude de la Sengle (1553–1557)
Jean de la Valette (1557–1568)
Pierre de Monte (1568–1572)
Jean de la Cassiere (1572–1581)
Hugues Loubenx de Verdala (1581–1595)
Martin Garzez (1595–1601)
Alof de Wignacourt (1601–1622)
Luis Mendez de Vasconcellos (1622–1623)
Antoine de Paule (1623–1636)
Juan de Lascaris–Castellar (1636–1657)
Antoine de Redin (1657–1660)
Annet de Clermont–Gessant (1660)
Raphael Cotoner (1660–1663)

Nicolas Cotoner (1663–1680)

Gregorio Carafa (1680–1690)

Adrienne de Wignacourt (1690–1697)

Ramon Perellos y Roccaful (1697–1720)

Marc'Antonio Zondadari (1720–1722)

Antonio Manoel de Vilhena (1722–1736)

Raymond Despuig (1736–1741)

Manuel Pinto de Fonseca (1741–1773)

Francisco Ximenes de Texada (1773–1775)

Emmanuel de Rohan–Polduc (1775–1797)

Ferdinand von Hompesch zu Bolheim (1797–1802)

Tsar Paul I of Russia [de facto 1799–1801]

Giovanni Battista Tommasi (1803–1805)

[Interregnum of the Lieutenants 1805–1879]

Giovanni Battista Ceschi a Santa Croce (1879–1905)

Galeazzo von Thun und Hohenstein (1905–1931)

Ludovico Chigi Albani della Rovere (1931–1951)

[Interregnum 1951–1962]

Angelo de Mojana di Cologna (1962–1988)

Andrew Willoughby Ninian Bertie (1988–2008)

Matthew Festing (2008–)

(Source: Horsler and Andrews 192–3)

Notes and References

Prologue
1. In Ulam, AB, *Expansion and Coexistence*, (New York, Praeger, 1968) p. 377n.
2. Luttrell, A, in 'The Hospitallers of Rhodes: Prospectives, Problems, Possibilities'.
3. Sire to author.

Chapter 1
1. Quoted in Asbridge, T, *The Crusades: The War for the Holy Land* (London, Simon & Schuster UK, 2010) p. 460.
2. Runciman, S, *The Crusades* III (London, Penguin, 1991) p. 47.
3. Reston, J, Jr, *Warriors of God* (London, Faber & Faber, 2001) pp. 199–200.
4. *Ibid.* 201.
5. Asbridge, p. 464.
6. Also known as al-Tawil, cf. Reston, p. 205.
7. Asbridge, p. 468.
8. *Ibid.* 472–4.

Chapter 2
1. *Daily Telegraph*, 4 March 2015.
2. Runciman I, p. 29.
3. Beltjens, A, *Aux Origines de l'Ordre de Malte* (Belgium, undated) pp. 39–43.
4. Jaspert, N, Nicholson, HJ and Borchardt, K, *The Hospitallers, the Mediterranean and Europe: Festschrift for Anthony Luttrell* (London, Ashgate Publishing, undated), op. cit.
5. Durant, W, *The Story of Civilization* IV, (New York, Simon & Schuster, 1949–1954) p. 585.
6. Montefiore, SS, *Jerusalem: The Biography* (London, Phoenix, 2011) p. 201.
7. Quoted in *Ibid.* 202.
8. Durant IV, p. 587.
9. Quoted in Beltjens, p. 119.
10. Nicolle, p. 16. *Knights of Jerusalem: The Crusading Order of Hospitallers 1100–1565* (Oxford, Osprey, 2008).
11. Komnene, Anna, *The Alexiad* (London, Penguin Classics, 2009) p. 276.
12. From a lecture by Dr Jonathan Riley-Smith, former Dixie Professor of Ecclesiastical History at Cambridge University, in March 2005, quoted in Horsler and Andrews, p. 18. The New Testament passage on which the modus operandi was based is Matthew 25:39–40.
13. Thompson, JW, *Economic and Social History of the Middle Ages*, (New York, 1928) p. 397.
14. Beltjens, p. 307.
15. The evidence for this is circumstantial. See Beltjens, pp. 198–201.
16. Beltjens: 'It is unfair to judge the mediaeval warrior-monks by modern criteria.' Op. cit. p. 309.

17. Runciman II, p. 116.
18. *Ibid.* 156–7.
19. Montefiore, p. 219.
20. Runciman I, p. 83.
21. Matthew 10:34 and Luke 22:36.
22. Gibbon, E, edited by Hugh Trevor-Roper, *The Decline and Fall of the Roman Empire* (London, Phoenix, 2005) pp. 540–2.
23. Durant IV, p. 593.
24. Nicolle, *Knights* pp. 17–18.
25. Runciman II, p. 199.
26. Durant IV, p. 593.
27. Gibbon/Trevor-Roper, p. 565.

Chapter 3

1. Durant IV, pp. 572–3.
2. Ferguson, WK, and Bruun, G, *A Survey of European Civilization* (Boston, Houghton Mifflin, 1962) p. 199.
3. Hitti, PK, *History of the Arabs* (New York, St Martin's Press, 1968) p. 545.
4. Komnene, p. 285.
5. Qahir was the name the Arabs gave to the planet Mars, 'the triumphant of Heaven'. The Venetians corrupted the name into Cairo. Hitti, p. 619*n*.
6. *Ibid.* 475.
7. *Ibid.* 640.
8. Montefiore, p. 216.

Chapter 4

1. Nicolle, *Knights* p. 21.
2. Montgomery of Alamein, *A History of Warfare* (London, Collins, 1968) p. 175.
3. Quoted in *Ibid.* 177.
4. *Ibid.* 176.
5. Runciman II, p. 317.
6. Montgomery, p. 178.
7. Quoted in Nicolle, *Knights* p. 104.
8. *Ibid.* 141.
9. Quoted in Asbridge, p. 177.
10. *Ibid.* 179–80.
11. Jaspert et al., op. cit.
12. Norwich, JJ, *Byzantium: The Decline and Fall* III (London, Penguin, 1996) p. 80.
13. Montefiore, p. 223.
14. Usama bin Mundiqh, quoted by Montefiore, p. 227.
15. In Asbridge, p. 210.

Chapter 5

1. Quoted from Hector Haratsis, *The Teutonic Knights*, (Athens, Eurobooks, 2010).
2. Leviticus 26:7–8, cited in Reston, p. 37.
3. Nicolle, *Knights* p. 186.
4. Durant IV, p. 593.
5. Runciman II, pp. 446–8.
6. The oft-repeated story that travelling with the caravan was Saladin's sister has been discredited by serious writers, cf. Runciman II, p. 450*n*.
7. Hitti, p. 644*n*.

8. Quoted in Reston, p. 40.
9. Durant IV, p. 597.
10. Reston, p. 40.
11. Montefiore, p. 243.
12. Reston, p. 43.
13. Quoted in Asbridge, p. 352.
14. Montgomery, p. 180. For the controversy that still swirls around the Battle of Hattin, see Runciman II, pp. 486–91.
15. *Ibid*. 466.
16. Durant IV, p. 689.
17. Reston, p. 93.
18. Asbridge, p. 371.

Chapter 6
1. Quoted in Asbridge, p. 375.
2. Runciman writes delicately that Richard's 'own tastes did not lie in the direction of marriage'.
3. Erickson, C, *Brief Lives of the English Monarchs* (London, Constable, 2007) p. 58.
4. *Ibid*. 62.
5. Quoted in Reston, p. 108.
6. Quoted in Montefiore, p. 259.
7. The phrase is Montefiore's, p. 260.
8. Reston, pp. 271–2.
9. *Ibid*. 277–8.
10. Reston, p. 288; the Biblical reference is 1 Samuel 13.
11. *Ibid*. 293.
12. Runciman III, pp. 77–8.
13. The phrase is Runciman's, III, p. 205.
14. Nicol, DM, 'Byzantium, Venice and the Fourth Crusade,' in *Southeastern Review* (undated).
15. Runciman III, p. 130.
16. Nicolle, *Knights* pp. 60–8.
17. Runciman III, p. 159. Runciman mentions Saint Francis in a cynical light as one of 'many good and unwise persons' having a naive belief in the power of peaceful institutions.

Chapter 7
1. Quoted in Durant IV, p. 715.
2. *Ibid*.
3. Cited in *Ibid*. 692.
4. Runciman III, p. 281.
5. *Ibid*. 392.
6. *Ibid*. 418.
7. Asbridge, p. 654.
8. A number of Templars stayed put on the fortified islet of Ruad off Tortosa for twelve more years.

Chapter 8
1. Quoted in Asbridge, p. 656.
2. Durant IV, p. 610.
3. Phillips, S, 'Hospitaller Relations with the Local Community on Cyprus,' available at www.academia.edu

4. Nicolle, *Knights* p. 123.
5. Nicolle, D, *Crusader Castles in Cyprus, Greece and the Aegean* (Oxford, Osprey, 2007), p. 24.
6. Nicolle, *Knights* p. 27.
7. See Luttrell, 'Prospectives ...'
8. Ferguson and Bruun, p. 275.
9. Quoted in *Ibid.* 303.

Chapter 9
1. Quoted in Nicolle, *Knights* p. 29.
2. Luttrell, 'Prospectives ...'
3. *Ibid.*
4. *Ibid.*
5. Description in Nicolle, *Knights* pp. 110–11.
6. Luttrell, 'Prospectives ...'
7. Nossov, K, *The Fortress of Rhodes 1309–1522* (Oxford, Osprey, 2010) p. 6.
8. Nicolle, *Knights* p. 197; other reports name the temporary replacement as Maurice de Pagnac.
9. See the *Destan of Umur Pasha*, a fifteenth century work cited by Nicolle, *Knights* p. 170,177.
10. Montgomery, pp. 190–1.
11. Nicolle, *Knights* pp. 177–8.
12. Quoted in *Ibid.* 185.
13. *Ibid.*
14. Ferguson and Bruun, I, p. 307.
15. Luttrell, 'Prospectives ...'
16. Nicolle, *Knights* p. 131.
17. *Ibid.* 119. Froissart, our main source for the battle of Poitiers, does not mention such an incident.
18. *Ibid.*; Luttrell, 'Prospectives ...'
19. Nicolle, *Knights* p. 93.
20. Norwich III, p. 355.
21. Nossov, pp. 9–10.

Chapter 10
1. Horsler, V and Andrews, J, *The Order of Malta: A Portrait* (London, Third Millennium, 2011) p. 24. The castle is now a Turkish-run underwater archaeology museum.
2. Nicolle, *Crusader Castles*, p. 50.
3. Brockelmann, C, *History of the Islamic Peoples* (New York, Capricorn, 1960) p. 284.
4. The troop figure most often given is 100,000, but most modern writers suspect it is a gross exaggeration. See Nossov, p. 46.
5. *Ibid.*
6. *Ibid.* 48*n.*
7. *Ibid.* 49.
8. *Ibid.*
9. Horsler and Andrews, p. 27.
10. *Ibid.*
11. Brockelmann, pp. 285–6.
12. Quoted in Nicolle, *Knights* p. 35.
13. Nossov, p. 45.
14. Cited in Durant VI, p. 704.
15. Nossov, p. 59.

Chapter 11
1. Nicolle, *Knights* p. 101.
2. Luttrell, 'Prospectives …'
3. Sire, HJA, *The Knights of Malta* (New Haven and London, Yale University Press, 1994) p. 102.
4. *Ibid.* 104.
5. Nicolle, *Knights* p. 41.
6. Barker, J, *England Arise* (London, Little, Brown Book Group, 2014) p. 234.
7. Nicolle, *Knights* p. 99.

Chapter 12
1. The description is by HG Wells in *The Outline of History* (London, Cassell, 1951) p. 784.
2. The Sant'Angelo Tower was destroyed in the Second World War, rebuilt, and since 1998 has served as the Order's embassy in Valletta.
3. Cited in Durant VI, p. 509.
4. Cited in a letter to the *International New York Times* by John Howard Wilhelm of Ann Arbor, Michigan, USA, quoting John Adams and Thomas Jefferson in a report of 1786. The 'cut-throat' description is by Thomas A Bailey in *The Diplomatic History of the American People* (New York, Meredith, 1964) p. 64. As late as 1805 the Barbary pirates seized US Navy ships and personnel, exacting a heavy ransom from President Jefferson.
5. Sire, p. 89.
6. Capponi, N, *Victory of the West: The Story of the Battle of Lepanto* (London, Macmillan, 2006) p. 208.
7. Other sources estimate the force at no more than about 20,000. Cf. Durant VI, p. 718.
8. Out of the several sources giving different figures I have preferred Henry Sire as prima facie the most reliable. Cf. Sire, p. 69.
9. Capponi, p. 89.
10. Sire, p. 70.
11. Quoted in *Ibid.*
12. French historians, however, blame Toledo for inexcusable slowness, and make the demonstrably false claim that he was dismissed from his post. Cf. Sire, p. 71*n*.
13. Sire, p. 72.
14. *Ibid.* 73.
15. *Ibid.* 89.
16. Capponi, pp. 134–5.
17. Montgomery, p. 260.
18. Capponi, p. 254.
19. *Ibid.* 282.
20. *Ibid.* Capponi avers that Giustiniani survived by bribing a Barbary corsair.
21. Montgomery, pp. 258–61.

Chapter 13
1. Sire, p. 92.
2. *Ibid.* 74.
3. *Ibid.* 76.
4. *Ibid.* 82.
5. *Ibid.* 83.
6. One of his paintings, the huge *The Beheading of John the Baptist*, hangs in the co-Cathedral of Saint John in Valletta.
7. List cited in Sire, p. 77.
8. Quoted in *Ibid.* 78.
9. Candia is the modern Heraklion in Crete.

Chapter 14
1. For the available details of the Knights' long conflict with the Barbary pirates, see Sire, pp. 91–8.
2. Sire, p. 95.
3. The figure is in *Ibid.* 234.
4. *Ibid.*
5. *Faust*, Part One, Scene 5.
6. Ferguson and Bruun, p. 547.
7. Sire, p. 236.
8. Written by Freiherr von Schönau and quoted in Sire, p. 238.
9. *Ibid.* 239.
10. In Ferguson and Bruun, p. 624.
11. Sire, p. 241.
12. *Ibid.* 242.

Chapter 15
1. Horsler and Andrews, p. 28. It was not the first time, nor would it be the last, that the Mother of God was seen in the front line of Christian battles.
2. Ferguson and Bruun, p. 624.
3. *Ibid.* 642.
4. Sire, p. 248.
5. The adjective is Sire's, *Ibid.* p. 249.
6. *Ibid.* 250.
7. *Ibid.* 252. Author's italics.

Chapter 16
1. *Ordine di Malta* p. 56.
2. *Ibid.* 111.
3. *Ibid.* 125.
4. *Ibid.* 133. Author's translation.
5. *Ibid.* 137.
6. Sire to author.
7. Quoted in Horsler and Andrews, p. 84.
8. Quoted in *Ordine di Malta* p. 170.
9. Sire to author; Horsler and Andrews, p. 176.

Epilogue
1. There seems to be no apparent connection with the British-made chocolate confectionery of the same name.
2. Horsler and Andrews, p. 28.
3. 'Crusader Hospital Unearthed in Jerusalem,' Discovery Channel, 5 August 2013.

Bibliography

The following are the chief sources I have used in writing this book.

Asbridge, T, *The Crusades: The War for the Holy Land* (London: Simon & Schuster UK, 2010).

Bailey, Thomas A, *The Diplomatic History of the American People* (New York, Meredith, 1964).

Beltjens, A, *Aux Origines de l'Ordre de Malte* (published in Belgium, undated).

Brockelmann, C, *History of the Islamic Peoples* (New York: Capricorn, 1960).

Capponi, N, *Victory of the West: The Story of the Battle of Lepanto* (London: Macmillan, 2006).

Durant, W, *The Story of Civilization* (vols. IV, V and VI) (New York: Simon & Schuster, 1949–1954).

Erickson, C, *Brief Lives of the English Monarchs* (London: Constable, 2007).

Ferguson, WK and Bruun, G, *A Survey of European Civilization* 3rd Edition (2 vols.) (Boston: Houghton Mifflin, 1962).

Gibbon, E, *The Decline and Fall of the Roman Empire* (London: Phoenix, 2005) (a one-volume condensed version of Gibbon's classic work edited by Hugh Trevor-Roper, cited in the notes as Gibbon/Trevor-Roper).

Hitti, PK, *History of the Arabs* 9th Edition (New York: St Martin's Press, 1968).

Horsler, V and Andrews, J, *The Order of Malta: A Portrait* (London: Third Millennium, 2011).

Jaspert, N, Nicholson, HJ, and Borchardt, K, 'The Hospitallers, the Mediterranean and Europe: Festschrift for Anthony Luttrell,' (London: Ashgate Publishing, undated).

Kollias, E, *The Knights of Rhodes* (Athens: Ekdotike Athinon, 2013).

Komnene, Anna, *The Alexiad* (London: Penguin Classics, 2009).

Luttrell, A, 'The Hospitallers at Rhodes,' in Setton, K, (ed.) (Vol. 1) *History of the Crusades* (University of Wisconsin Press, 1969).

Luttrell, A, 'The Hospitallers of Rhodes: Prospectives, Problems, Possibilities,' at www.uni-heidelberg.de

Montefiore, SS, *Jerusalem: The Biography* (London: Phoenix, 2011).

Montgomery of Alamein, *A History of Warfare* (London: Collins, 1968).

Nicol, DM, 'Byzantium, Venice and the Fourth Crusade,' in *Southeastern Review* (undated).

Nicolle, D, *Crusader Castles in Cyprus, Greece and the Aegean* (Oxford: Osprey, 2007).

Nicolle, D, *Knights of Jerusalem: The Crusading Order of Hospitallers 1100–1565* (Oxford: Osprey, 2008)

Norwich, JJ, *Byzantium: The Decline and Fall* (London: Penguin, 1996).

Nossov, K, *The Fortress of Rhodes 1309–1522* (Oxford: Osprey, 2010).

Phillips, S, 'Hospitaller Relations with the Local Community of Cyprus,' at www.academia.edu

Reston, J, Jr, *Warriors of God* (London: Faber & Faber, 2001).

Runciman, S, *The Crusades* (3 vols.) (London: Penguin, 1991).
Sire, HJA, *The Knights of Malta* (New Haven and London: Yale University Press, 1994).
Sovereign Military Order of the Hospitallers of Saint John of Jerusalem, Rhodes and Malta,
    Ordine di Malta / Ordre de Malte: Fotografie Inedite 1880–1960 (Rome: Gangemi, 2015).
Thompson, JW, *Economic and Social History of the Middle Ages*, (New York: 1928).
Wells, HG, *The Outline of History* (London: Cassell, 1951).

Index